BILD-ING a MEMORY MODEL of GOD

BILD-ING a MEMORY MODEL of GOD

A Wesleyan and Neuroscientific Prospect

KWANG-JIN OH

PICKWICK *Publications* · Eugene, Oregon

BILD-ING A MEMORY MODEL OF GOD
A Wesleyan and Neuroscientific Prospect

Pickwick Publications
An Imprint of Wipf and Stock Publishers
199 W. 8th Ave., Suite 3
Eugene, OR 97401

www.wipfandstock.com

PAPERBACK ISBN: 978-1-6667-7536-5
HARDCOVER ISBN: 978-1-6667-7537-2
EBOOK ISBN: 978-1-6667-7538-9

Cataloguing-in-Publication data:

Names: Oh, Kwang-Jin, author.

Title: *Bild*-ing a memory model of God : a wesleyan and neuroscientific prospect / Kwang-Jin Oh.

Description: Eugene, OR : Pickwick Publications, 2024 | Includes bibliographical references and index.

Identifiers: ISBN 978-1-6667-7536-5 (paperback) | ISBN 978-1-6667-7537-2 (hardcover) | ISBN 978-1-6667-7538-9 (ebook)

Subjects: LCSH: Mind and body—Religious aspects—Christianity. | Theological anthropology—Christianity. | Cognitive science—Moral and ethical aspects. | Image of God. | Theology, Doctrinal. | Christian life—Methodist authors.

Classification: BT741.3 .O17 2024 (paperback) | BT741.3 .O17 (ebook)

05/01/24

Contents

Acknowledgments

EVERY BOOK IS A winding journey, forays into the corners of academia, to "find" what I'm looking for. It can be a brutal slog, hacking through the material to come up with new ideas and refreshing old ones, but there is also the exciting prospect of contributing something new. This book is no different in the long journey that others have taken, and this short space acknowledges those who have helped me complete this task.

How does the saying go? Family first? Not only have they been there since the beginning, but they have been a source of strength, finance, and well-being. The Apostle Paul talks about ceaseless prayer, and I know they have been doing that on my behalf. To Myung-Jin Oh, my brother, for being the only in-person family connection for most of this journey, someone who I can rely on to keep me accountable for my health, and my needs around the city. To Sung-Hee Oh and Sung-Kown Oh, my mother and father, who most of the time are in Korea, for all the prayers and encouragement, advice, and inspiration along the way. To remain strong in faith, in mind, and in heart and to pray.

Lastly, I would like to thank Dr. Brent Waters, my advisor and my dissertation committee members for their patience and insightful comments in crafting this book.

Abbreviations

DLPFC   dorsolateral prefrontal cortex

GAPS   general abstract processing system

MTL   medial temporal lobe

WJW   Wesley, John. *The Works of John Wesley*. Edited by Albert Outler. 4 vols. Bicentennial ed. Nashville: Abingdon, 1984–87

Introduction

THIS BOOK ATTEMPTS TO build a memory model of the Christian image of God, blending philosophy and theological language in order to understand better how memory might be embodied and to give insight into the "mind of Christ" (1 Cor 2:16). While neuroscientific psychological theories of memory are important, theology takes precedent here. This means that this book will not be using scientific proof for how theology "exists" in the world, as if one could locate a God in a "spot" in the brain, or mind. In this respect, the context of the book is a theology of nature, not of natural theology. Therefore, the topic of discussion is principally the theological concept of the image of God or the *imago Dei*, the former referring to the human and concept in general, while the latter specifically to Christ. Yet, the character of theology will look through the lens of memory. Taken together, theology will offer how memory embodies a "natural" interpretation of the image of God in a Wesleyan theological anthropology.

In chapter 1, modern interpretations of the image of God will be discussed to assess what we currently seem to mean by the image of God. This beginning is offered as the collective opinions of various theologians as they have wrestled with the question of being made "in the image of God, according to our likeness" (Gen 1:26–27). The important words are "image" and "likeness" and what each seems to represent. In general, image appears to be something more objective while likeness takes on a certain quality. Depending on the theologian, different emphasis is placed on either term, with some preferring a single concept of image-likeness while others make a distinction in the terms. A sketch of language analysis serves to highlight either case, whether they are synonyms and can be used interchangeably or if there are markers to make a distinction. In the end, interpretations of the image of God can be largely classified into substantial, functional, or relational approaches.

Because of the diversity of meaning found in the image of God, however, interpretations are blended, even if a particular interpretation is favored. This book will point out the popularity of the relational approach. Most proponents of this approach do so at the expense of the other two, which are more problematic. For instance, John F. Kilner points out the dangers of making the image of God about how human attributes are like God.[1] Since the image of God is often relied on for human dignity arguments in the ethical treatment of others, Kilner's concern is certainly warranted if attributes are revoked, as history has shown to be the case. The same concern applies to human ability to steward creation. Due to the fall, internal human characteristics and abilities are suspect. Only Christ is the *imago Dei*, to which humans are to conform. Thus, instead of an image, which some, such as Karl Barth and Emil Brunner, think the Bible says little about, the image of God must be outside the human person. There is a switch from what an image is to what can be imaged. Whether this takes the form of a relationship between God and humanity or some dialogical approach in speech, a relational approach is less dangerous than either the substantial or functional approaches because "likeness" is a quality.

Given the weight of opinion in favor of relational approaches, this book points out the importance of the body, especially since memory will be used later. This does not deny the important points brought up by relational advocates. In fact, much of what they desire in rightly ordered relationships is the ethical goal of theological models. However, as an external phenomenon, it has a noetic quality that betrays the importance of the body which Christianity has maintained in the incarnation and resurrection of Christ. To this end, some remarks will be made about "glory" and how that relates to weight, both bodily phenomena in what can be seen and felt. Then Jacques Fantino's work on Irenaeus's Christology and soteriology will be extremely helpful in emphasizing the body as a physical "quantity" in the image of God. In creating human beings, one is imprinted by the Holy Spirit, thus not only creating an impression, but imparting a weight that can be felt.

1. Kilner, *Dignity and Destiny*, 79.

As such, image is no longer a static quantity but a dynamic one that causes one to "pass through" it in a gesture to something else. Such symbolism is not new by any means, but it raises the question of what image is. Combined with a theological anthropology, a theology of image results, questioning what that image represents *in* a human being. It is here that memory enters the book. For all the talk about impressions, it was Plato and Aristotle who started the conversation about a tablet of wax.

In chapter 2 the ancient notion of memory will be examined in order to get a philosophical appreciation for the dynamism found in memory and eventually move to the *imago Dei*. First, however, there needs to be a working definition of memory and the starting point is in Plato's *Theaetetus*. It is here that the famous wax tablet comes up in a dialogue about epistemology. Does what one perceives count as knowledge? In the ensuing discussion, memory is likened to a wax block that holds the impression of a percept, but there is the rub. The resulting impression is only an intermediate which cannot count as knowledge. However, upon such realization, one is "reminded" that true knowledge is of the thing itself. Therefore, in memory there is the necessity of sensory input *through* which the soul knows particulars, but memory is more than just a unidirectional pass-through object. The impression is also indicative of the soul's desires and affections to reach out, becoming "fastened on" to memory and establishing a relationship between soul and object. In effect, a person makes a judgment about an object, which are the roles played by the scribe who writes onto the soul, and the painter who paints what has been written in Plato's *Philebus*.

Memory's multidimensional and multidirectional properties are also found in the word "image," creating a tautology reminiscent of the question of the one and the many. Some word analysis from the work of David Ambuel on the *Sophist* and related works will be important here in distinguishing *eidolon*, *eikon*, and *phantasma*. All refer to the general concept of image, but the directionalities of each word are nuanced. *Eidolon* refers to differences in the image whereas *eikon* refers to similarity. *Eikon* also looks to the past in that similarity whereas *phantasma* is creative and is more about the future. Thus, *eikon* is the preferred term as it relates to memory because there would be no recourse to the past without a sense of similarity. In addition, these directional cues also point to memory's "usage." One possesses *eikon* whereas one has a *phantasma*, lending an interpretive frame not only to the wax tablet but also to the aviary model of memory in the *Theaetetus*. These differences are important because of the specific use of *eikon* in the image of God.[2] Thus, in looking at the tautology, one is able to link together image and memory and apply them to the image of God and *imago Dei*.

The theological piece to this chapter will draw heavily on Chris Kugler, who argues for a wisdom Christology for the *imago Dei*. His work also integrates what image meant to the ancients and incorporates the Second Temple and intertestamental periods when Jewish wisdom theology developed. This is important because it provides evidence for how the word *eikon* could have changed in meaning *between* the Hebrew Scriptures and the New Testament, refuting the claims of scholars who insist on the exclusion of Greek influence in the New Testament. For Kugler, Paul appropriates Jewish Sophia tradition to make the claim that Christ is the cosmogonical agent (*protokos*) in all creation. By taking image analysis of the word *eikon* and relating it to logos (a coalescing), the *charakter* of the *imago Dei* is revealed. Christ as divine logos is the coalescing of God's wisdom as written or engraved on the heart (letters of Christ). Recalling the written nature of memory leads to an ethical outlook as one "reads" memory. It is the beginning of understanding what having the mind of Christ might be like.

Chapter 3 attempts to assemble everything together in the construction of a Wesleyan theological anthropology involving memory. While the intent of the book is to develop a memory theory of the *imago Dei* consistent with biblical times, it is possible that modern ideas would be incorporated by the time of Wesley. That said, the "feel" of this chapter will still rely on the language analysis developed in the preceding chapters, especially with regard to words like "impressed" and "written," and as they pertain to memory. Here, the concept of divine illumination from Lydia Schumacher's work will provide the "content" for the *imago Dei* as the knowledge/wisdom of Christ. But as the chapter progresses, more will be drawn on the functions of the Holy Spirit and with regard to being "sealed" with the "weight" and "glory" of memory's affective properties. Ultimately, the constructive process of this chapter moves from Augustine through to Bonaventure and ends with Wesley, taking unique features of theology along the way.

To begin, Augustine provides the theological heritage from which subsequent theological anthropologies drew their inspiration. The tradition of divine illumination, God's enlightening influence on the human mind, is typically traced to Augustine and his understanding of human psychology

---

2. Aristotle's *De Memoria* will also be used here but more as piece on *phantasma* than *eikon*. For this, Richard Sorabji and Sophie-Grace Chappell will provide insight.

in the Trinitarian powers of the soul: memory, intellect, and will. Following Schumacher, these powers reflect God in an abstractive process of the mind, which then indirectly reflects God's Goodness as ordered in creation. Thus, in an act of remembrance one "recovers" the image of God *in the intellect* (commonly called understanding), which is enlightened to be able to "think" like God as one consults the "inner teacher."

Paige Hochschild notices, however, that while Augustine's famous Trinitarian constructs of the image of God have been studied, mostly in his *Confessions* and *De Trinitate*, memory has not been systematically studied. One of her arguments is that memory functions to "graft" God onto the human. Thus, distinct from Schumacher, Hochschild puts the image of God in memory. As a source of knowledge, it is only in memory that a grafting can occur, that is, memory is the only place where an image can be "fixed" in time and act as basis for discourse to occur. Memory anchors the image of God, and one can move toward the idea of the *imago Dei* as possession. This is a claim Schumacher and Hochschild do not make, but one specific to this book. The *imago Dei* as *eikon* is a memory pattern that counts for knowing God that is the knowledge of Christ.

From Augustine, this book travels to St. Bonaventure. This is not to deny the importance of St. Thomas Aquinas his contemporary or to argue who was the more faithful Augustinian. Rather, Bonaventure was chosen for what this book considers the unique theological views on "contuition," the divine-human agreement, and *synderesis*, the impeccable power and love of God, the Holy Spirit. T. Alexander Giltner's book will be the launching point since Giltner also discusses divine illumination as well as the two previous authors already mentioned. Importantly, divine illumination is *in memory* as opposed to the intellect because the intellect can only grasp what is stored in memory. Christ the light in the tabernacle of the human being points to a divine access of the *imago Dei* and through the image of God in its triumvirate of mental powers, "triangulates" to the pattern of God, or the memory of God. Contuition, then, is a stronger form of participation with God because "certitude" found in "agreement" is how God sees and knows creation.

To get to *synderesis*, however, some explanation is required of "likeness" since, following the distinction in Irenaeus, scholars such as Philip L. Reynolds and Jinyong Choi prefer to place all affective qualities of the soul into likeness rather than the "value-neutral" image. Their arguments are not without merit and, in fact, are very traditional in an Eastern Orthodox sense. The distinction of image and likeness allows a certain preservation of the image while likeness is restored. More importantly, the likeness is a "superadded" grace that then brings the image into participation with the divine. This infusion of grace from the Holy Spirit is what allows for the reception of all the virtues. This all sounds good in theory, but it also seems to be too qualitative an answer, to the point of being a disembodied feature. Instead, as this book has argued, the image of God must truly have a physical component upon which the Holy Spirit acts to bring out a likeness, not merely provide a likeness.

Thus, rather than a "noetic" addition to the image, Robert Glenn Davis offers an account of Bonaventure's *affectus* through *synderesis* as the weight of the will. The definition of *affectus* is difficult, so at base, it will be the immanent ability to experience God, and as such refers to the physicality of the body. Davis, however, looks at *synderesis* as the weight of the will, here the appetites or desires of the body, rather than choice. This weight or *pondus* is an affective power that moves one naturally and rightly and cannot err. As such it is the grace of the Holy Spirit that orders us in God, self, neighbor, and body, through charity. Therefore, *synderesis* is the weight of love, the spark of conscience rather than a natural conscience that performs judgments. In essence, the Holy Spirit impresses on the body through grace and ordered appetites. This imprint is the love of the Holy Spirit or *charakter* of God that we experience. Then, it is contuition and *synderesis*, the cognitive-affective together, that count for moral judgments as one transforms into Christ.

This last section puts everything together into a Wesleyan theological anthropology of memory. John Wesley's tripartite structure to the image of God are the natural, political, and moral images. The natural image contains the powers of the soul: understanding, will, and liberty. While memory is not specifically listed in the natural image, memory was nevertheless important for Wesley. Much of his philosophy was in context with philosophers, scientists, and medical professionals of his time, and where applicable, extracted their thoughts and commented on them. Therefore, while Wesley does mention memory in his sermons, his "natural philosophies" in conversation with John Locke provides insight into ideas, which for Wesley were called memories.

However, since Wesley did not believe in innate ideas, building a memory model poses a significant challenge. Nevertheless, because of Wesley's belief in the unity between revelation and empiricism, a memory model can be drawn out, particularly as it relates to his doctrine of the image of God. Barry Bryant's dissertation on "John Wesley's Doctrine of Sin" will provide much anthropological content as it relates to Wesley's empiricism but also to the image of God itself. Importantly, memory as part of the image of God will be drawn from the *language* Wesley used, words such as "impressed," "engraven," "written," or "sealed" within the person and typically on the heart, an ongoing theme of the book. For Wesley, spiritual matters of the heart were always in the purview of the Holy Spirit's affective function in revelation. Thus, one of the key arguments of this book that follows the cognitive-affect discussion found in Bonaventure, argues for a "Wesleyan" *synderesis* that impacts the knowledge of Christ as moral law. In so doing, the "supernatural grace" of the Holy Spirit imprints the body through love that once realized and accepted makes for understanding, or the filling of moral law, "the pattern of our great Master."[3] In effect, one awakens (recollects) a memory of a Memory, or perhaps, an image of God of the *imago Dei*.

Of course, this is somewhat a difficult case to make since there is no evidence that Wesley read Bonaventure, though he did read Aquinas. Furthermore, there is significant disagreement among Wesleyan scholars—Young Taek Kim, Kenneth Collins, and Theodore Runyon—centering on what is "natural." As a result, there are interpretive differences on conscience, while *synderesis* is not mentioned by any of the above scholars. Wesley himself only mentions it once in his sermons. If, however, the book has made its case with language analysis, its use, and relation to memory, a memory anthropology can be "revealed" at the center of Wesley's natural, moral, and political images as one moves through them, recapitulating the way human beings were intended to be ordered. Thus, in being able to peer into the "mind of Christ," one lives an ordered life through: 1) loving God, 2) self-knowledge, 3) loving neighbor, 4) *transformation of the world*, and 5) perfection of the body, that is, the meaning of the political image as it relates to all of creation.

Chapter 4 is arguably the hardest one to write. First, there is already the tension between science and religion, and how each may or may not influence each other. Scholars throughout the ages have argued about which has primacy over the other, which is the handmaiden of whom, and if the two can be brought together in some interdisciplinary fashion. Obviously one possibility is Stephen Jay Gould's non-overlapping magesteria, but there is

---

3. "On Working Out Our Own Salvation," in *WJW*, 3:208, §3.5.

considerable debate as to where those boundaries are or even if they can (or should) be maintained. This chapter will not go into those debates, but since this book is principally a theological work, it will privilege theological claims *into* what is revealed by science, from "poetics" to science. In this respect, this chapter is a theology of nature rather than a natural theology. It speculates on what might be a possible physical instantiation of the image of God as revealed by scientific data.

Second, there is considerable argument in philosophy on how to characterize memory. One position is the more familiar "archivist" model or "structural analog," where memory is likened to what is stored on a computer hard drive and then retrieved. Most of this book, in its Greco-Roman and theological context, is this form of memory, where some kind of image or representation serves as content for a person to retrieve. Another position is the distributed memory model, where one locus does not contain memory, but that memory results from the instructions sent from neurons to each other in a connected network. This newer model considers the nuances of the *process* of memory formation, or how memories are constructed rather than simply retrieved. While interesting and important in attempting to define memory, these discussions do not speak directly to the most germane feature, the memory engram, which might provide a basis for a hypothetical image of God in the brain. Thus, while mentioned here for the sake of completeness, these philosophical arguments will not be discussed in this book. For those interested, however, Sarah Robins's arguments for a casual theory of memory can be compared to Sven Bernecker's and Michaelian Kourken's arguments for distributed memories.[4]

Finally, the key piece of scientific data that could provide for a potential manifestation *for* (as opposed to *of*) the image of God in the brain is the memory engram. First coined by Richard Semon in 1921, the memory engram provides potential substrate in memories as well as their recall. It should be noted, however, that at the time, there was no evidence for an engram, and in that context, served as a hypothetical, much like what the ancients "poetically" supposed in a wax tablet. Of course, the field of neuroscience has had many advancements since then, and along the way, have discovered brain structures for different types of memory. These include the medial temporal lobe and associated regions for *episodic* memories of experience as opposed to *sematic* memories of facts. Here, there is little

---

4. Robins, "Representing the Past"; Bernecker, *Memory*; Kourken, "Generative Memory."

choice but to use neuroanatomical taxonomy in describing brain regions important for memory.

Having gone through some basic neuroscience of memory, the next section looks at two different attempts at linking God and neuroscience together. The first is the more outdated work of Carol Rausch Albright and James B. Ashbrook. These authors adapt Paul D. MacLean's triune brain, three evolutionarily distinct brain regions with specific cognitive and emotional functions, into their own Trinitarian image of God. The science here is admittedly outdated but is worth mentioning because it seeks to resolve the theological in what is scientifically found. Patrick McNamara takes a more general approach to God but with more detailed neuroanatomy as it relates to the self and "decentering" events. The gist is that religious experiences are a process of decentering and recentering a self as various selves compete in building a "new" self. Obviously, the brain areas for emotion and memory are involved in this process. Yet, it appears that none of the authors think of the image of God from an ontological standpoint. Rather, the image of God results from evolution or are mental concepts.

Therefore, a neuroscientific understanding of the memory engram provides a plausible physical candidate for the image of God. This will be demonstrated through the use of optogenetics, a technique that uses light to switch genes on and off in rodents. By using this technique, Susumu Tonegawa and others were able to establish how engrams cells were created and how engram cells become "silent" or latent. Depending on the stimulus, these latent engrams can become activated. Thus, the memory engram can also serve as a physical site for theological action, as described in chapter 3. It also fits the theology of *eikon* and serves as an anchor of godly possession.

1

The Meaning of the Image of God

A Theological Overview

INTRODUCTION

> 26 Then God said, "Let us make humankind in our image, according to our likeness; and let them have dominion over the fish of the sea, and over the birds of the air, and over the cattle, and over all the wild animals of the earth, and over every creeping thing that creeps upon the earth."
> 27 So God created humankind in his image, in the image of God he created them; male and female he created them. (Gen 1:26–27 NRSV)

> 26 Then God said, "Let us make humanity in our image to resemble us so that they may take charge of the fish of the sea, the birds in the sky, the livestock, all the earth, and all the crawling things on earth."
> 27 God created humanity in God's own image, in the divine image God created them, male and female God created them. (Gen 1:26–27 CEB)

THE IMAGE OF GOD or the *imago Dei* might be one of the most challenging topics on which to write for any theologian. From a Christian standpoint, it lies at the intersection of a Trinitarian doctrine of God, an anthropology, and the subsequent existence as human beings in the world. In addition, 2 Cor 4:4 clearly states that Christ is the image of God, so one must also consider Christology, which also impinges on anthropology. To take topics even further, Col 1:15 claims that Christ is the "image of the invisible God, the first born of all creation," bringing in a doctrine of creation. So, too, are connected facets of soteriology since part of Christian anthropology involves a fallen creation and its redemption through Christ.

To write completely on all of these theological doctrines is not possible within the scope of this book, so the doctrine of God and doctrine of creation will be given precedence with connecting features of other theological doctrines when appropriate. This is for two reasons. First, the *imago Dei* is foremost about God. This is clear in Gen 1:26–27. Whatever the divine image might be, humankind was created "in" or "according to" that image. Thus, the flow of theological anthropology begins with God and runs through to humanity, not the other way around. The latter is a key distinction to make because of the risks and potentially damaging consequences of idolatry. Along those lines, however, the question of "likeness" must be addressed within the New Testament claim that Christ is the image of God but also with respect to the Hebrew Scriptures' understanding. While image suggests some form of resemblance, likeness suggests the degree to which the human image resembles the divine image. Historically, this has been a classic distinction, which is prefaced by a doctrine of God and a doctrine of creation.

The distinction between image and likeness is all the more readily apparent in modern theological anthropology because of the problematic association of the divine image as a human possession. As John Kilner's recent scholarship on the image of God points out, interpretive mistakes have harmfully played out to various people of color, to women, and to those with mental disabilities because they have been deemed as lacking the *imago Dei*.[1] It is unsurprising that scholars have thus deconstructed the traditional image of God to probe the depths of what the *imago Dei* means. This had led critical work to reappropriate and rehabilitate the traditional interpretations of the *imago Dei* to incorporate a greater sense of justice and responsibility. From a theological point of view, these new interpretations

---

1. Kilner, *Dignity and Destiny*, 49.

place the emphasis on likeness with the assumption that well-ordered likeness results in conformation to the divine image.

While this certainly is the case, and historically as well, an emphasis on likeness becomes an interpretive feature of the divine image; that is, moral rectitude is the result of being made according to the image, but is not the image itself. Of course, because of the fallen nature of humanity, no one is claiming that moral behavior constitutes the divine image. It is, after all, the purpose of distinguishing between image and likeness. If, however, one is to speak about the degree to which humanity reflects the *imago Dei*, then there must be a divine image from which one must start. Clearly the New Testament provides the language in Christ, but here, too, most modern theological analysis is not of Christ as image, but of Christ as moral exemplar and how closely one can mimic or "follow" Christ. Again, one is drawn to the behavioral consequences of what it means to be made according to the image of God.

Thus, the main purpose of this section is to counterbalance the emphasis on likeness with the weight of the divine image represented in the physical human body. One could fairly critique this move as being retrograde to outdated thinking on the image of God. It will, after all, traverse the border between divine attributes and human possession, one that has been painted over again and again with the dangers of divine similitude. This exercise, however, is not to deny those dangers, but to bring the body to the fore, which, despite the dualism of flesh and spirit endemic to traditional theological anthropology, was an important defining characteristic of the *imago Dei*, one that has been overbalanced by likeness rhetoric.

IMAGE OF GOD CLASSIFICATIONS AND INTERPRETATIONS

In this seesawing action of interpretations, the image of God scholarship has been categorized into several groups. For instance, Beth Felker-Jones introduces the image of God in three categories: 1) substantial, 2) functional, and 3) relational.[2] The substantial interpretation has some "physical" components, which, as have been mentioned, have been interpreted as human attributes. Rationality has typically been the focus of the image of God, but a more generic interpretation is anything that pertains to the human body. The functional view entails how the divine image may define

2. Felker Jones and Barbeau, *Image of God*, 13.

a human role, usually one of some representation, but also stewardship of creation. The relational view of the divine image takes on an ethical approach since it seeks to understand human relationships with others and with God. Felker-Jones advises that these categories can be reductionistic since scholars tend to blend some of these categories together as one flows into another. This makes the image of God more of a hybrid term in taking what is understood as "image" to ultimately what it means to be human. What the image *is*, however, remains a problem.

Although this book is not intended to be a complete textual analysis of the word "image," it will nevertheless examine the historical usage of the word and the ways that various scholars have situated it in its different contexts. To that end, some remarks will be made on the words *tselem* and *demuth* and their Hebraic usage, followed by remarks on the Greek translations of the Hebrew, *eikon* and *hoimosin*, respectively. As will be shown, the ancient Near East (ANE) context ranges from functional approaches to more substantive ones; by the time of the New Testament authors, however, the Greek meaning of "image" takes on a more cosmological role as it pertains to Christ, who *is* the *imago Dei*.

As any biblical scholar knows, the cultural currency of New Testament ideas cannot be retrojected into the authorial intent of Old Testament authors. They would not have had the concepts available while crafting their work. Of course, one could take the caveat that the writers of Hebrew Scriptures were divinely inspired so that they "knew" what was to transpire, but usually this interpretive approach is employed by scholars who must bridge the gap of time and space. They must take what has been revealed into claims of what is now foreshadowed. This means that while a Christian approach takes into account Paul's claim that Christ is the image of God, such a concept does not figure into the language and meaning of the image of God before its translation and usage during Hellenistic times.

In fact, the Jewish idea of God is mainly a mystery because to claim that God has one particular form is idolatrous. Therefore, the difficulty lies primarily in the lack of determinative characteristics "found" in God since the Bible does not land on any one particular characteristic. God has been described as being plural (Gen 1:26), as exhibiting emotion (jealousy [Exod 20:5]), as being spirit (John 4:24), and as being love (1 John 4:8). Moses was able to see the back of God but not God's face while in a cleft of rock, since God blocked Moses's sight with God's hand as God walked past (Exod 33:17–23), yet previously, Moses "spoke to God face to face as one speaks to a friend" (Exod 33:11). Jacob wrestled with a man who later revealed himself as God, so that Jacob said that I have seen God face-to-face but did not perish (Gen 32:30). Job argued with God, who spoke out of a whirlwind (Job 42). And of course, there is the specific prohibition to not cast idols. In the vein of apophatic theology, the "responsible" theologian would be wise to declare that God is not one thing.

Since theological anthropology "overlays" the divine image on top of the human being, the danger is to quantify a human attribute, for instance human reason, as composing the divine image, which then qualifies whether one does or does not have it. Kilner extensively details this interpretive failure, principally on the lack of close attention to Scripture. He blames the importing of "powerful cultural influences" rather than "biblically sound instruction."[3] In fact, Kilner argues that the image of God does not "refer to actual current likenesses to God,"[4] meaning *any* current human attribute cannot be considered as being the image of God. This includes human reason or mental capacities, which developed early in Christianity as the defining character for the divine image.[5] To a large extent, the influence of Greek cultural artifacts can be found in Clement of Alexandria, Origen, Athanasius, Cyril of Alexandria, Gregory of Nyssa, Augustine, and Aquinas, who, working in the dualistic context of anthropology, found the locus of divine image in the "highest" parts the human being, namely the "immaterial" soul. Their thinking on "intellectual capabilities" or "rationality" left its mark into modernity where reason (or the mind) became part and parcel of the image of God. Those without such rationality could be excluded from having the image of God and deemed "subhuman." For Kilner, a close look at Scripture does not suggest that the divine image refers to reason at all.[6] In fact, in line with Kilner's arguments against the "importing of cultural influences" mentioned above, Karl Barth makes an even harsher critique, arguing that "authors merely found the [image of God] concept in the text and then proceeded to pure invention in accordance with the requirements of contemporary anthropology."[7] Indeed, Vladimir Lossky cites the same passage to make the general argument that "certain Protestant

---

3. Kilner, *Dignity and Destiny*, 180–81.

4. Kilner, *Dignity and Destiny*, 119.

5. Kilner, *Dignity and Destiny*, 178–89.

6. Kilner, *Dignity and Destiny*, 182, referring to Gen 1:26–27; 5:1; 9:6.

7. Barth, *Doctrine of Creation*, 193.

theologians who like to exclude the 'theology of the image' from the essentials of Christianity"[8] do so based on what can be found in Scripture.

To Barth's point, scholars have noted the "rarity of the *imago Dei* language in the Tanakh, appearing exclusively in the book of Genesis and then exclusively in texts usually assigned to the so-called Priestly Source or Priestly Redaction (Gen. 1.26–27; 5.3; and 9.6)."[9] This paucity of textual references has caused scholars to speculate that theological anthropology concerning the image of God must not have been important for Jewish thinking. For instance, Lossky cites Anders Nygren, who thinks that the concept should have been frequently employed in describing the relationship between God and human beings. Instead, the "Old Testament is completely silent and did not appear until Greek language was making its way into Jewish religious literature."[10] For Nygren this suggests that it was Greek language that precipitated the image of God language, so along with Barth, Emil Brunner,[11] and Kilner, there is a decided tilt against Greek anthropological constructs as foreign to the Bible.

Other scholars have a more nuanced interpretation. For example, Chris Kugler acknowledges the few scriptural passages that use image of God language, but rather than assume the lack of evidence as indicative of unimportance, argues instead that Jewish Scriptures do not mention the *imago Dei* as part of anthropology because of a "forcefully expressed resolute and aniconic Jewish monotheism."[12] This makes sense considering the widely practiced Asherah-pole idol worship during preexilic times, but then why do the scriptural passages in Genesis mention the possibility of being created in God's image if there are prohibitions against it? Edward Curtis is also surprised by the Priestly authors' choice of words and speculates that because there is no "biblical understanding that would give content to the meaning of the Image of God beyond that which the context passages suggest . . . any further understanding of the Image of God must

---

8. Lossky, *In Image and Likeness*, 126. Lossky considers the image "in its two-fold acceptation—the image as the principle of God's self-manifestation and the image as the foundation of a particular relationship of human beings to God."

9. Kugler, *Paul and the Image*, 61. Note that these are the same three passages referred to by Kilner.

10. Lossky, *In Image and Likeness*, 127.

11. Lossky, *In Image and Likeness*, 126–27. Lossky quotes Emil Brunner as saying "the doctrine of the *Imago Dei*, if one equates the phrase with the truth for which it stands, does not play a very important part in the Bible."

12. Kugler, *Paul and the Image*, 62.

come from outside the biblical material."[13] Thus, the concerns of previous mentioned theologians seem warranted. How then does an "aniconic Jewish monotheism" translate to a "bold adaptation of Jewish Idol polemics"[14] involving the image of God?

Curtis and others may be correct in their assertions that understandings of the image of God have come from material outside of Scripture, but the aforementioned concerns primarily have to do with the image itself. As Curtis also notes, the ANE context of image is still relevant to understandings of the image of God because "the primary purpose of image was not to describe god, but to use qualities or attributes that would show the primary places where god manifests Godself."[15] A prominent example is the Egyptian opening of the mouth ceremony, where a statue is magically effected with a deity's presence (presumably through the mouth).[16] Stephen Wright takes the image argument further by saying that statues were "made of *gods*,"[17] which makes sense in light of Curtis's citation since a statue would then be an embodiment of a god. Yet, it was not only statues that held such power, but also people. Both Curtis and Wright agree that people believed that kings or rulers themselves were gods and that their domination over the lands they ruled was reflective of a nation's deity.[18]

It is within this context that Scripture was interpreted, providing the impetus for *analogia entis* long before Aquinas made it popular and before Barth offered his scathing critique. If indeed biblical people thought that people could be images of god, then some sort of substantive interpretation, that there is *something* of the divine image in human beings, is valid and is not simply some anachronism overlaid on top by interpretive mistakes made by future theologians. In fact, this seems to be the approach of Curtis and Wright who translate Gen 1:26–27 to say that human beings are made "as God's image" as opposed to "according to God's image" or "in God's image."[19] Thus, despite the biblical materials' reluctance to de-

---

13. Curtis, "Image of God (OT)," 3:390.

14. Kugler, *Paul and the Image*, 62.

15. Curtis, "Image of God (OT)," 3:390.

16. Curtis, "Image of God (OT)," 3:390. See also McLeod, *Image of God*, 45–46.

17. Wright, *Growing into God*, 32 (emphasis original).

18. Curtis, "Image of God (OT)," 3:390; Wright, *Growing into God*, 33.

19. Curtis, "Image of God (OT)," 3:389; Wright, *Growing into God*, 33. Curtis argues specifically against "according to" while Wright says that "as the image" is more precise than "in God's image."

fine exactly "what" God's image consists of, there was nevertheless some "thing" upon which humans were created as an image. In other words, how people thought about image per se figures into how people thought about the image of God.

Catherine McDowell expands upon this point in her interpretation of the image of God as she moves to her arguments for "kinship" with God. Significantly, McDowell notes that in rabbinic theology, God has some form and that the human body resembles it.[20] Evidence of this comes from an anthropomorphized God who exhibits human characteristics. Moses is able to see a "backside" as God "walks by" or that God has emotional characteristics. These are human elements used to describe God even though God is completely transcendent. In this light, the image of God language in Gen 5:3 denotes some "in kind" resemblance that is passed from father to son. Indeed, McDowell cites Theodor Nöldeke, as evidence for this physical representation since his analysis of *tselem* and the Arabic cognate *salama* ("to cut" or "to cut off") points to sculpture.[21] The allusion is even more tantalizing with reference to Gen 2:7, where Adam is created from the dust of the ground, as mentioned previously in Curtis and a point to be explained later below.

In any case, McDowell then interprets the "kind for kind" retribution in Gen 9:6 and connects it with "kin" language expressed in Gen 5:3.[22] Since human beings are created in God's image, all human beings are kin and to murder is akin to fratricide. In addition, kinship represents "sonship" as found in Gen 5:3, so together with various "kind for kind" language found in the creation story, "to be created in the Image of God is to be created as a 'son' of God the Father."[23] To be sure, McDowell is careful to assert that nowhere does the Bible claim that humanity is described as "God's son" or even "like God's son,"[24] but that the wealth of kinship imagery suggests a particular *relationship* between God and humanity, that of "sonship" as described in the relationship between Adam and Seth. This kinship argument is popular as a common denominator in pleas to human dignity and

---

20. McDowell, "In Image of God," 31–32.

21. McDowell, "In Image of God," 32. See also, McLeod, *Image of God*, 47. McLeod cites Porteous, who makes the same physicality argument.

22. McDowell, "In Image of God," 36–37. See also Kilner, *Dignity and Destiny*, 116–17n121.

23. McDowell, "In Image of God," 38–39.

24. McDowell, "In Image of God," 39–40.

perhaps is the impetus behind being called "children of God" (1 John 3:1) or being "adopted" sons and daughters (Eph 1:5). In this particular context, Jewish people are royal children ("sons") and are God's representatives and example for living God's intent for creation, even for God's eschatological redemptive purposes.[25]

Note, however, how McDowell makes the move from the substantive to a functional/relational hybrid. Even though there is some "thing" which gets passed from God to human beings, it is sonship or kinship that provides meaning to the image of God. This is consistent within the context of ANE image theology where royal representatives ruled or dominated territory and is supported by the scriptural mandate to have dominion over creation.[26] This is also how Diodore, John Chrysostom, and Theodoret of the Antiochene school interpreted the image of God "qua males." Even though these theologians came much later, Frederick G. McLeod points out the overall consistency that the Antiochene school exhibits with Semitic interpretation of Scripture as opposed to the allegorical and "spiritual" methods employed by the Alexandrian school.[27] Related here is the more "ecologically friendly, stewards of creation" motif as opposed to outright human rulership, which instead acknowledges God's sovereignty.[28] Either way, the representation of God's power on earth is a common functional theme.[29]

That power, however, is usually held by the social elite, namely the rulers,[30] so to claim that humankind is created *as* the image of God could be interpreted as a "bold adaptation of Jewish idol polemics"[31] and could also explain the relative lack of image of God language in the Tanakh. It was only after the Exile, when "idolatry was no longer a major problem," that positive descriptions of the image began to surface.[32] It was because of the Israelites' emergence from Babylonian captivity and the ANE's context

---

25. McDowell, "In Image of God," 43, 46.

26. Curtis, "Image of God (OT)," 3:391; Wright, *Growing into God*, 33; Kilner, *Dignity and Destiny*, 199–200; referring to Gen 1:28.

27. McLeod, *Image of God*, 44, 59, 61, 82.

28. Milford, "Substantive or Relational," 98, 101; Kilner, *Dignity and Destiny*, 200–201.

29. McLeod notes this theme in the Antiochene theologians Theodore and Nestorius but with more symbolism. McLeod, *Image of God*, 82.

30. Kilner, *Dignity and Destiny*, 121.

31. Kugler, *Paul and the Image*, 61.

32. Curtis "Image of God (OT)," 3:391; Kugler, *Paul and the Image*, 61.

of image that the idea of the image of God "universally"[33] applied to all of humanity, not only to rulers. Thus, the establishment of the Second Temple solidifies an anionic polemic *against foreign rule*, that theologically wrestles not so much with the substance of God's image, but with the locus of God's power in the created order.[34] Again, this is a functional outcome from a relatively universalized substantive position.

Yet, being royal representatives embodies a certain relationship with God's creation, other human beings included, and may be the most popular approach in "recent" times. Certainly, the beginnings of the relational approach can be traced back to the Reformation, Cappadocian fathers, and Augustine, depending on Christian traditions,[35] but as many scholars will attest, Karl Barth seems to be the foremost recent proponent.[36] As mentioned above, rather than an *analogia entis*, the meaning of the image of God is an *analogia relationis*,[37] and that has to do with a "Living God of Israel,"[38] who speaks to God's children. Indeed, Lossky makes the same assessment. Given the unbridgeable gap between God and creation, God nevertheless has "personal relationships, living intercourse with men, with a people; speaks to them and they reply . . . understanding that life is a dialogue between human beings and God."[39] To be sure, Barth's interpretation of the image of God hangs on that unbridgeable gap, that nothing can be known about God unless God reveals Godself through the Word, Jesus Christ. In the "let us" of Gen 1:26, there is a divine "I" and "Thou," which then mirrors the same relationship among human beings.[40] As a result, what is *imaged* in a human being is not anything of divine substance, but the relationship revealed from the "dialogue" within the Godhead. The

33. Wright, *Growing into God*, 33.

34. Curtis, "Image of God (OT)," 3:391; McLeod, *Image of God*, 47.

35. Kilner, *Dignity and Destiny*, 211.

36. Kilner, *Dignity and Destiny*, 211; Blomberg, "True Righteousness and Holiness," 70; McDowell, "In Image of God," 33; Welz, "*Imago Dei*," 80–81; Gonzalez, *Created in God's Image*, 64.

37. Barth, *Doctrine of Creation*, 143.

38. McLeod, *Image of God*, 47–48; citing John McKenzie who notes the personality of a God who "plans, desires, achieves, and responds personally to the words and deeds of men. In this 'living' quality man resembles Him."

39. Lossky, *In Image and Likeness*, 129.

40. Welz, "*Imago Dei*," 81; Barth, *Doctrine of Creation*. Note that for Barth, relationships were also ordered in the male and female.

image of God becomes one of divine encounter with a human counterpart just as God speaks to Godself.[41]

Brunner takes this adaptation of Martin Buber's I-Thou in a more concretely dialogical direction when he characterizes the *imago Dei* as "man being called into existence."[42] Whereas the *imago* emerges from the speech within the plurality of the Godhead for Barth, Brunner interprets the *imago* in the form or being addressed. Rather than the "unlikeness" in the analogy of relation for Barth;[43] that is, what can only be a facsimile of divine relationship imaged onto people, for Brunner, is the Word of God, which bridges that gap, making the conditions possible for human existence. In this respect, the transcendence of God is maintained and when Christ "calls" to humanity, it "answers."[44] Thus, Brunner's interpretation of the *imago Dei* emerges figuratively and cosmologically into a "responsible human existence from love, in love, and for love,"[45] through the linguistic property of divine speech.

William Dyrness notes this as a unique ANE creation story in which direct conversations take place between God and humanity but also notes another characteristic of God's plurality, that of self-reflexivity.[46] Citing Barth, Dyrness views the "concert of the mind and act and action in the divine being itself"[47] as being "imaged" onto the human being, allowing people to "transcend themselves and imagine a possible future."[48] To be sure, this appears to be a mental construct of some sort, but the focus is not on the mind from a substantive point of view. Rather, continuing in the vein of Barth and Brunner, self-reflexivity translates to the ability to transcend the self in the network of relationships people have with each other and with the rest of creation *for* some future. In fact, Dyrness goes on to layer the divine linguistic property onto the human, saying that "God wanted

---

41. Welz, "*Imago Dei*," 81.

42. Brunner, *Man in Revolt*, 97. Brunner comments that this call, in its "literal sense, only applies to man," which then gets transferred to the rest of creation. This perhaps means "scripturally," which then translates to a more functional interpretation of the *imago* rather than a hierarchical ordering between man and woman which one finds in Barth.

43. Hutabarat, "Exploring Karl Barth's View," 128.

44. Brunner, *Man in Revolt*, 97.

45. Brunner, *Man in Revolt*, 97–99; McDowell, "In Image of God," 33.

46. Dyrness, "Poised," 48–49; Welz, "*Imago Dei*," 81.

47. Barth, *Doctrine of Creation*, 192.

48. Dyrness, "Poised," 49.

to see what Adam would *call* the creatures, to make culture."[49] Daniela C. Augustine uses similar language when she draws upon the concept of *logoi*, that human "words" are added to the divine Word to complete creation.[50] In this way, human beings are creative artisans of the world, bringing new significance to the function of "dominion."

This artistic quality to the image of God has found popularity in the term "created co-creator" in some liberal strands of theology. "To be made in the Image of God means that human beings are a part of a creative process,"[51] in building their reality. Ted Peters views this as an evolutionary process, symbolized in a rescued Barthian *imago Dei* of a "unified interaction of the feminine and masculine."[52] Much like the Chinese yin and yang, there is a balance between order and disorder in the world to bring about creation in a fruitful, dynamic homeostasis. Process theology aligns well within this interpretation, for human beings themselves are a part of the evolutionary process given by God.[53] They are created in the sense that they are contingent beings within an "evolutionary matrix" but are free to make choices within nature herself. Thus, while Philip Hefner does not explicitly use Gen 1 (at least in *The Human Factor*), he refers to an "image which becomes genuinely theological because it is given its place in the process by God."[54] Interestingly, Hefner also considers technology a part of nature, since human influence has now created a techno-nature, which according to Hefner is the *only* nature humans now have.[55] Therefore, while human beings are created by God within the bounds of nature, they attempt to "cooperate" with God in the directing of evolution. This also fits within the broader category of natural theology in a "humanization of nature."[56]

Whether one considers created co-creator or dialogical interpretations valuable, however, finds an end point in moral claims about relationships. Kilner notes that rather than the possibility of relationships, scholars

49. Dyrness, "Poised," 52 (emphasis added).

50. D. Augustine, "Image, Spirit, and *Theosis*," 185–86. Augustine follows Lossky in her interpretation of the *imago*. Interestingly, Lossky passingly mentions Origen's *logikos* as defining of the "theology of image." See Lossky, *In Image and Likeness*, 126.

51. Peters, "Image of God," 121.

52. Peters, "Image of God," 121. Peters also goes as far as to say that God *is* evolution (113).

53. Hefner, *Human Factor*, 42–43.

54. Hefner, *Human Factor*, 36.

55. Hefner, *Human Factor*, 154.

56. Hefner, *Human Factor*, 154; Peters, "Image of God," 124.

favor actual embodied relationships.[57] This means that for all the damage that substantive interpretations have done, one is forced to acknowledge that *in* those relationships there is a physical dimension that one must be responsible toward. Indeed, one can say that human beings as "the embodiment of evolution at the cultural level, have the responsibility to sustain the work of the creative process at the physical-chemical and biological levels of existence."[58] This nod to the "natural image" is to accede to humanity's existential nature, and without having to go all the way to Paul Tillich's existential fall, one can make the theological claim that "something" in the image is represented in right relationships. After all, regardless of whether one ascribes to a substantive, relational, functional, or some hybrid, ethical human behavior is always the end point in choices made.[59]

Given the popularity of relational interpretations, however, caution should be exercised in defining such interpretations as the image of God. Certainly, Barth was correct in his critique of the "theology of image" since the categories previously described are only implied in the language of the image of God and not directly about it. His critique is also warranted since determining the image of God is primarily about God and not human beings, as Kilner repeatedly stresses in his critique.[60] Consequently, even good relationships with people and with creation suffer the same critique: the result of being created in the image is confused for the actual image. To be sure, being created in the image of God should engender right relationships, but to state that one "has" the image only when in right relationships is problematic. In reducing the image to relationships, being created in the image of God avers on whims of human behavior.[61] In fact, Brunner, a firm proponent of the relational interpretation, has said that the "protections of the image of God cease without true living,"[62] referring to mental stability. However, how one defines "true living" as reflective of Christian behavior might provide pause to whether or not one is or remains in the image of God. Woe to those who fail at right relationships![63]

57. Kilner, *Dignity and Destiny*, 213.

58. Peters, "Image of God," 121.

59. Related to the idea of self-reflexivity is the idea that human freedom is the image of God. While also a popular theory, this will not be directly addressed here.

60. Kilner, *Dignity and Destiny*, 150.

61. Kilner, *Dignity and Destiny*, 213, 219.

62. Brunner, *Christian Doctrine of Creation*, 57; Kilner, *Dignity and Destiny*, 20.

63. This book was being written at a time when Donald Trump incited an

Why has the relational interpretation gained so much traction in recent times? It certainly cannot be the fact that other interpretations are not scriptural, that is, passages that directly mention a particular interpretation in the language of the image of God. For as much criticism that the substantive interpretation has gotten, the functional and relational approaches are *also* ascriptural. For example, while McDowell points out the relationship between Adam and Seth in terms of likeness and image, the "general" message becomes one of kinship, which is implied rather than direct. Kilner makes the same observation, noting that the parent-child image ignores the particulars of the passage and applies it holistically to other passages where "sonship" is not in view.[64] In fact, the limited number of passages makes scriptural generalization difficult since each speaks of the image in different ways. Thus, for Kilner, the image of God refers to the lowest common denominator consistent with Scripture: a "special sense of connection"[65] between God and humanity. Since Scripture does little to describe what the image consists of, that is the substantive approach, the functional and relational approaches have taken prominence.

IMAGE VERSUS LIKENESS

In addition, the terms "image" and "likeness," and the preposition as well conjunctions between the two terms, have caused great debate among scholars. Even more, there is the translation of the Hebrew into Greek and then Latin and other languages. Since some detail of the prepositions have already been covered above, it is worth reiterating the "negative force of the Hebrew governed by the *be* and *ke*," which limits whatever similarities might exist between God and humanity.[66] It is consistent with an aniconic Jewish theology and the radical break between God and creation espoused by the Neoorthodox position found in Barth. Therefore, *because* Hebrew Scripture is ambiguous in defining the image of God, there is no choice but

---

"insurrection" on Capitol Hill during his lame-duck period following the 2020 presidential election. There have been many claims questioning his mental fitness. Should Trump not be considered to be created in the image of God?

64. Kilner, *Dignity and Destiny*, 221.

65. Kilner, *Dignity and Destiny*, xi, 41, 53–55, 57, 132, 138, 288, 330.

66. Lossky, *In Image and Likeness*, 128. For the terms *tselem* and *demuth*, respectively, Lossky also translates the Hebrew as "in our image, after our likeness." Brunner uses "in our image, in our likeness." See Brunner, *Man in Revolt*, 96. Barth uses "in" and "after." See Barth, *Doctrine of Creation*, 92.

to extract what is *imaged* (a verb rather than a noun). Lossky would describe this as the positive force of the Greek words "according to,"[67] which coordinates with the economic revelation of God (the only way God reveals Godself).[68] In fact, Greek language, per se, is a mode of revelation with what it can convey as opposed to the Hebrew.[69] Thus, there is the possibility that Greek ideas are not necessarily cultural contaminants but a part of God's revelation. To anticipate, the importance of Greek notions of image figure prominently in the intertextual period as well as in the New Testament.[70] Before getting there, however, there remains the issue of whether image and likeness should be considered a single or double concept.

As the terms separately suggest, image *and* likeness appear to be two different concepts. As Lossky notes, there can be a matter of degree in its usage. "After our likeness" is a softening of "in our image,"[71] consistent with an apophatic direction. Bruce Vawter agrees in that "*tselem* seems like an exact reproduction whereas *demuth* denotes a resemblance."[72] Since human beings cannot be exact copies of God, the second in sequence, *demuth*, seems to be a qualifier. Similarly, Walter Vogel's interpretation aligns the "harder" attribute of power which human beings share with God in *tselem* as opposed to the "softer" role human beings play as procreators. Coupled with the eventual Latin rendition of *imago* and *similitudo* for "image" and "likeness," one can see its popular usage to theologically denote something that remains in the image of God and something that is lost in the fall. Irenaeus is often credited with making this distinction, and as Brunner notes, this was "a simple and brilliant solution to the central question of Christian anthropology."[73]

---

67. Lossky, *In Image and Likeness*, 128.

68. Lossky, *In Image and Likeness*, 15.

69. Lossky, *In Image and Likeness*, 128.

70. Strangely, Kilner considers a pre-Genesis understanding of the word "image" as "providential" but then argues that Greek cultural influence was detrimental to the meaning of image. Kilner, *Dignity and Destiny*, 119.

71. Lossky, *In Image and Likeness*, 128.

72. Vawter, "Genesis 1:1—11:26," 175; see also McLeod, *Image of God*, 44–45.

73. Brunner, *Man in Revolt*, 93. Here, the question is how human beings could simultaneously have been created with some original intent, justice or otherwise, and with the fall, have a sinful nature. For Irenaeus, rationality and freedom remain "godly" images, but the ability to be righteous had been lost.

That all said, Brunner himself cast aside the dual notion of the image in favor of a single concept that applies to the entirety or "man."[74] It is this application to the whole person that is the most consistently applied by scholars who favor the single concept of the image. For instance, even though Vawter above argued for a difference in the words *tselem* and *demuth*, the application nonetheless applies to "the person itself, not merely nature; that the image and likeness of God is conceptually existential not essential."[75] Barth notes the difference in "representation and imitation," respectively.[76] Furthermore, Kilner cites a wealth of scholarship refuting the apparent differences in words, showing the fluidity in the Greek translations for the image and likeness themselves as well as the prepositions used.[77] For example, while in Gen 1:26 *tselem* is translated into *eikon* (the favored translation), *eikon* becomes the translation for *demuth* in Gen 5:1. This show of "synonymous parallelism" occurs frequently in biblical Hebrew and in the wider context of the ANE in other countries.[78] As a result, the words "image" and "likeness" are interchangeable because they mean or apply to the same single image-likeness concept.

If indeed, however, "either term is sufficient to refer to humanity's status bestowed through creation by God,"[79] then why are two terms used? While this could simply be an issue of randomness, that words were just picked to express some concept, this hardly seems to be case when translating. In contrast to a spontaneously written piece of writing, translating requires a previous concept and a deliberate choice to convey the meaning of the words as they move across from one language to another. It may have been true that there were synonymous parallelisms in Hebrew language, but that could easily have been lost in the conceptual differences in the translators' choice of words. To be fair, there is an amount of similarity, but the choice to use *eikon* for *demuth* could be deliberate and influenced by Greek concepts already in use during the translation of Hebrew into the Septuagint. If Israelites were aware of what image meant in the ANE during the crafting of Genesis, then surely the Jewish diaspora was aware

74. Brunner, *Man in Revolt*, 96. Brunner describes the image as being a "parable."

75. Vawter, "Genesis 1:1—11:26," 175.

76. Barth, *Doctrine of Creation*, 195. Barth makes reference to plastic or painted representation for *tselem*, whereas *demuth* means copy or duplicate.

77. Kilner, *Dignity and Destiny*, 124–25. See 89–91 for preposition analysis.

78. Kilner, *Dignity and Destiny*, 124; see also McLeod, *Image of God*, 44.

79. Kilner, *Dignity and Destiny*, 124.

of their Hellenistic culture. So, could it be possible that a translator used *eikon* specifically for *demuth* in Gen 5:1 to convey what was thought to be an allusion to God's image in Gen 1:26? After all, in Gen 5:3, where both *tselem* and *demuth* return, *eikon* once again assumes *tselem* while *demuth* takes on "idea" not likeness.

Part of this debate is a matter of hermeneutics, of authorial intent in what the writers of Genesis meant by image and likeness. Originality, however, is not as much the issue as is trying to show the consistency of the meaning of the image-likeness concept through time. For example, Kilner cites 1 Cor 11:7 and Jas 3:9 in their use of the terms "image" and "likeness," respectively. His intention is to show that when referring to creation, either term suffices for the image-likeness concept as he does with the Hebrew *tselem* and *demuth*.[80] Yet, this assumes that the concept of image has not changed between the writers of Genesis and the New Testament. As will be explained shortly, this is simply not the case. Kilner himself even references the possibility that "Jewish intertestament speculation may have changed the meaning of 'image and likeness' to depart from the teachings in Genesis."[81] And if he is aware of the possibility of nuances in Greek prepositions, then it would not be a stretch to consider that "image" and "likeness" meant different things by the time of the New Testament, not to mention a difference in diction between Paul and James.[82]

The other part to the debate of the image-likeness concept is the *necessary* collapse of the image-likeness concept entirely into its likeness "part." As has been mentioned before, if there is such a radical break between God and creation, then little if anything can concretely be said about God *as it pertains to image*. For Greek thinkers like Lossky, this is a matter of common substance shared among the Trinitarian hypostases that counts toward "image."[83] Obviously, human beings do not share in the same "substance" as the Trinity, and so do not share in the same "image." Given such an orthodoxy, knowledge of God is limited and follows *via negativa*, which can only

---

80. Kilner, *Dignity and Destiny*, 124.

81. Kilner, *Dignity and Destiny*, 126.

82. Interestingly, James refers to "likeness" as something that people curse. This perhaps could suggest that there is a difference between "image" and "likeness" because of the weaker term of the latter. Human beings can curse a likeness of God, but not the *imago Dei*, Godself.

83. Lossky, *In Image and Likeness*, 92. Lossky quotes Cyril of Alexandria: "The Son is the image of the Father and the Holy Spirit is the image of the Son."

approach God to some intelligible fashion of what "God is not,"[84] that is, the *imago Dei* properly *is* and belongs to God. Placed within the context of theological anthropology, the divine image cannot be a human possession, which then places the weight of interpreting the *imago Dei* completely on "likeness." To be sure, the above orthodoxy is already interpreted in light of the New Testament and early Christian theology, but in contrast to Kilner's attempt at showing what "image and likeness" meant in Hebrew Scriptures by drawing on New Testament examples, this argument traces a theological abstraction on the nature of God which has been largely resilient through time: the unknowability of God.

In fact, this theological abstraction foreshadows the arrival of New Testament teachings where the image of God is made clear. In contrast to the ambiguous nature of interpretation found in Hebrew Scripture, Paul states: "In their case the god of this world has blinded the mind of the un-believers, to keep them from seeing the light of the gospel of the glory of Christ, *who is* the Image of God" (2 Cor 4:4). Coupled with deutero-Pauline Col 1:15—which states: "He is the image of the invisible God, the firstborn of all creation"—Jesus Christ is the clear person to whom the image of God applies. As Kilner notes, while human beings are created "according to" or "in" the image of God, Christ simply *is* that image.[85] This is a pivotal theological move from the Christian standpoint as Christ becomes involved in both the creation and the destiny of human beings and the importance of declaring Christ as the image of God cannot be underestimated. An actual image exists upon which specific claims can be made.

It is here that most scholars hang their hats for interpreting the image of God and what that *means* for human beings. The arguments over Hebrew semantics become reinterpreted in light of what is christologically revealed in the New Testament. Some scholars interpret the image of God with the benefit of centuries of theological debate over the nature of Christ. While importing those theological views onto what the biblical authors thought might be an overstep, the nature of image language can still be consistent. Christ can only be the image of God if Christ is consubstantial with the Father. In fact, scholars have noted the Greek word *charakter* (rather than *eikon*), which means perfect image or imprint, appears only once in the New Testament to significantly characterize Christ as the image of God

---

84. Lossky, *In Image and Likeness*, 19–21.

85. Kilner, *Dignity and Destiny*, 88.

(Heb 1:3).[86] Similarly, Craig Blomberg, along with Kilner, observes that Christ's very being (hypostasis) is what constitutes this stamp or imprint of God.[87] Taken together, Christ becomes the singular, *visible* image of God, and where certainly God had interacted with humanity through dialogue, in Christ, there is a *person* to which people can *see*, interact, and relate.

Thus, the stage is set for the crucial dialectic which results in human beings' conformity to the image of God. If people were "merely" created "according to" the image of God, then Christ is the standard which people are created *in*, *by*, and *through* so that human beings can reflect the image of God *for* Christ (Col 1:15–20; Heb 1:3; 2 Cor 4:3–6).[88] In the single-concept of the image of God, "Christ both is and illustrates human destiny,"[89] that is, he exhibits the connection between God and humanity while also enabling human destiny. This means that Christ as template, model, prototype, paradigm, norm, or ideal for humanity includes all the previously discussed human attributes typically associated with the divine image (reason, rulership, righteousness, relationships).[90] Only in Christ, who reflects God's intentions for humanity, can those attributes be faithfully employed for God's intended purposes for humanity.[91] Being created according to the image of God thus means an intended likeness, only fully seen in Christ, to which humanity is to be conformed, a goal to be attained, but not yet.

IMAGE OF GOD AND GLORY

Therefore, conformation to the image of God is of a transformation process that figuratively turns human beings into "mirrors" who can reflect God. Christina Bieber Lake notices this in Hans Urs von Balthasar where "as a totality of spirit and body, man must make himself into God's mirror and

---

86. Kilner, *Dignity and Destiny*, 66–67. Kilner contrasts with likeness-image versus imprint-image. Both are single-concepts, but whereas likeness-image shows similarity, imprint-image refers to identicalness. See Kilner, *Dignity and Destiny*, 59; Wright, *Growing into God*, 38.

87. Blomberg, "True Righteousness and Holiness," 76. Blomberg also notes a synonymous parallelism with "likeness" and "morphe" to mean an exact nature. Similarly, Lossky sticks with the patristic arguments of Christ's consubstantial nature in the hypostasis as defining what be an image. See Lossky, *In Image and Likeness*, 136.

88. Wright, *Growing into God*, 37; Kilner, *Dignity and Destiny*, 53, 75.

89. Kilner, *Dignity and Destiny*, 73; see also 78.

90. Kilner, *Dignity and Destiny*, 72–80.

91. Kilner, *Dignity and Destiny*, 119, 277.

seek to attain to that transcendence and radiance that must be found in the world's substance if it is indeed God's image and likeness."[92] For Bieber, this mirror language suggests that human beings continually have a "form, picture, or image in some way of God" capable of reflecting God's radiance.[93] While Kilner might not exactly agree about the constitution of the image, he shares Lake's assessment in how biblical writers employ the term "glory" to denote the "radiance" apparent in one's appearance.[94] Drawing upon Paul in 2 Cor 3:18–4:6, Kilner observes that one must first see Christ, the image of God, as in a mirror to begin the transformation that allows human beings to also reflect God. In so doing, people become "mirrors," or "likenesses of God," allowing human beings to reflect the image of God *to each other* in "tri-directional direction," so that everyone can *see* God's face.[95]

Importantly, the visual language used above becomes a measure of the image. One can see glory. This is not to say that glory is necessarily equivalent to the image. In fact, Kilner warns against this association, that, while connected in some respects, distinctions remain.[96] Glory does not seem to be one particular "thing" since it can characterize both what one can see as well as "functional" attributes like power or dominion. In translating the Hebrew word *kabod*, a sense of weightiness or importance is conveyed which can evoke a sense of awe or praise. In this respect, the Greek translation *doxa* applies quite well, in that what is revealed is praiseworthy. In these circumstances, however, one cannot escape the visual nature of the word "glory," so that in the generic sense of "image," glory refers to some kind of appearance. Paul mentions this in the celestial bodies having different glories and in Christian transformation, one is changed from one glory into another (1 Cor 15:41; 2 Cor 3:18). Within the framework of theological anthropology, glory changes, and for Kilner, it is the damaging effects of sin which then hinders human abilities to the reflect God's image. The problem is not with a damaged image, but with glory, which is indicative of

92. Bieber Lake, "Carrying the Fire," 142; referring to Balthasar, *Seeing the Form*, 21–22. .

93. Bieber Lake, "Carrying the Fire," 145.

94. Kilner, *Dignity and Destiny*, 247–48; Wright, *Growing into God*, 41.

95. McFarland, "Icons and Identity"; Bieber Lake, "Carrying the Fire" 175, 188. This is probably an allusion to Moses seeing God face-to-face and Paul's commentary on it. An important note missing from this discussion is that it is the work of the Holy Spirit that allows recognition of the image. For instance, Clement of Alexandria says that it is God's grace that allows one to see God face-to-face. See Lossky, *In Image and Likeness*, 22.

96. Kilner, *Dignity and Destiny*, 63–65, 156.

human "manifestations of God's attributes."[97] What one "sees" measures the image, however undefined it might be.

Other scholars make a stronger connection between image and glory.[98] Although a part of the Qumran community and within a dualistic anthropology, Kugler cites the work of Crispin Fletcher-Louis and George Van Kooten who think that the "glory of Adam" in the Qumranic text represents an embodiment of the glory of the Lord or its visual splendor as found in Ezek. 1:28.[99] This aligns with the "image" of God in Gen 1:26. Here, Kugler takes a more moderate position, much like what Kilner says about image, in that the "glory of Adam" means the intended glory God meant Adam to have, since Qumran anthropology was also an eschatological one where Adam refers to the Qumran community.[100] Later, Kugler makes a tighter association of "image" and "glory," citing rabbinic exegetical tradition in which Moses has "access to God via a mirror,"[101] that is, Moses actually sees an image of God. The same rabbinic commentary also mentions Isa 40:5 where the glory of Lord shall be visible to everyone. Taken together, there is a functional equivalence of image and glory.[102] Along this line of interpretation, Kugler then argues that Paul reappropriated glory/image language to assert that Moses saw Christ, which applied to "everyone," comes to a head in "beholding the glory of the Lord" (NRSV uses "reflecting") in a mirror as one is transformed in that same "image," one glory into another (2 Cor 3:12–18).[103]

It is worth pausing here again to note how the discussion so far has only reinforced the popular notion of relationships as the image of God. Part of this has to do with the inescapable fact of human plurality and the need to communicate in order to get anything done. Actual relationships

97. Kilner, *Dignity and Destiny*, 65; see also 142, 145, 277. Kilner consistently says that the image of God is not damaged. See Kilner, *Dignity and Destiny*, 160–76, for arguments to the contrary throughout Christian interpretation.

98. See also Kilner, *Dignity and Destiny*, 63, where he mentions authors who think image and glory are synonymous.

99. Kugler, *Paul and the Image*, 75. The passage in Ezekiel references the fiery appearance of God in God's "chariot" where God displays a "rainbow" brilliance in the "appearance of the likeness of the glory of the Lord."

100. Kugler, *Paul and the Image*, 78. The idea here extends to the two creation stories, where the Adam in Gen 1 is "spiritual" whereas the Adam in Gen 2 is "fleshy."

101. Kugler, *Paul and the Image*, 134.

102. Kugler, *Paul and the Image*, 134; citing David Litwa.

103. Kugler, *Paul and the Image*, 133, 136.

do matter in the moral sphere, and the quality of relationships is a valued attribute in the social fabric of society. However, another part particular to this book is the visual nature of morality as described above. If indeed "glory" is how well one shows godly attributes, then how one behaves shows how well one is like or unlike God. In fact, Kilner's preferred terminology to the divine image is likeness-image[104] as opposed to image-likeness, or even likeness-glory, the latter of which might have been better for his arguments. With likeness factoring so prominently with reference to Christ, *the image of God*, one's ability to conform cannot escape the necessity of good relationships imbedded in human existence. Thus, likeness-image, even though Kilner denies that the image of God is anything a human being *has*, becomes a measure of that image as it translates to a morality that can be seen in the actions, or nonactions, of people. If "God predestined human beings to be conformed to the image of Son" (Rom 8:29), then it means that Christ is the ultimate exemplar in being and behavior.[105]

IMAGE OF GOD AND BODY

To be sure, most of the single concept approach can be attributed to a wholistic anthropology typical of Semitic interpretations, as mentioned above in the word analysis of *tselem* and *demuth*, but the wholistic anthropology also extends to perceived dualities like what one finds in Paul's writings about the body. For instance, Susan Eastman, while acknowledging that there are dualisms in the ancient world (i.e., "flesh" and "Spirit"), follows Dale Martin's assessment that "retrojecting all Cartesian oppositions onto ancient language is misleading."[106] For her purposes, Paul's "body" does not necessarily refer to human beings but to higher-order realities that hold sway over the person.[107] What results is more of a functional dualism (according to the flesh, according to the Spirit) rather than an ontological one, much like how *tselem* and *demuth* provide a function for the divine image. This functional nature of Paul's "dualism" can be seen in Paul's rhetorical arguments in Rom 7–8. Eastman notes that Paul's "I" in Rom 7:15 is not

---

104. Kilner, *Dignity and Destiny*, 48, 59, 69.

105. Kilner, *Dignity and Destiny*, 52–53.

106. Eastman, *Paul and the Person*, 92; D. Martin, *Corinthian Body*, 1–14. Eastman notes that in Paul there definitely is a dualism between "flesh and Spirit."

107. Eastman, *Paul and the Person*, 87–88.

exactly singular since the agency ascribed to it is the "flesh."[108] Rather, the rhetorical feature employed asks Paul's audience to identify with the "I," who is a "bound" by the everyday power of the "flesh." In identifying with the "I," the hearer shares ("we know" in 7:14) a "felt experience" to this bondage which seeks its resolution in the Spirit of Christ in Rom 8. No ontological dualism is at work here, but rather a "hierarchy of essences" that drive the body.[109]

So why this little detour on the body? Based on the discussion thus far, it seems that while relationality is certainly important in the way the image of God functions, it seems to make the human body accidental in nature. The body is just a sheer existential fact rather than an integral part of created order, which has some implications for the image of God. Of course, no one denies the body in the traditional Platonic way, and no one would deny the importance of the body as it pertains to the individual. However, the language embedded in relational interpretations is "exocentric."[110] The "I" is dependent on the "you." The individual is dependent or defined by the community. As the postmodern might say, "Individuality presupposes relationality."[111] As such, the body, while not synonymous for the person, becomes merely technical in those relationships. The image of God becomes technical language, and the meaning must be pulled out from its use, which is not based explicitly in biblical text.

To be fair, and as previously described, the substantive position fares no better with the ever-present risk of claiming a human attribute solely as the image and what can only be implied from godly character. This tension between the substantive and relational positions and the circles one must travel has caused some scholars to question whether either position is viable. Stephen Milford, for example, claims that in trying to explain the "what" of the image of God, both sides use the same approach wrapped up in different theological garb, leaving a "counterfeit choice" if picking a side.[112] Even many of the hybrid approaches, some discussed above, tend to favor or collapse to one side or the other. In Milford's estimation, a "nonfoundational," "postliberal" hermeneutic needs to be employed so as to

---

108. Eastman, *Paul and the Person*, 112.

109. Eastman, *Paul and the Person*, 92. Eastman again quotes Dale Martin here.

110. Pannenberg, *Anthropology in Theological Perspective*, 62.

111. Eastman, *Paul and the Person*, 16. Eastman quotes from Timothy Chappell, *Knowledge of Persons*, 3–4.

112. Milford, "Substantive or Relational," 86–87, 101–2.

take into consideration the "primary theology" that occurs within communities, based on its own assessment of "wholeness."[113] Only then can theologians proceed to "secondary theology," and as they "critically reflect on this primary theological experience of wholeness, it produces a range of descriptive doctrines."[114] The result is a pluriform *imago Dei* that accounts for various interpretations of "divine communities" that reflect the social Trinity. Viability of a particular interpretation is not at issue. Rather, its validity is expressed as communities wrestle with their own interpretations of the image of God.

Milford's hermeneutic has some appeal in the scholastic sense since validity, rather than viability, is being critiqued. How a community does its interpretation is being analyzed instead of the concept itself. Communities do not operate within a vacuum, though, so to say that a substantive or relational interpretation "works" for a community still invites one to consider the concepts being used. Furthermore, the work of primary theology does not necessarily adjudicate moral principles. That occurs more often in secondary theology. To bring this to a contemporary example, Jesus as the image of God has been shown to be race specific. Some have argued the harmfulness of a "White" Jesus because it promotes White values. This shows a bent toward a substantive interpretation which harms, rather than, perhaps, a relational approach, which, regardless of race, shows how people should act toward one another.

Given all the various interpretations of the image of God, in all its forms, and the momentum of religious ethics in the direction of human relationships, where does one move toward in assessing the image of God? The importance of relationships has been amply demonstrated, especially when contrasted with the divine image a person "owns" that, when determined to be missing in other people, gives people a reason to harm them. As discussed, however, this can be turned on its head by making the argument that relationships themselves become a human attribute. Furthermore, such a relational interpretation functionally implies that the image is only active when good relationships are enacted. Relationships, and therefore the image of God, become a "privilege of believers"[115] that must rely on "destiny" to bring to fruition God's intentions at creation. This teleological drive seems to have its foundation in Christ being the end point for

---

113. Milford, "Substantive or Relational," 107–8.

114. Milford, "Substantive or Relational," 111.

115. Milford, "Substantive or Relational," 94.

humanity, made more real because of the incarnation. But with Christ's death and resurrection where does that end point lie except with continued human development, one that will always be tainted by original sin? And while theologically one can say that all good action only comes from the grace of God, it is human striving for good moral outcomes that ends the day. In this case, Christ becomes moral exemplar and human evolution is based on the degree to which one is able to or not conform in *using* the image.[116]

Perhaps the last sentence was a bit too technical since, in effect, Christ as image must be used in some way (more on that much later). However, the open-endedness of destiny, especially if one never attains the image of God until "after Christ returns, the dead are resurrected, and sin is gone,"[117] seems to overemphasize the eschaton and overstates human ability to conform to Christ. In this forward-looking trajectory of humanity, the importance of the body is lost since relationships exist outside the body, even if it does so between two bodies in the relational I-You. One's "relationship with Christ," however that may be defined, thus exists outside oneself as well, at least in the relational setup where moral behavior accounts for one's conformity to the image. It would not be too far a stretch to say that Christ's example is in effect lifted out of his body, just as relationships are lifted out of the text, and eaten whole while tasting of Pelagius. Admittedly, the previous statement is a bit tongue in cheek, but it is intended to highlight the power of original sin and not as much to detract from Christ as moral exemplar. To speak of destiny is to acknowledge an end point, but does its open-endedness of *humanity* seem too long of a time and too distant a future to be meaningful as far as how the image of God might operate?

Matthew Petrusek asks a similar question, assessing whether the image of God is practical in guiding moral behavior. For Petrusek, the image of God must be "morally vulnerable, that it can be harmed by human action."[118] Why? In order for something to be practical, it must have an "ought" that goes beyond a descriptive claim. If the image of God cannot be harmed, then one is "incapable of coherently providing the grounds for

---

116. For instance, Helmet Thielicke is quoted as saying "the imago is . . . not a residual condition, a property in the sense of a habitus, but something which actively happens in the moment. It has the quality of an event [and] must be constantly realized afresh." See Petrusek, "Image of God," 61, 72; citing Thielicke, *Theological Ethics*, 163.

117. Kilner, *Dignity and Destiny*, 273.

118. Petrusek, "Image of God," 65. There are both personal and interpersonal vulnerabilities that are necessary.

determining which actions compromise the integrity of the imago, and thus ought to be avoided, and which actions protect the imago, and thus ought to be performed."[119] Petrusek analyzes Helmut Thielicke's interpretation of the image of God, or "alien dignity," as a test case. He concludes that since human action cannot affect dignity, the image of God cannot not provide a moral obligation by itself. Even with the prospect of divine command, the practicality of the image fails because it is the command—not the description of the image itself—which provides guidance. Consequently, moral guidance must be sought *outside* the image of God, in relationality, or some other moral imperative.[120] In contrast, the Catholic interpretation maintains the divine relationality of the image of God in humans but uses various language to indicate that the image has been "damaged" in some way, following Church tradition. As a result, there is practical application for "given that human beings are made in the image and likeness of God, humans ought to perform any action that respects that image in the form of providing protection from, or removing, any obstacle that frustrates its realization in oneself or others."[121]

To be sure, Petrusek's analysis is only one particular interpretation of the image of God, but as has been the case for most of the relational proponents discussed so far, the image of God is something that cannot be lost nor be affected in any way. Kilner moves the locus of vulnerability to glory while emphatically denying that sin can damage the image.[122] Barth locates the divine image in the plurality of God from which an I-Thou relationship is analogously spoken, but because of the radical break from creation, the image, as proper to God, cannot be affected in any way. In addition, as Claudia Welz observes, "Before human beings can say anything, God has already addressed them and called them to live a life in dialogue with him and with each other, questioning whether human beings can contribute anything to the formation of God's image."[123] Brunner insists that that human responsibility to God cannot be lost despite sin. In the same vein, other scholars point to some relational or functional aspect that exists

119. Petrusek, "Image of God," 65.

120. Petrusek, "Image of God," 77.

121. Petrusek, "Image of God," 80.

122. Kilner, *Dignity and Destiny*, 65, 113, 135–36. To be fair to Kilner, he does argue against good relationships as composing the image of God since it would then make the image a human attribute.

123. Welz, "*Imago Dei*," 83. This is also in line with Petrusek's argument.

outside the image. In the end, people can be damaged, but not the image, which is some sort of connection to God.

To be sure, God is ever present to God's creation, and in this respect the connection can never be broken or lost. (Nothing separates us from the love of God.) But simply to state that the likeness-image is a connection to God explains very little, especially the semantic reduction of image/likeness into a single concept means that, in some way, whatever is meant by "image" is touched by "likeness" or "glory." The divine image may be proper to God, but its representation in human beings is distorted, effaced, worn away, as glory is "conducted" back to likeness/image. But, for a moment, let us assume that relationships represent the *imago Dei* and the relationship with God. With the track record of humanity's attempts at good relationships with each other and the rest of creation, is not the relationship between God and humanity broken in some way, just as the Hebrew Scriptures depict from time to time? Is not sin's effect on people a root cause for failed relationships in humanity's attempt at conforming completely to Christ in the New Testament? Is this not what the bulk of Western Christianity has attempted to put into words when they speak of the image of God as being erased, effaced, and worn?

TOWARD A PHYSICAL INTERPRETATION OF THE IMAGE OF GOD

Indeed, the problem with a single-concept likeness-image is that a confused picture of image, likeness, and glory results that still relies on some pseudo-duality in order to make semantic sense of image/likeness. For what reason would the Priestly writers use two words that seemingly mean two concepts? Why not use just one unless there is some dual aspect to image and likeness? Case in point, Brunner had to "divide" the image of God into "formal" and "material" instances. The "formal" described a human responsibility that could not be lost while the "material" described the lost ability to carry out loving relationships. Yet, this distinction only exists from the viewpoint of humanity, not God, and, so, only "wrongly exists."[124] Whatever may be the case, this division is very similar to the distinction Irenaeus made, which is all the more ironic since Brunner attempts a wholistic anthropology after denying *imago* and *similitude*. Similarly, Thielicke had to divide the *imago* into a negative and positive aspect, neither of which

---

124. Brunner, *Christian Doctrine of Creation*, 61.

were actually "ontic," to describe humanity's sinful existence.[125] And while Thielicke's "alien dignity" subsists within the Lutheran tradition of the complete loss of the image, the constant struggle with the dual nature of image and likeness is clearly present. This begs a number of questions.

First, is the single-concept approach the better alternative to a dual-concept approach if one needs to resort to some pseudo-duality? It would seem that returning to a dual-concept would be the simpler thing to do. Arguments have already been assessed as to the "biblical" nature of a dual-concept, but these can largely be addressed by Greek influences as part of God's revelation, per Lossky, especially by the time of Paul. Concepts can change with time. So while Paul certainly drew on his Jewish heritage for his concept of image-likeness, it is entirely plausible that *eikon* meant something specifically Greek in meaning. Scholars note, however, the dualism that is apart from Christian anthropology. To refer to image *and* likeness only encourages dualism. This, however, seems to play on a Cartesian anthropology rather than a "dualism" (duality?) that related the inner being to the outer.

Second, if the locus of the image of God lies outside the human, either with God or in relationships, is it "unreal" in the sense that it has no material reference? God is largely "invisible" in Hebrew Scriptures, and while Christ is the image of God, Christ is no longer physically present. Relationships exist *between* people. All these suggest an air of uncertainty, perhaps too much so. After all, does not the prospect of "which" Jesus one follows, or any number of policy decisions based on what Jesus tells you to do, present multiple images? If Christ is the standard to which people are to conform, it is problematic if there are multiple images. It would make sense, then, if there is some material representation to which Christ acts as an anchor. Indeed, it is only after Christ is anchor—yes, in the Christian symbolic sense even[126]—that Christ is also human destiny. Christ as anchor is necessary *before* good relationships can be forged. For this reason, one must take a step back and reconsider the "substance" of the image, which brings us to the third question.

Why does it seem that the body is underappreciated when it comes to the *imago Dei*? One answer might be the aforementioned dualism and the

---

125. Petrusek, "Image of God," 71.

126. Early Christian art during the persecution used the fish but also the anchor to represent Christian identity. Consider Heb 6:19–20: "We have this hope, a sure and steadfast anchor of the soul, a hope that enters the inner shrine behind the curtain, where Jesus, a forerunner on our behalf, has entered, having become a high priest forever according to the order of Melchizedek."

propensity to locate the *imago Dei* in reason or the soul. Michelle Gonzalez observes that historically *imago Dei* has been in the male domain, setting a contrast with the female body.[127] In addition, the move toward transcending the body through thought and culture has been, again, assigned to males rather than females.[128] What cannot be underappreciated here is that the *experience* of God, of Christ, which must happen through the body; if human beings are created for grace, then the possibility must exist within human nature.[129] This seems such a simple concept that perhaps it is taken for granted. With respect to the *imago Dei*, one must *feel* it after looking at the image and "see" before reflecting it.

The importance of the body leads to one of the central features of this book. Contra most scholars examined here, the image of God is located within the human body. This argument is not entirely new, since it can be traced to patristics, but the *imago*'s substantive form is anchored in the body. This will eventually make its way into the mind via memory, but, for now, the image refers to the body. Note that this is a stronger statement than the either "human" or "humanity," and while the image certainly applies to humanity in the collective, the personable expression of the image is being brought to the fore here. That must include an attempt at explaining why the body is important for the image, even if it runs the risk of "damaging" the image. Since many scholars point to Irenaeus as the first to create a theology of image,[130] retracing some of his concepts will be useful as a starting point and provide a basis from which to reclaim the importance of the body for this book.[131]

IRENAEUS AND THE IMAGE OF GOD

Some scholars note that Irenaeus uses the words "image" and "likeness" as synonyms.[132] While this may have been true, Irenaeus makes distinctions between the two, especially when arguing against the gnostics. For Irenaeus, the primary meaning of "image" was to "express the fact that a

127. Gonzalez, *Created in God's Image*, 121–24.

128. Gonzalez, *Created in God's Image*, 121; quoting Mary Ann Zimmer.

129. Gonzalez, *Created in God's Image*, 71; referencing Karl Rahner's transcendental anthropology.

130. McLeod, *Image of God*, 53, 58; Kilner, *Dignity and Destiny*, 196.

131. While true that Irenaeus's ideas came much after Paul, as will be shown, the ideas remain consistent with Paul's ideas about "form" and "shape."

132. McLeod, *Image of God*, 53; citing Jules Gross.

subject possesses the features of another being, which supposes form and substance."[133] This is important in two regards. First, by form, Irenaeus means that some "constitutive element" exists in the image.[134] As Jacques Fantino explains, Irenaeus's arguments against the gnostics prompts him to define the image as supposing form because only a material being can be an image.[135] The spiritual being, which one cannot see, has no form and thus cannot be an image. Thus, there is some "measurable" continuity between image and exemplar. The exact nature of this element is unclear. Irenaeus has no great love for Plato, and he is not promoting some sort of Aristotelean hylomorphism. In fact, Irenaeus seems to argue for exactly the opposite. Since a spiritual being can only be made visible by uniting with the material world, "it is the body which gives form to the spiritual (soul), not the other way around."[136] Thus, while the image of God could be, "a material reality possessing a visible form either the same as or similar to one present in its exemplar,"[137] the image reveals the intent of reproducing the "shape" of the exemplar.[138]

Second, and more importantly, the flesh, and by extension the body, is the substance that is the image of God. Of course, Irenaeus is discussing the spiritual and bodily components of human beings in terms of a unified whole. For the "perfect man consists in the commingling and the union of the soul receiving the spirit of the Father, and the admixture of that fleshy nature which was molded after the image of God."[139] No one component, be it flesh, soul, or spirit in itself, is what makes for a "man." Note, however, that in the same passage, Irenaeus also says that "if anyone takes away the substance of the flesh, that is, the handiwork of God, then what exists is purely spiritual."[140] If the above is correct, then the spiritual certainly cannot be the image. Furthermore, if the "Spirit be wanting to the soul, he, left carnal, is imperfect but possesses the image of God in his

133. Fantino, *Homme, image de Dieu*, 91.

134. Fantino, *Homme, image de Dieu*, 91.

135. Fantino, *Homme, image de Dieu*, 87.

136. Fantino, *Homme, image de Dieu*, 88, 91–92.

137. McLeod, *Image of God*, 53.

138. Fantino, *Homme, image de Dieu*, 89. It is important to note here that this is opposite to what will come later when theologians posit that the image of God is in the soul or mind. In this respect, Irenaeus follows the Antiochene rather than the Alexandrian school of thought. See also McLeod, *Image of God*, 9, 48.

139. Irenaeus, *Adversus Haereses* 5.6.1.

140. Irenaeus, *Adversus Haereses* 5.6.1.

39

formation."[141] What makes a human being imperfect? It is the lack of the Holy Spirit. Importantly, however, this does not strip a human being of the divine image. In fact, the Spirit is what allows a human being to be made in the *likeness* of God but is not the image of God. Irenaeus is being precise here. When he writes about the likeness or similitude, he refers to the Spirit, but when he writes about the image, he refers to the flesh. The image in the flesh provides the reality of being.

Thus, we arrive at the classic distinction between image and similitude. "Resemblance designates the relationship established between two beings while image itself insists on the subject who bears the similitude."[142] The image is proper to the material reality of the subject, while similitude, or likeness, exists between the two subjects. Thus, if a relationship is to be forged between two subjects, some comparative feature must first exist. As has been discussed, one direction of interpretation can be that of relationships, either in the Godhead or in human relationships. Note, however, that relationships presuppose a body.[143] Simply asked, if one is being transformed *into* the image of God, then what is being transformed? Reason, righteousness, rulership, relationships? The entire person? People in general? All of these are abstractions and cannot exist without a physical body, which is the image that reveals intention. It is this "*secondary,* or *derived* meaning, used to represent the existence of a correspondence between two beings or realities that 'image' *then* joins the meaning of similitude."[144]

It is important to note that Irenaeus's insistence on the flesh as image results from his Christology. It is the incarnated Word that is the perfect image of God. According to Fantino, Irenaeus refers to the image of God in one text, *The Demonstration of the Apostolic Teaching*.[145]

> For He made man the image of God; and the image of God is the Son, after whose image man was made: and for this cause He appeared in the end of the times that He might show the image (to be) like unto Himself.[146]

---

141. Irenaeus, *Adversus Haereses* 5.6.1.

142. Fantino, *Homme, image de Dieu*, 89.

143. Note that this is different than saying that individuality presupposes relationships.

144. Fantino, *Homme, image de Dieu*, 106 (emphasis added).

145. Fantino, *Homme, image de Dieu*, 153.

146. Irenaeus, *Demonstration of Apostolic Preaching*, 22.

Notice that Irenaeus says both human beings and the Son are images of God. It is qualified by human beings made according to that image, so in this respect, is in line with most scholarship. It stands apart, however, because Irenaeus presupposes that the flesh is the substance of the image. In effect, Irenaeus is reversing Old Testament thinking. One does not need to wonder about what God "looks" like because Christ's flesh is the image of God. Therefore, the starting point for the image of God is *not* some abstract concept but is "taking from Himself the substance of the creatures [formed], and the pattern of things made, and the type of all the adornments of the world,"[147] that makes for "let Us make man after Our image and likeness."[148] In concert with what is the "perfect man," "image points to the whole human *nature* that Adam and all other humans share with the incarnate Word's humanity."[149] Thomas Weinandy agrees, saying, "It is of singular significance that the body of human beings bears the *imago Dei* . . . that if we are made in the image of the Father's Son, and if we are bodily, then, for Irenaeus, our very bodies must manifest the Son's image."[150] In fact, for Weinandy, it is not just the body of Christ, but the "*risen humanity of Jesus* that most fully manifests the Son's divine likeness to the Father."[151]

Irenaeus's Christology, then, is necessarily tied to his soteriology through a comparison of images that shows resemblance. One can clearly see this in *Adversus Heresies* 5.16.2 when Irenaeus refers to the creation of human beings according to the "image of God in a time long past."[152] Because the "invisible Word" had not yet taken on flesh, human beings "easily lost their similitude." With the incarnation, however, the Son confirms the fleshy image since "He became Himself what was His image," *and* "reestablishes the similitude by assimilating man to the invisible Father through means of the visible Word."[153] At face value, this assumes that there is a difference between the image of God in human beings and the image of God in Christ, namely, only the latter is perfect. Yet, aided by the Holy Spirit, one is able to be assimilated to God (note similitude). In fact, Irenaeus poses that very question of "how one is to be a God. It is through faith

---

147. Irenaeus, *Adversus Haereses* 4.20.1.

148. Irenaeus, *Adversus Haereses* 4.20.1.

149. McLeod, *Image of God*, 55 (emphasis added).

150. Weinandy, "St. Irenaeus," 21.

151. Weinandy, "St. Irenaeus," 29–30 (emphasis added).

152. Irenaeus, *Adversus Haereses* 5.16.2.

153. Irenaeus, *Adversus Haereses* 5.16.2. See Fantino, *Homme, image de Dieu*, 154.

and subjection to Christ that one will receive His handiwork and will be a perfect work of God."[154] In this fashion, the mediating function of the incarnate Christ "recapitulates in Himself His own handiwork,"[155] redeeming a fallen humanity. Only by "carrying the Image in Christ's flesh"[156] and thus also in the flesh of created human beings, can there by a "typological order in the correspondence of a common form between two beings."[157] And it is only "preserving this framework that one shall ascend to that which is perfect."[158] One could say then that it is through the flesh that one "sees" in order to become assimilated into becoming like God.[159]

THE LANGUAGE OF MEMORY: CREATION AND THE IMAGE OF GOD

Taking the christological and soteriological aspects together, for Irenaeus, the image of God is inscribed into the human body by God's creative power. Here, however, the emphasis shifts from reading Gen 1 to Gen 2. While it is true that the words "image" and "likeness" do not appear in the text of Gen 2, the text of Gen 2 show a material reality more so than its more abstract counterpart. Scholars will note that there is no need to harmonize the two creation accounts, but given the concept of image in the ANE as previously described in the Egyptian mouth-opening ceremony, the creation of Adam out of the dust of the earth is very much germane to this discussion. Not only does it follow in the Antiochene tradition of identifying the image of God with "the person of clay fashioned in the 'second' creation,"[160] but it also gives a heavier, more personal, meaning to being created in the image that is physically borne by the body. This "bearing of the image" can go back to the previous discussion about *kabod* and *charakter*. Whereas *kabod* has

154. Irenaeus, *Adversus Haereses* 4.39.2.

155. Irenaeus, *Adversus Haereses* 4.22.1. See Weindandy, "St. Irenaeus," 28; see also McLeod, *Image of God*, 57–58.

156. Fantino, *Homme, image de Dieu*, 154.

157. Fantino, *Homme, image de Dieu*, 106. This is also consistent with the Antiochene school of thought regarding archetype and type. See McLeod, *Image of God*, 20.

158. Irenaeus, *Adversus Haereses* 4.39.2.

159. Fantino, *Homme, image de Dieu*, 113; McLeod, *Image of God*, 55; Welz, "*Imago Dei*," 83.

160. McLeod, *Image of God*, 51. Irenaeus is identified as being in the Antiochene tradition.

been discussed in the more abstract sense of the meaning's "importance" or "weightiness" in what one sees in "glory," here *kabod* has the literal sense of the "weight" of the flesh in being created by God.

Irenaeus uses anthropomorphic language in describing God the Artificer when God creates human beings:

> But man He formed with His own hands, taking from the earth that which was purest and finest, and mingling in measure His own power with the earth. For He traced His own form on the formation, that that which should be seen should be of divine form: for (as) the Image of God was man formed and set on the earth. And that he might become living, He breathed on his face the breath of life; that both for the breath and for the formation man should be like unto God.[161]

In a clear allusion to Gen 2, Irenaeus points to being created by "God's hands" in the shaping of earth into a human being that shows divine form, and "by the hands of the Father," Irenaeus means by the Son and the Holy Spirit.[162] Interestingly, the "Finger of God" that "writes" the law of God in stone is described as being "that which is stretched forth from the Father in the Holy Spirit."[163] Coupled with a direct reference to 2 Cor 3:3, "salvation [is] written on hearts by the Spirit, without paper or ink."[164] Later, Irenaeus says more explicitly, that the "Spirit lays hold on the flesh," before quoting the rest of 2 Cor 3:3, that "ye are the epistle of Christ inscribed not with ink, but with the Spirit of the living God, not in tables of stone, but in the fleshly tables of the heart."[165] All this comes after "bearing about the dying of Jesus that the life of Jesus might be manifested in our body."[166] Thus, it is not only in a Trinitarian creation "in the beginning," but an ongoing creation of a person as well. For as "God's workmanship, one is to await the hand of our Maker . . . whose creation is being carried out."[167] In this respect, Irenaeus shows his well-known developmental anthropology, as one "grows into the *imago Dei* and matures in his likeness."[168]

---

161. Irenaeus, *Demonstration of Apostolic Preaching*, 11.

162. Irenaeus, *Adversus Haereses* 5.6.1.

163. Irenaeus, *Demonstration of Apostolic Teaching*, 26.

164. Irenaeus, *Adversus Haereses* 3.4.2.

165. Irenaeus, *Adversus Haereses* 5.13.4.

166. Irenaeus, *Adversus Haereses* 5.13.4.

167. Irenaeus, *Adversus Haereses* 4.39.2.

168. Weinandy, "St. Irenaeus," 22.

The body, and therefore the image of God, is something that can be molded. Again, Irenaeus alludes to the creation of human beings in Gen 2:

> Offer to Him thy heart in a soft and tractable state, and preserve the form in which the Creator has fashioned thee, having moisture in thyself, lest, by becoming hardened, thou lose the impressions of His fingers. But by preserving the framework thou shalt ascend to that which is perfect, for the moist clay which is in thee is hidden [there] by the workmanship of God. His hand fashioned thy substance.[169]

Two things are important here. First, the malleability of the flesh is dependent on moisture. Moisture represents the ability to be shaped by God in one's receptivity and does not represent bodily fluids literally. A moist clay can be *impressed* by the workmanship of God. Second, and to the contrary, a hardened or dry clay will *lose* the impression. A straightforward interpretation suggests that if one does "dry out," then one can lose the image of God. This, however, seems unlikely given the previous analysis and the general idea that "the image refers to what is natural to human beings and was not lost with Adam's sin."[170] In fact, when taken within the context of receptivity, hardness shows the lack of the ability to be impressed by the Holy Spirit. One can see this in Irenaeus's discussion about divorce being permitted because of the hardness of heart, Pharaoh's hardening of the heart, or God reproving "Adam and Eve for being hard-hearted and disobedient."[171] When adding Paul's words of the circumcision of the heart with the Spirit writing on the tablet of the heart, the hardening of the heart is but a temporary "shell" that needs to be "moistened" by the workmanship of God already hidden in the heart itself. In effect, the "body" is always ready to be impressed upon by God's divine action and intention.

Therefore, in Irenaeus's christological, soteriological, and anthropological aims, the flesh that receives God's fingerprints, and this *imprint* is what marks the image of God. As such, the body is pressed and so *feels* the weight of God. After all, glory or *kabod*, is not just a visual phenomenon, but one that impacts the senses to give rise to awe or majesty. Thus, while glory is usually referenced with respect to what can be outwardly seen, it is tied to the material reality of the body, which is the image of God. This is what Irenaeus fought so hard for in his arguments against the gnostics

---

169. Irenaeus, *Adversus Haereses* 4.39.2.

170. McLeod, *Image of God*, 55. This is not to say that the image may be damaged.

171. Irenaeus, *Adversus Haereses* 4.15.2; see also 4.29.2. In the latter reference, the finger of God is mentioned again as that which leads the Israelites out of Egypt.

when developing his theology of image. Something that "appears" to be a body is not enough. The body must have "weight" so that it will be able to take the shape of the divine. In this respect, the image found in the flesh is the receptive aspect that allows communicating with God. As mentioned previously the body communicates with the soul, not the other way around. Therefore, in feeling the "pressure" of God, one bears the weight of the image and directs oneself toward the shape, or likeness of God. And this, in the positive sense, is the meaning of *charakter*, or God's imprint.

Irenaeus was not alone in his thinking that image pertains to the body. Justin Martyr also alludes to Gen 2 when he claims, "It is evident that man made in the image of God was of flesh,"[172] since God created human beings from the dust of the earth. It is not surprising, then, that Irenaeus would have similar language, having read Justin Martyr. Moreover, Irenaeus's thoughts on imprint and developmental anthropology could also have been influenced by Justin Martyr. For he says, "God the artificer, to wit, a *potter*" works with "clay or wax to make the form of a living animal, and if his handiwork be destroyed it is not impossible for him to make the same form by working up the same material and fashioning it anew."[173] In following these strands, one envisions God as the divine artist, a potter, who fashions matter, or flesh, into an image.

The image of God as potter is a recurring biblical theme. One finds references in Isaiah, Jeremiah, Sirach, Wisdom of Solomon, and in Romans. The important takeaway is the link between what is left behind in the image and its source. In claiming that "fingerprints" are God's imprints on human beings is to say that they have been specially marked for covenant. Here, both sides of the relational and substantive divide can agree. Brunner, for example, notes that human beings have "not been merely created by God and through God, but in and for God."[174] McDowell observes that, "unlike animals, human beings can enter into a covenant relationship with God."[175] Therefore, it is in covenant that the rubber meets the road, substance meeting relationality. For if there is one purpose for being the image of God, it is to point to God first. In bearing the mark of the Artificer, one is "called" *even before* one hears.

Thus, the divine image functions symbolically. This is not a new idea, by any means. Paul Tillich is often credited with symbolism in his

---

172. Justin Martyr, *On the Resurrection*, Fragment 7.

173. Justin Martyr, *On the Resurrection*, Fragment 6 (emphasis added).

174. Brunner, *Man in Revolt*, 92.

175. McDowell, "In Image of God," 33.

systematic theology, but the apostle Paul makes use of creation in general as a pointer to God in Romans. Such a gesture plays off the old idea of the "intelligence" behind the ontological argument. Irenaeus also says that "for by means of creation *itself*, the Word reveals God the Creator but also by means of the world and formation [of man], the Artificer who formed him."[176] Taken all together, the image of God in the reality of human flesh points to God. The question for the remainder of this book is "how," as it pertains to the "theology of image."

CONCLUSION

As a start, the relatively new perspective of *Bildwissenschaft* might point us in the right direction. Jason Gaiger gives a working definition of the term by addressing the words *Bild* and *Wissenschaft* separately, and then analyzing whether *Bildwissenschaft* as a field of "image science" "can pass a unified comprehensive treatment of its subject."[177] This book will not address the philosophy of image, or *Bildtheorie*, and will not go into the debates of what might constitute a universality to image science. Both are beyond the scope of this work. What is evident from the field, however, is a willingness to be multidisciplinary in an attempt at universality beyond what historically has been in the purview of art history. Gaiger notes Hans Belting's anthropological approach to "image," "body," and "medium,"[178] while Claudia Welz notes that "*Bildwissenschaft* originates at the intersection of semiotics and visual studies."[179] Thus, in methodology, there is a fusion of ideas of what *Bild* can mean as it extends into cognitive science, neuroscience, psychology, and various forms of art, "sculpture included (the German word for sculptor is *Bildhauer*, literally an 'image hewer')."[180] Artistically, the latter seems especially relevant given Gen 2 and potter references, but the other disciplines will factor into this book later.

More precise to this discussion, Welz not only reviews different models of the image of God, but also wrestles with the question of how an image can represent something that is invisible.[181] While the theological answer

176. Irenaeus, *Adversus Haereses* 4.6.6. (emphasis added).

177. Gaiger, "Idea of Universal *Bildwissenschaft*," 209.

178. Gaiger, "Idea of Universal *Bildwissenschaft*," 211.

179. Welz, "*Imago Dei*," 75.

180. Gaiger, "Idea of Universal *Bildwissenschaft*," 209.

181. Welz, "*Imago Dei*," 74, 85.

is the incarnation, Welz takes an image theory approach that incorporates the "iconic" or "pictorial" turn in what image represents in a human being. For Welz, "To call a human being an 'image,' must take into account an embodied image that is both material and immaterial, both visible and bearing references to the invisible."[182] If Welz is right, then she seems to agree with Irenaeus's distinction between image and likeness. "Contained" in the *imago* is the reference to the divine. Thus, the image of God is a "complex sign that is at once, iconic, indexical, and symbolic, signifying through deixis and thereby pointing beyond itself."[183] It is iconic because it shares characteristics between image and model. It is indexical because some sort of causal function exists between them. And it is symbolic in what the image can represent outside itself.[184] Taken together, the image "gestures" by pointing rather than "talking,"[185] inviting those who see the image to look toward God.

The image, then, is something that cannot be reduced to one thing but exists like Janus, both looking forwards and backwards. It like "a border, poised between likeness and unlikeness."[186] Paradoxically, the image of God in human beings is contained in the flesh, but also transcends. For all these reasons, people have been interpreting the image of God for millennia. Yet, God's creation of human beings, not just initially but continually, is the one anchor for them all. In this respect, bearing the weight of the image in one's body is to feel the impression of God. The reader is reminded here of Justin Martyr's reference to clay or wax impression, but by the Middle Ages, Mechthild of Hackeborn describes a similar experience. As quoted by Caroline Walker Bynum, Mechthild of Hackeborn saw Christ place his hands on hers and give her "the imprint and resemblance like a seal in wax."[187] Clearly, the physical impression is an image, but if the concept of *Bildwissenschaft* is correct, then there is more than just the impression. In this gesture to God, one must turn to the mind, which, despite its seemingly dualistic property, works to remember God. That is the topic of the next part of this book where we explore *memory* as the image of God.

---

182. Welz, "*Imago Dei*," 75.

183. Welz, "*Imago Dei*," 74; see also 86–87.

184. Welz, "*Imago Dei*," 86. Of note, Welz does not think that an actual comparison can be made between image and model in the iconic case since the invisible by its nature cannot be fully represented. This is decidedly different than Irenaeus's interpretation.

185. Welz, "*Imago Dei*," 87.

186. Lossky, *In Image and Likeness*, 139.

187. Bynum, *Jesus as Mother*, 210; see also Gonzalez, *Created in God's Image*, 48.

2

From Ancient Concepts of
Memory to Christ as Memory

INTRODUCTION

THE PREVIOUS CHAPTER COVERED some of the theological background of
the image of God, ending in Irenaeus's interpretation of "image" and "likeness." This separation, while bifurcating the "image" into two components,
focused heavily on the material reality of the human body (flesh) as the image. Because, however, image resembles and is not the exemplar itself, the
modern notion of *Bildwissenschaft* was employed to gesture to the source of
the image. This chapter will attempt to show that the image consists in the
memory of God. At the surface, this seems paradoxical since "mind things"
seem separated in nature from the body, but as the rest of the book will show,
the classic Cartesian dualism does not hold. Rather, even memory is tied to
the body, and in that respect is part of the image. In order to arrive at the
argument that the image of God consists of the memory of God, however,
the previous argument that the image is the physical imprint needs to be expanded to include imprint as memory, after which, memory pertains to God.

Thus, a survey of Greek thought on memory, something the apostle
Paul might have been familiar with, is necessary to establish the character of

ancient memory. Admittedly, this takes on a more philosophical approach in attempting to define memory within an ancient anthropology. Greek dualism is a given for Plato and Aristotle, who both locate memory in the soul. While there is some room for a physical understanding of memory in Aristotle, to interpret ancient anthropology in some wholistic fashion (for instance, some form of emergentism) is mostly modernist. Instead, memory exists in the immaterial soul or mind.

Given this framework of how memory exists in the soul, *what* memory is like will invoke various words that involve memory in some capacity. These include *eikon, typos, phantasia,* and *phantasma.* Note that these words refer to some kind of image. This is important given the nature of the image of God, some of which was previously described in the discussion of *eikon* in the previous chapter. Here, the argument will be made that imprint gives rise to the concept of memory. Only after memory has been described can one proceed to describe how memory functions, which is to broach the ancient distinction between memory and reminiscence.

Having discussed the difference between memory and reminiscence, the explicit link among memory, imprint, and the image of God will be made, drawing upon Chris Kugler's research on intertestamental Jewish wisdom literature, and how such texts provide resources for a creational wisdom Christology. In connecting wisdom Christology to memory, Paul may have used Jewish wisdom speculation to create a transcendent concept of memory.[1] As a result, memory bridges the more dualistic Greek anthropology to a Christian wholistic one.

To this end, several authors will be engaged in trying to piece together what is meant by memory. Some of these authors, such as Mary Carruthers and Michelle Karnes, are literary critics and theorists, while others, such as Richard Sorabji and Paul Ricoeur, are philosophers. Janet Coleman is a historian, while yet others, such as Paige E. Hochschild and Chris Kugler, are theologians. This assemblage of scholarly material shows the foremost attribute of memory: it is of the past. As such, memory unsurprisingly provides the foundation from which various, if not all, fields build upon. Memory is a part of the nature of scholarly work but also a key to understanding the human person, and arguably how to live.

---

1. Hochschild does not make the argument that Paul is creating a transcendent concept of memory. Rather, she speculates that Aristotle leaves room for a transcendent concept because "knowledge itself does not include the passage of time." Hochschild, *Memory,* 64.

First, however, what *is* memory? The answers to this question have been a thorn in the side of anyone who attempts to define it, from the ancient Greeks to moderns.[2] Is it an object? Is it physical, or is it a purely intellectual outcome? Where does memory belong in the person? How does memory work? Most importantly, how does memory relate to image? Through the centuries, historians, philosophers, poets, and scientists have all tried to answer this question, so the research on memory is vast and complex. Largely, however, questions and therefore answers about memory can be divided into two: the epistemological and the practical. Since the two are related, one cannot escape discussing only one of them, so for the purposes of this book, epistemological and practical questions will be addressed as they relate to the theological concept of the image of God, which is still considerably large.

PLATONIC MEMORY

In Plato, memory is discussed within the larger question about knowledge. In this regard, Janet Coleman is correct to point out that, contextually, memory "is linked intimately with the problem of how we know what we know, and what the object of knowing essentially is."[3] For example, in the *Theaetetus*, the first instance of memory is characterized as a "something,"[4] but is used to illustrate why perceiving (seeing in this case) is not knowing. *Presuming* that one already has in memory knowledge *of* an external object, Socrates asks Theaetetus to close his eyes. Of course, even without a visual perception, one seems to have knowledge of what is no longer being perceived,[5] that is, one remembers. At least here, memory is a knowable something that has a place inside one's thoughts or soul, even if memory is used more as a rhetorical device.

That said, the development of memory as a theme can be traced *indirectly* in the *Theaetetus*. After the first mention of memory as a something, Socrates asks whether someone can both know and not know something at

---

2. For the time being, Western concepts of memory will be assessed since they are the most germane to the question of memory during Paul's time. This is not to say that there might have been other cultural influences but that the writing of the Bible arises out of Greco-Roman and Jewish cultures, Western as opposed to Eastern.

3. Coleman, *Ancient and Medieval Memories*, 4.

4. Plato, *Theaetetus* 163e.

5. Plato, *Theaetetus* 164a.

the same time, which is essentially an extension of the memory argument *if* perceiving is knowledge.[6] Theaetetus responds by saying that it is impossible, to which Socrates moves to a somewhat tongue-in-cheek Protagorean defense. In mimicking what Protagoras might say, Socrates notes an objection that:

> To begin with, do you think anyone is going to concede to you that when we have a present memory of things that have happened to us, this is the same sort of experience as the one we had originally, if we're no longer experiencing the things in question? Far from it. Or, conversely, that anyone will hesitate to concede that it's possible for the same person to know and not know the same thing?[7]

The answer to the first question is a resounding no, that just because one no longer sees an object does not mean that one does not know some form of knowledge. Protagoras seems to be picking on an assumption that when Socrates asserts that not-seeing is not-knowing, he is including a concept of what-is-not since one no longer sees an object.[8] Later, Socrates discusses what-is-not in the context of seeing and not seeing, which seems to refer to the earlier discussion about not-seeing and not-knowing.[9] The second answer, if converse to the first, must be a yes, that it is indeed possible to know and not know the same thing. Since Socrates has already admitted that memory is a "something," then he must be able to explain memory as knowledge if a present memory is not the same thing as the one originally experienced. Clearly, something is being known in memory that relates to what has been perceived. Otherwise, why would it be important to stress that a remembered experience is not the same as what was first experienced?

From an epistemological view, the obvious distinction is a difference between the "sensible and the thinkable."[10] There are some things which are purely thoughts that do not have a given percept, for instance, mathematical or geometric concepts. Surely, one can see "five" and "seven" objects but not see the object of "twelve" after performing addition. Similarly, when Socrates asks, what is clay, the answer is not to be found in the particulars of clay, such as whose clay (a potter's clay, for example), but in a general

6. Plato, *Theaetetus* 165b.

7. Plato, *Theaetetus* 166b.

8. Plato, *Theaetetus* 164b. Contrast with "As befits knowledge, then, perception is always of what is, and never plays us false" (152c).

9. Plato, *Theaetetus* 188b.

10. Coleman, *Ancient and Medieval Memories*, 8.

characteristic of earth mixed with water that is *thought* to be clay.[11] There is some interpretive room here. Socrates appears to use an observation, so even here, this particular mixture of earth and water is clay as opposed some other mixture that would equally be clay. The point, however, is that when it comes to knowing what clay *is*, the answer cannot simply be in what one perceives, has a belief about, or have a belief with an account (logos) because of the changing nature of the percept itself. While one can have knowledge *of* something, it is not knowledge itself and can be prone to error or false beliefs.[12] Knowledge itself can only arise from *knowing* something itself, and this can only occur in the realm of thought, independently from perceived reality, and what any scholar of Plato will recognize as Forms.

Interestingly, scholars have noted the lack of any mention of Forms specifically in the *Theaetetus*, and have argued the exact opposite, that the *Theaetetus* does not mention Forms because they are "irrelevant to the subject discussed,"[13] namely what knowledge *is*. A number of reasons support this premise. First, even though *eidos*, or *idea*, words used in other Platonic works to denote Forms, appear in the *Theaetetus*, they do not seem to "have the same technical sense"[14] employed in those works. Second, even if the *Theaetetus* were to borrow the mention of Forms (μέγιστα γένη, greatest kind) from its companion piece, the *Sophist*, its use in the *Sophist* is not used to explain error and cannot subsequently be applied to the explanation of error in the *Theaetetus*.[15] Finally, in a more technical argument, should μέγιστα γένη mean Forms, one cannot make the argument that Plato purposely excludes mention of it.[16] There would be no reason to appeal to the Forms to resolve the aporia of what knowledge is. But even if that were the case, just because the *Theaetetus* ends in aporia does not necessarily lead to

---

11. Plato, *Theaetetus* 146–47.

12. Plato, *Theaetetus* 146e5–e10.

13. Robinson, "Forms and Error," 16.

14. Robinson, "Forms and Error," 3.

15. Robinson, "Forms and Error," 11.

16. Robinson, "Forms and Error," 10. Robinson is ambiguous on his stance on translating "greatest kind" into Forms. He acknowledges as much by saying he has not formed a "confident opinion" not once, but twice, acknowledging that is "quite possible" but then denying it to form an argument against Francis Cornford's view. In any case, Robinson sees the point as moot since he argues that Forms are not brought into the discussion to describe error in the *Sophist*.

the conclusion that knowledge must be Forms, even if Plato himself would have made that inference.[17]

Despite this controversy, Christopher Rowe is likely correct to observe that Forms are central to both the *Theaetetus* and *Sophist*. Contra Richard Robinson, Rowe cites the "single acknowledged reference" to Forms in the *Sophist* as something "forever as they are" as being consistent with how Forms are described by Socrates in the *Republic*.[18] This reference to Forms occurs in a "conversation" with the "friends" of the Forms and is contrasted with things that are constantly coming-into-being. Just as Robinson supposes that there need not to be a jump to implicate Forms with language that seemingly describes forms, Rowe suggests that there need not be any reason to depart from Platonic convention. Thus, even in the case of multiple words for form (*eidos*, idea, *genos*), they all refer to the form of something, and so, rather than a "volte-face" on his position of Forms, Plato is changing the emphasis of Forms from what they are to how they might "share in" particulars.[19] After all, everyone must begin with perception.

This discussion on Forms has an important bearing on memory, more specifically on recollection. By Aristotle's time the distinction between them becomes more apparent, but for now, memory is collapsed into recollection. Why? Since all perceptible objects are in a constant state of flux, there can be no knowledge about them. As a result, true objects of knowledge exist independently in Forms, which, according to Socrates in both *Meno* and *Phaedo*, existed in preexisting souls before human birth.[20] Since the immortal soul has seen and learned everything there is to know, when someone remembers, he or she is recollecting, or perhaps more accurately, recognizing the content in the soul. In fact, it is *wisdom* that is in the soul before birth.[21] From a mental standpoint, recollection crosses the gap between conscious and unconscious,[22] reawakening our knowledge of the Forms.

Thus, in a way, the seeming hostility between body and soul has also been mitigated, even though Plato consistently refers to the external,

17. Robinson, "Forms and Error," 14.

18. Christopher Rowe, in Plato, *"Theaetetus" and "Sophist,"* xiii.

19. Christopher Rowe, in Plato, *"Theaetetus" and "Sophist,"* xi–xiii.

20. Plato, *Meno* 81c–d; *Phaedo* 75c—76a.

21. Plato, *Phaedo* 76c.

22. Chappell, "Plato," 387. Chappell notes the original problem in the *Meno*. The problem with inquiry is that one must *already* know what one is looking for. In the mind, there is no gap as in a physical search for something (for instance, a lost sock) where "location" is the problem.

independent existence of Forms as true knowledge. As Sophie-Grace Chappell notes, in the *Phaedo*, perception is a "necessary condition of knowledge that *reminds* us of the absolute standards," or Forms.[23] In seeing an equal number of sticks and stones, one sees the difference between the equal number of sticks and stones themselves and is led to the abstraction of the Equal itself.[24] One, however, must first *see* the sticks and stones to come to that conclusion, that is, through recollection. As Christopher Rowe observes, "The theory of recollection, advanced in *Phaedo* and elsewhere, provides a mechanism whereby the process [of apprehending the Forms] can start: we begin to see things *as* beautiful or ugly, equal or unequal."[25] Thus, the body and soul cooperate in coming to knowledge in a process of recollection which closes the "gap" between body and soul.

Recollection, however, is "the *experience* of the soul alone of things originally apprehended by the soul and body together"[26] and is not memory itself. As the *Philebus* points out, recollection, memory, and perception are all different, with the *end point* being recollection. Prior to recollection, "memory and perception meet with one feeling and motion," which accounts for consciousness.[27] If, however, the "shocks of the body" do not reach the soul, it is called unconsciousness, or what Socrates describes as the "affections of the body that are extinguished before reaching the soul."[28] Plato is also careful to distinguish between unconsciousness and forgetfulness here, the latter being an "exit of memory." If memory were to exit, it could have done so only after it had acquired something through perception. Yet, this does not mean that memory holds only the *objects* of perceptions, which seems to be common parlance among Platonic scholars.[29] To be fair, memory must represent something, and by the time of Aristotle,

---

23. Chappell, "Plato," 391. Interestingly, Chappell chooses to use the absolutes standard as a generic F-ness and the perception as F instead of Equal and equal number in the *Phaedrus* section she cites. One later encounters whiteness and white in the Protagorean theory of the "measure of a man" in the *Theaetetus*.

24. Plato, *Phaedrus* 74b–d. There are some interpretive issues here. It is unclear what makes for the sticks and stones to be equal. I have chosen here to say that they are equal in number.

25. Christopher Rowe, in Plato, *"Theaetetus" and "Sophist,"* xiv.

26. Hochschild, *Memory*, 25 (emphasis added).

27. Plato, *Philebus* 39a.

28. Plato, *Philebus* 33e.

29. For instance, Hochschild notes, "Plato [is] saying that memory, is the 'preservation' (*soteria*) of sensation, or sense images." Hochschild, *Memory*, 24.

this takes the form of images. But before getting there, one must consider what memory might be and hold, with respect to perception.

Indeed, Socrates does not question memory at first but perception:

> Socrates: I must first of all analyze memory, or rather perception which is prior to memory, if the subject of our discussion is ever to be properly cleared up.
>
> Protarchus: How will you proceed?
>
> Socrates: Let us imagine affections of the body which are extinguished before they reach the soul, and leave her unaffected; and again, other affections which vibrate through both soul and body, and impart a shock to both and to each of them.[30]

The question is, however, what does Socrates mean when there is a shock to both the body and the soul *and to each*? One interpretation is that "perception defined as 'motion' occurs when soul and body are jointly affected and moved by one and the same affection."[31] Similarly, Hochschild describes "sensation as an 'upheaval' (*seismos*) that 'penetrates' both the body and soul in a way that is 'peculiar to each but also common to both'; this is properly called a single movement and therefore a single affection."[32] It would seem a single perception must be "strong" enough to pass through both the body and soul. Moreover, this is a *unidirectional* flow of motion since it is possible that an affection of the body can be "extinguished" before reaching the soul. Why then does Socrates include "to each of them"? Given the current context, should not the imparting of a shock be sufficient to affect both soul and body without regard to each?

Part of the difficulty of interpretation might have to do with Socrates's definition of consciousness as the "union or communion of soul and body in one feeling and motion."[33] It is here that perhaps commentators are conflating consciousness with perception in assuming the single movement of an affection. If Socrates had stopped at consciousness, one could assume that whatever affection the body was able to "transmit" would reach the soul somehow, and then the soul would apprehend the sensed object. This generally agrees with most interpretations that separate "understanding"

---

30. Plato, *Philebus* 33d—34a.
31. Deretić, "ΨΥΧΗ as Biblion," 72.
32. Hochschild, *Memory*, 25. She cites *Philebus* 33d–34a.
33. Plato, *Philebus* 34a.

from "sense objects,"[34] or knowledge from perception as one finds in the *Theaetetus*. The potential problem with this kind of interpretation is that it does not adequately consider the role of memory in consciousness. In fact, the very next statement from Socrates concerning consciousness refers to memory as its preservation.[35]

If memory is the preservation of consciousness, then memory as a thing must occur after perception and *with the soul*. The latter part is especially important because memory "belongs" in the soul, and while perception has been discussed with external objects, internal objects have not. In the *Philebus*, Socrates recalls the recollection puzzle in the *Meno*: "But how can a man who is empty for the first time, attain either by perception or memory to any apprehension of replenishment, or which he has no present or past experience?"[36] Socrates answers that the soul, not the body, must apprehend the opposite of emptiness, that is, replenishment, *with the help of memory*. In fact, "an impulse [of replenishment] is generated of the opposite experience [emptiness] which proves that there is memory of the opposite state."[37] Furthermore, it is memory that attracts us toward the objects of desire, proving that such impulses, desires, and moving principles have their origin in the soul.[38] In direct opposition to what has been discussed with external perception, there is an *internal* movement that impinges on memory. Thus, if consciousness is of *one* feeling and motion when soul and body combine, it must be after both the soul and body have contributed their "shocks" to memory that the one feeling arises, that is, the soul perceives and makes a judgment.[39]

While this may be open to interpretation as a single movement, direct evidence of memory's involvement comes shortly later in the internal "scribe" and "painter."

34. Coleman, *Ancient and Medieval Memories*, 9.

35. Plato, *Philebus* 34a.

36. Plato, *Philebus* 35a.

37. It should be noted that Socrates does not explain where this opposite came from. One could think of it as some Form that fits within the larger recollection theory, but this is not necessary to explain the role of memory in consciousness.

38. Plato, *Philebus* 35d.

39. M. F. Burnyeat makes the similar conclusion that conscious perception is one where judgment is made, otherwise simply being "conscious" of what is out there offers no idea to what it is. Arguing that one sees "through" as opposed to "with" eyes suggest that there is a soul (reaches out) that does the perceiving and, in so doing, makes a judgment. See Burnyeat, "Plato on the Grammar," 42, 46, 50.

> Socrates: Memory and perception meet, and they and their at-
> tendant feelings seem to almost to write down words in the soul,
> and when the inscribing feeling writes truly, then true opinion and
> true propositions which are the expressions of opinion come into
> our souls—but when the scribe within us writes falsely, the result
> is false.
>
> Protarchus: I quite assent and agree to your statement.
>
> Socrates: I must bespeak your favour also for another artist, who is
> busy at the same time in the chambers of the soul.
>
> Protarchus: Who is he?
>
> Socrates: The painter, who, after the scribe has done his work,
> draws images in the soul of the things which he has described.[40]

In the very first statement of the quoted section, the combination of memory and perception is composed of not one, but multiple feelings. Clearly
this is inconsistent with one feeling and motion said to be of *perception*.
Instead, it must refer to what the soul and body bring independently of
each other but with their "attendant feelings." It is only after these combine
and are written by the "inscribing feeling"[41] that the plurality of feelings
is lost, and true or false beliefs result. It is only after this combination and
formation of belief has occurred that the idea of one feeling and one motion
can become consistent with Socrates's earlier description of consciousness.
And it is only after something has been written into their soul, that is, having thought about the perception, can it become conscious. Memory, in effect, is the soul's endeavor to judge, of which Socrates, invoking the scribe,
can say that "belief and the endeavor to form a belief always spring from
memory and perception."[42]

What about the painter? As Irina Deretić observes, the painter's action of drawing images occurs after the scribe has written, so is dependent

40. Plato, *Philebus* 39a.

41. The scribe as a character is not mentioned here, only an inscribing feeling. Irina
Deretić, "ΨΥΧΗ as Biblion," notes that Plato must have thought of the symbolic figure of
the scribe as being able to coalesce dispositions into beliefs and words (72). Furthermore,
even though it is "merely" a feeling (*panthema*), Deretić cites the cognitive functions
found in the *Republic* that make use of *panthema*. Deretić settles on "intellect" as the
cognitive agent represented by the scribe (74).

42. Plato, *Philebus* 38b.

on the scribe's words.[43] As such, the painter has no access to the outside word. It does not have "eyes" to see through (lacks perception), so it must "reinterpret" only the scribe's words in making an illustration. The result, as Socrates says, is to see in his mind the images what were once there. Hannah Arendt defines this process as "de-sensing," which is a necessary product of thinking itself.[44] In fact, once cannot think about an object without first turning away (withdrawing) from it. Therefore, in creating an image (*phantasma*), the painter re-presents words and belief in pictorial form, that is, "a mixture of belief and perception"[45] to be used in thinking. Whether this counts as another form of judgment since there is a translation from words to art may be anachronistic. It is clear, however, "these pictures are like judgements"[46] and used as such, even if it may be different than the scribe's. But why is this second "judgement" necessary and for what purpose?[47]

One potential reason may furnish the answer to Socrates's question in the *Theaetetus* about memory and knowledge. The question of "how judgements, or beliefs, can emerge from immediate sensory awareness,"[48] that is, knowledge, is answered by and through what memory captures in an image. Earlier in the *Philebus*, Socrates defines "recollection and reminiscence as recovery of herself the lost recollection of some consciousness or knowledge."[49] Notice that Socrates says a recovery of lost recollection. This suggests that one has already gone through the sensory process in coming to create a painting, representative of whatever conscious experience was felt at the time. Thus, in a way, the painting is stored in memory and acts as a form of knowledge that can be used in comparative tasks *within oneself*. This is the situation found when Socrates asks whether something in the distance is a man or an image made by shepherds,[50] which is *not* the same as what is

---

43. Deretić, "ΨΥΧΗ as Biblion," 74.

44. Arendt, *Life of the Mind*, 75–77. Deretić chooses to point out the empirical nature of an image as being "away from" and less than the original percept. Arendt is more personal in a deliberate turning away from a sense object (cf. 75).

45. Deretić, "ΨΥΧΗ as Biblion," 75.

46. Plato, *Plato's "Philebus*," 73.

47. Deretić asks the same question. "ΨΥΧΗ as Biblion," 77.

48. Chappell, "Plato on Knowledge in the *Theaetetus*." In *Theaetetus* 186d, knowledge is reasoning about experiences, which is what exactly happens in anticipatory desire as well as comparative analysis.

49. Plato, *Philebus* 34b. Hackforth translates only "recollection" but notes the alternative translations. Plato, *Plato's "Philebus*," 65.

50. Plato, *Philebus* 38c.

found in the *Theaetetus* where Socrates asks whether distance can confuse the identities of both Theaetetus and Theodorus while perceiving them.[51] In the *Philebus*, imagination must have created "a man" and "a figure of a man" and in the thinking process, pulled those images from memories in order to make a judgment about what was being seen. And by creating an image, the painter creates a thought thing that becomes a part of memory.

What does memory exactly capture, however? Verity Harte asks this very question after noting that immediately after *Philebus* 34a10, Socrates does not initially say what has "been preserved."[52] Harte's solution, through Socrates's desire argument, claims that there are preserved representations of desire, which are fastened on (*ephaptesthai*) in memory.[53] Indeed, Harte's analysis agrees with what was discussed earlier. Ignoring for now the modern notions of memory and its various forms, the *Philebus* states that there are "shocks" or "attendant feelings" and that these need to reach the soul for it to be perceived. The fact that a shock needs to be able to reach the soul suggests that the soul, or whatever is in the soul, needs to be "impressionable." Since percepts that do not reach the soul are "unconscious," that is, have not entered memory, seems to suggest that the shocks or feelings are made upon memory. Thus, what is preserved in memory is not simply the sensory data, as if one is talking about the features of a picture. Instead, it is a more complete sensory experience.

In fact, for Deretić, "the intensity and vividness of anticipatory pleasures can only be fully experienced by internal, mental images, or in other words, though imagination about their content."[54] In other words, the painter's image "holds" the emotional valence necessary for something to even be called a desire, representing the shocks to the body in conscious perception. Thus, while true that the painter's role "reinterprets [the scribe's] words and belief in order to connect perception to memory,"[55] for it to be called a desire is to "trap" or represent an experience or *pathos* in something that can be put *into* memory. Interestingly, in a more Aristotelean fashion, then, the painting *itself* acts as a form of memory, so that one particular experience can then be *compared* to another. That is the point of anticipation and its use in thinking. So, as Arendt notes, when "an image stored

51. Plato, *Theaetetus* 193–94.

52. Harte, "Desire, Memory, and Authority," 46:52.

53. Harte, "Desire, Memory, and Authority," 46:53, 55.

54. Deretić, "ΨΥΧΗ as Biblion," 77.

55. Deretić, "ΨΥΧΗ as Biblion," 78.

in memory becomes 'vision in thought' when the mind gets ahold of it, it shows that thinking always implies remembrance,"[56] but in an addendum, remembrance is also the soul moving to feel.

The soul moving to feel is another important facet of memory. If the painting is a form of knowledge (not all might agree here), and it incorporates affections, then it also expresses the relationship of objects to the perceiver in the pursuit of judgment and knowledge. Harte notes this active, as opposed to passive, ability of the soul, when she mentions that it is the soul which perceives, even though the body is instrumental in acquiring information about the world.[57] Similarly and perhaps more poignantly, M. F. Burnyeat's analysis of Plato's use of "through" as opposed to "with" in *Theaetetus* 184c shows that the soul reaches out to objects *through* the apertures of the senses and that there actually is a single subject that receives the sensory input.[58] Once again, the soul perceives and in making a judgment, perhaps a double one at that, "fastens on" feelings in memory to sense objects, establishing the relationship of object to perceiver. Moreover, this *memory* as a kind of knowledge, represents the relationship between the world and the soul. It makes possible to some degree that "under normal circumstances, with the body functioning properly, the senses relay data reliably."[59] To illustrate, the shadows on the wall of Plato's cave allegory take the form of the objects from which they come, so even if the shadows are images of the "real" objects, one can still perceive and judge the images themselves. And perhaps, through memory, recollect the objects as well.

IMAGE AS MEMORY

In the previous section, the Platonic concept of memory was discussed in an attempt to define memory. Starting with the *Theaetetus*, memory was discussed within the context of an epistemological problem that was reflective of the Forms, of which ultimately one "recollects" through dialectic and being reminded of "absolute standards." "To know then, is effectively, to remember; living must be a process of coming to know and therefore remembering what has always been true and worth uncovering with the

---

56. Arendt, *Life of the Mind*, 77–78. Arendt is referencing Augustine's thoughts on memory in the Trinity.

57. Harte, "Desire, Memory, and Authority," 46:69.

58. Burnyeat, "Plato on the Grammar," 33, 37, 46.

59. Hochschild, *Memory*, 15.

help of memory."[60] This kind of memory is the latent variety, which, as a reminder of the Forms, is "impersonal."[61] The contents in memory are universal and must be to be able to point toward the Forms. By contrast, what people normally experience through the senses and store in "personal" memory does not qualify as knowledge. In keeping with such distinctions, Coleman can say:

> The Platonic process of recollection requires no explanation of how we interact with our environment precisely because the particularity of this world is forgotten in the recollective process. In discussing memory, Plato forgets sense data as such and therefore implies that any conscious recollection is not the retrieval of images but rather what, logically, must have been the essence of an earlier situation of which one was previously aware and then the reworking of these elements into a rational pattern.[62]

And if one abides by the impersonal definition of memory in that epistemological context, memory can only ever be secondary and can provide no real basis for judgment upon the particulars of the world that depend on a measure of stability. The *Philebus*, however, directly refutes "impersonal memory" in 1) how conscious recollection occurs, 2) the creation of an image, 3) the retrieval of that image in future judgment, and 4) memory as a kind of knowledge. Memory is *more* than simply recollecting, so the collapse of memory into recollection may be premature, though, recollection could simply be describing "personal" memory.[63] Are these distinctions simply a Platonic accident or could there be an intermediate state that applies to memory? The answer might lie in what has already been discussed in defining image and how that relates to memory.

Returning to the *Theaetetus*, the first description of image as it relates to memory is found in the famous wax tablet passage:

> Socrates: I want you to suppose, for the sake of argument, that our souls contain a waxen block. It is larger in one person, smaller in another, of purer wax in one, filthier in another; in some it is too hard, in others too soft, while in still others it is as it should be.

60. Coleman, *Ancient and Medieval Memories*, 14.

61. Coleman, *Ancient and Medieval Memories*, 9.

62. Coleman, *Ancient and Medieval Memories*, 11.

63. Clearly there seems to be some differentiation of memory here since "personal" memory refers to personal episodes, historical facts even, which would not have a record until after one's birth. Not every memory can be explained by recollection.

> Theaetetus: Done.

> Socrates: Let's say, then, that it is a gift from Memory, mother of
> the Muses, and that we imprint on it whatever we wish to remem-
> ber from among the things we see or hear or the thoughts we our-
> selves have, holding it under our perceptions and thoughts as if we
> were making impressions from signet rings; whatever is imprinted
> on the block, we remember and know for as long as its image is in
> the wax, while whatever is wiped off or proves incapable of being
> imprinted we have forgotten and do not know.[64]

The first thing to note is that the wax tablet includes some impression in
the wax (image), whose state depends on the condition of the wax, something elaborated on in the ideal states of wax opposite "shaggy"[65] ones later
in the dialogue. Second, there is a relationship impressed into the wax by
whatever is sensed. This seems consistent with the discussion of what can
be captured through the "apertures" of the body above. Yet, because the
Theaetetus does not mention the strength of the impression, but, rather, the
condition of the wax, the focus of the *Theaetetus* is on the impressions as
prospective pieces of knowledge. Regardless, what indelibly remains, is a
"record" or "image" of perception and is supported by Socrates supposing
that he has a memory of what Theodorus and Theaetetus are like, that is, he
has images of them in his memory.

Therefore, the discussion of memory flows into one of knowledge in
the aviary model of memory:

> Socrates: So, just as in the preceding discussion we installed some
> sort of contraption in souls that we'd moulded out of wax, now let's
> make a sort of aviary in every soul, containing birds of all different
> varieties, some of them in flocks separate from others, some in
> small groups, others flying about wherever it might be on their
> own in among them all.

> Theaetetus: Done. What's next?

64. Plato, *Theaetetus* 191d. Note that here, in a work that predates the *Philebus*, Plato
refers not only to the senses but also to the thoughts we might have as things we can
impress into memory. Clearly, memory is of something, suggesting that it is a kind of
knowledge.

65. Plato, *Theaetetus* 194c1—195e1.

> Socrates: We're to say that when we are little children this contain-
> er is empty, and think of pieces of knowledge instead of the birds.
> If someone comes to possess a piece of knowledge and confines it
> in the cage, we're to say he has learned or discovered the thing this
> knowledge was originally of, and that is what knowing is.[66]

Here, rather than in image, memory is likened to an aviary where knowledge is "stored" and flies about like birds. Yet, no actual mention of memory
is given as is stated in the wax tablet. In fact, one is to suppose that the
aviary is initially empty and upon learning something, one catches a "bird"
and puts it into the aviary. Once this "hunt" has been completed one has
come to "possess" knowledge. There is, however, another hunt, one that
involves the catching of the bird in the cage those which have been already
acquired. Only when one "has a bird in hand" does one recover knowledge
and recollects. Thus, in the distinction between "possessing" and "having"
knowledge, a model for remembering emerges.[67]

There are some important differences between the two models, however. First, in the aviary, gone is the relationship of signet ring to the imprint left in wax. Instead, one finds the generality of knowledge as thought
things, which are necessary to explain the difference between knowledge
one "possesses" or "has."[68] Second, the aviary model layers on top of "a con-
traption" (memory) that houses knowledge with a process in retrieving that
knowledge (recollection). The latter is something one finds eventually in
Aristotle, but before getting there, there is a reason for the difference, which
is not sufficiently paid attention to by many scholars.

Again, most scholars view the stories about the wax tablet and aviary as attempts at epistemology, and since Plato consistently states that the
dialogues are about defining knowledge, this appears to be true. Chappell
mentions this scholarly bent in two groups, those who view the *Theaetetus*
as a failure to identify a positive account of knowledge and those who see
a successful attack of knowledge assumed by those Plato rejects.[69] Failure
is in the eye of the beholder. At the same time, however, Chappell notes
that it is the *Theaetetus* which attempts to answer the *Meno*'s paradox of
searching for something one has forgotten. Additionally, after Socrates

66. Plato, *Theaetetus* 197d–e.

67. This distinction between possessing and having will return when talking about
the image of God.

68. Chappell, "Plato," 394.

69. Chappell, "Plato," 393.

rejects perception as knowledge, he brackets "learning and forgetting," the intermediate state between knowing and not-knowing, only to come back to memory in the analysis of false belief.[70] Obviously memory is still important, but it is ancillary to knowledge. Or is it?

Chappell states that "Plato certainly makes no obvious attempt to salvage anything from the refutation of the Wax Tablet," even though she does think that it can give a general account of mental life, including memory.[71] Furthermore, she seems to value how the model could explain knowledge and memory, even if it might not be what Plato himself might have believed. It would then seem ironic that Plato would write a section dedicated to false belief only to really believe it. Hence, he moves on to a "new, wholly independent, account for false belief" to test thoughts by themselves,[72] which was the weakness of the wax tablet model since it relied on perception. But what if rather than focusing only on the epistemological context of false beliefs (one that Socrates denies anyway), one looks at how the wax tablet and aviary models are connected?

To start, even before the wax tablet is brought up, perception has been ruled out as being knowledge. Yet, by the time the dialogue arrives at the wax tablet, perception is being employed in creating impressions into memory. But why is Socrates employing perception if he has already ruled it out as being knowledge? Some "thing" must be being "imprinted" in the soul that can potentially act in the acquisition of knowledge. Nothing more is given other than its "physicality," but in the aviary we are to *suppose* that whatever is "inside" is knowledge. The two models are not independent but are linked together. In addressing knowledge as thoughts, Socrates implicitly relies on the actual content of memory via perception. Even though he tells Theaetetus to think of "five" and "seven" by themselves (which occurs in the wax tablet passage), there is no way to escape the imagery to perform the arithmetic needed to come to "twelve" (which occurs in the aviary passage). In fact, the reliance on the imagery of the wax tablet is why confusing an eleven-bird for a twelve-bird does not provide an answer for false belief. It is memory that must serve as the basis for knowledge. Thus, even

---

70. Chappell, "Plato," 392. Chappell translates 188a as "For the moment, I am not going to consider learning and forgetting, which are so to speak intermediate states between knowledge and ignorance." Rowe translates the same passage as "I recognize that there's learning, and forgetting, in between these, but I'm passing over them at the moment." The "in between" refers to the "intermediate" state between knowing and not-knowing.

71. Chappell, "Plato," 393.

72. Chappell, "Plato," 393–94.

though "Plato does not put them [wax tablet and aviary] to any constructive use anywhere outside these passages,"[73] at least in writing, one still gets the sense that taken together, the two models actually show memory used to make judgments, or what Socrates does think gaining knowledge can be, that of forming and having beliefs. In this process, one must use imagery to provide the content, so despite either model not being mentioned elsewhere, they are implied in what is found in the *Philebus*. Conscious perception is 1) written in souls, and 2) painted with emotional valence, so that 3) judgments can be made.

MEMORY AS IMAGE

Having demonstrated that imagery cannot be avoided in the *Theaetetus* and that its use is pivotal to memory's role in knowledge acquisition, how memory can point to something else has yet to be established. To the chagrin of many, the *Theaetetus* ends in aporia. Knowledge is never defined, only gestured at. But in a foreshadowing of what is to come in the *Sophist*, the dialogue in the *Theaetetus* questions whether Socrates and Theaetetus should have been talking about being and not-being (or what is and what is-not) instead of knowing and not-knowing. True, the question of knowledge remains, but it is approached ontologically instead of epistemologically. As a result, the "rescue" of the *Theaetetus* circles back to the wax tablet and memory. As Ricoeur notes, it is "the problem of *eikon* developed in the *Sophist* that comes to the aid of the *Theaetetus* in the recognition of the imprint."[74] Image presents the possibility of something that both is and what-is-not in "an ontological distinction between paradigm and image, that becomes the basis for the theory of participation as an account of reality and meaning."[75] It is an intermediary state that allows for a sharing-in or *koinonia* of paradigm and image.

In the previous chapter, the question of image as it related to how "image" was used related to its theological use. The covered material included its ancient Near East context and its function and substantive roles, with some analysis of the Greek, specifically *eikon*. The analysis below will return to this, but other Greek words that can be translated as "image" come into play in the *Sophist* and the rest of the Platonic corpus. For instance,

---

73. Chappell, "Plato," 394.

74. Ricoeur, *Memory, History, Forgetting*, 10.

75. Ambuel, *Image and Paradigm*, xiv–xv.

eidolon can mean "image," and is the word used in the wax tablet story.[76] David Ambuel's work on the centrality of image in the *Sophist* provides a summary of similarities and distinctions among the words used. Here, the point of word analysis is not necessarily its theological use, but its ontological use and how that might connect with memory.

Ambuel admits that for the most part, the words used for image—*eidolon, phantasma,* and *eikon*—all have the same meaning and in many cases, act interchangeably.[77] Yet, there are distinctions if pressed, which can be significant for interpretive purposes. *Eidolon* seems to be a general term that has historical meanings as "ghost" or "phantasm," in Homer's usage; but more commonly in the Platonic, the word is used to denote a "visible but unreal vestige of reality."[78] One is prompted to think of mirrored objects or reflections, which are visible, but not "real." There is a deficiency in the copy that depends upon the original, which shows some degree of removed reality. Therefore, the general "feeling" of *eidolon* is one of contradistinction. In recognizing what something is like in the image, the emphasis is placed on how it is not like the original.

Phantasma is proximate to *eidolon,* both in its usage and meaning. Ambuel notes that Plato often uses the two words interchangeably and near each other.[79] The similarity between the two words seems to have the same historical context, given that Homer's *eidolon* also means "phantasm." But while there is a sense of dependency from model to copy in *eidolon, phantasma* seems to be more general, as in "appearance" or "apparition." This is most likely due to the added nuance of the "image (*phantasma*) of the imagination (*phantasia*),"[80] lending a feeling of creative mental imagery (or dream) that lands even more heavily on the side of dissimilarity than the original. In fact, some philosophers discount the availability of a model (picture) from which *phantasma* is produced, only that an image "appears" after the completion of a mental process.[81] In other words, no mental picture exists upon which to draw. Consequently, there is an even greater sense of the "unreal" in *phantasma.*

---

76. Ricoeur, *Memory, History, Forgetting,* 9. Interestingly, when Ricoeur mentions the problem of *eikon* as the rescue of Theaetetus, he had previously cited *eidolon* as the word used.

77. Ambuel, *Image and Paradigm,* 70–75.

78. Ambuel, *Image and Paradigm,* 71.

79. Ambuel, *Image and Paradigm,* 73–74.

80. Ambuel, *Image and Paradigm,* 74.

81. Sorabji, *Aristotle on Memory,* xi–xiv.

AN ARISTOTELEAN DETOUR?

Of course, the difference between *phantasia* and *phantasma* is more Aristotelean in this debate, but there is substantial evidence for the objectivity of images, or, at the very least, the "representations" of images. For instance, Richard Sorabji makes the distinction between *phantasia* and *phantasma* and argues that *phantasia* is what appears, while *phantasma* is the object of memory.[82] Quoting Aristotle, "The affection in soul and body is like a sort of picture, the having of which, we say, is memory. It is an imprint of *aisthema* [perception] like the mark of a signet ring."[83] Similarly, Chappell sees *phantasma* as memory *of* something, that it is just as "real" of a perception, that is, as an object itself, as when it is first perceived.[84] Discussed within the context here, it is the process of *phantasia* that creates *phantasmata*. Thus, what we have here is similar to what is found in the story of the scribe and the painter in the *Philebus*. It seems both are involved, as the *Philebus* would imply, in its comparative function. Thus, not only is there a memory of perception in an image, but there is also a memory of judgment.[85]

All this, of course, brings us back to the discussion and puzzle of memory found in the wax imprint and, yes, to the third word used for image, *eikon*. According to Ambuel, when pertaining "to the copy of an original, *eikon* overlaps in meaning with *eidolon* and *phantasma*," but "emphasizes the resemblance that the image bears to the original, as opposed to difference."[86] This much has been covered in the theological chapter previously. Here, it is mentioned again with regard to memory because, for Aristotle, *eikon* is how mental object can be manipulated.[87] In order to create a mental object that is a reliable indicator of the sensory world, and something one can use, it must retain its likeness in some way. Therefore, Aristotle calls sense impressions *eikons*, which is contrasted with Plato's more generic use of the word *eidolon* in the wax tablet passage. While it may be true that *eikon* and *eidolon* share the sense of dependency a copy has on its exemplar, it is *eikon's* likeness which allows for memory to take place.

82. Sorabji, *Aristotle on Memory*, xvi–xvii.

83. Sorabji, *Aristotle on Memory*, xvi; quoting Aristotle, *Memory and Recollection* 450a25.

84. Chappell, "Aristotle," 401–2.

85. Chappell, "Aristotle," 397, 400. Chappell parenthetically notes that Aristotle seems to have deliberately referred to the *Philebus* in *De Memoria*.

86. Ambuel, *Image and Paradigm*, 74–75.

87. Chappell, "Aristotle," 402.

In fact, for Aristotle, there would not *be* an image if it were not for likeness because the "pathway" to get to the exemplar would not evident, that is, there would not be a passage of time.[88] Since memory is of the past, the imprint must serve "as a reminder." Otherwise, one would only get to as far as the imprint. Chappell notes this exact conundrum in *De Memoria*: "If there is in us something like an impression (*typos*) or an inscription (*graphe*), why would perception of *this* very thing be memory of some *other* thing, rather than of *it* [the impression]?"[89] Aristotle's answer is that an image is both a copy and a thing itself in its own right.[90] A painting can be viewed *as* a painting, but it can also capture something beyond what is just the painting itself. The image can serve as *reference* for whatever is the absent thing brought to mind.[91] It is here that the Aristotelean balance between *eikon* and *phantasma* is tilted in favor of the latter, for "in memory, knowledge or perception is retained in us by the retention of *phantasmata*. In recollection, knowledge or perception is recalled by way of *phantasmata*."[92] As the *Philebus* only implies, but Aristotle specifically states, the passage of time imposes a judgment, and with that judgment, the memory of perception (imprint) is "passed through" to that of a memory of judgment.

Therefore, recollection is a *search* for memory, and in a way, obviates the need for mental pictures (representations for those less inclined to pictures). Images can be manipulated in order to arrive at a particular memory. They can be ordered, giving a structure to memory that later becomes the familiar mnemonic technique of moving through various places.[93] Depending on a particular motion (*kinesis*) or even motions, images are "activated" and move on to the associated or linked image that is the target. If asked "what did you eat for breakfast," one might first see an image of their kitchen in the morning before moving to a bowl of oatmeal. This process can either be "necessary or habitual,"[94] marking the type of "relationship between images."[95] One remembers the bowl of oatmeal because

---

88. Sorabji, *Aristotle on Memory*, 7.

89. Chappell, "Aristotle," 401; Sorabji, *Aristotle on Memory*, 9; referring to *De Memoria* 450b.

90. Aristotle, *De Memoria* 450b20.

91. Chappell, "Aristotle," 402.

92. Chappell, "Aristotle," 403; referring to *De Memoria* 453a16.

93. Sorabji, *Aristotle on Memory*, 22–23.

94. Chappell, "Aristotle," 404.

95. Sorabji, *Aristotle on Memory*, 45. Sorabji makes a philosophical distinction here

one consumes it (habitually) in the kitchen (but not always). One could also respond by saying, "I had burnt bacon for breakfast," in which the image of fire on a stove (or heating element) can come before the bacon, demonstrating the necessary relationship between heat and burnt food. Regardless of whether the process was habitual or necessary, a starting point in a search leads to another representation, if not the target memory itself. In this scanning of memory, images are "read," as if reading a book, or in the case of Cicero, reading the words on a *wax tablet* or papyrus.[96] And in leafing through the "pages" one can show the mark of good memory, the ability to "move material about [manipulate] instantly, directly, and securely."[97] It is a bit ironic that it was Plato who likened the soul to a book in *Philebus* 38e, and the writings of the scribe and paintings of the painter to its pages.[98]

Thus, the crucial difference between Plato and Aristotle comes in what is meant by recollection. Even though Plato refers to the distinction between memory and recollection himself in the *Philebus*, recollection is a grasping of *a priori* ideas or Forms, in a general theory of knowledge.[99] For the most part, remembering is a reawakening of things already learned, accessing previous lifetimes of knowledge. As such, the functional significance of memory is recognition of the universal connections found through dialogue and judgment, in the face of distrusting perception. By contrast, Aristotle's theory of memory is much more neutral in that recollection can be of any ideas which show a connection or order in the past.[100] An image does not necessarily lead to Forms, but can be more of the mundane kind of knowledge one accrues through history, i.e., impersonal memory. Thus, Aristotle does not need to resort to a preexisting soul. Rather, recollection is learned material, that is, knowledge "seen" or learned for the first time, not before one's birth, and then accessed later in time.

---

in the relationship, whatever that might be, not of the images, but between them. It is the difference between "what" makes two images similar as opposed to "how" two images are similar.

96. Carruthers, *Book of Memory*, 33.

97. Carruthers, *Book of Memory*, 21–22.

98. Deretić, "ΨΥΧΗ as Biblion," 70, 78.

99. Chappell, "Aristotle," 405–6.

100. Chappell, "Aristotle," 406.

BACK TO PLATO

Consequently, the difference between Platonic and Aristotelean recollection also appears in the difference between possessing and having *memory*. Interestingly situated in a discourse between the wax tablet and aviary models of memory, the difference in possessing and having a cloak is in its use. One can possess a cloak but said not to have it "in hand," much like what the aviary model will propose by saying one has knowledge "in hand" by catching a bird. In so doing, one has "caught" a piece of knowledge, which was stored in memory. This "hunting down" and catching is Aristotelean, as one searches for a *phantasm*. Memory is *used* in the sense of *having* a mental picture and can only be called so if it goes beyond an imprint in the first place to something that can be "caught." Plato, however, only implies that the aviary is a model for memory since he only explicitly mentions "memory" in the wax tablet. Here, the imprint *is* memory and is something one possesses. In fact, one could say that the wax tablet necessarily precedes The aviary in how memory can be characterized. One needs to first possess a memory before being able to use it. This seems to be the resolution in the *Philebus*, which Aristotle picks up on. The picture (*eikon*, not *phantasma*) created by the painter is then later used by the person as *phantasma*.[101]

The potential problem with the painter and *eikon* rears its ugly head because in most of the Platonic writings, painting is associated with imitation in the negative sense. In *Republic* 10, the painter is a third class of artisan in the line of "bed maker," who only paints the *appearance* of a bed. This is carried over to the *Sophist* where the painter is classed with the appearance-makers, those who "say goodbye to the truth, and instead create those proportions in their images that seem beautiful instead of the actual proportions."[102] Furthermore, painting is an "imitator's art," which creates images that pose for things that are not.[103] This is significant because one of the major themes of the *Sophist* is to define what a sophist is through a splitting of opposing classifications. Since the painter is a creator of *phantasmata*, the painter, along with the sophist, is placed into the category of *phantastike* or art of appearances (as opposed to *eikastike*, or true to original), which as imitation, deceives one into thinking it is real. Eventually, the

---

101. Plato, *Philebus* 39b, 40a. Hackforth notes that Plato uses *phantasmata* in 40a as a synonym for *eikones*. Plato, *Plato's "Philebus,"* 72. It would seem that there is distinction in how the two words function.

102. Plato, *Sophist* 236a5.

103. Plato, *Sophist* 234e.

sophist is ultimately defined as an imitator of the philosopher, or one who pretends to be wise.[104]

The potential solution to this painter's problem might be in the same vein as the distinction between possessing and having found in the analysis of memory. In all the examples given, the painter *has* the original from which to make an imitation but cannot be said to possess it. The visitor sets a trap by mentioning "true proportions," and it is sprung precisely because a painter cannot be completely faithful in creating a copy of a "large-scale work." This is evident from the perspective of looking up at a large statue, the Colossus of Rhodes perhaps, where painting it "as is" will incorporate the said deception. In this case, the painter *must* imitate, that is, paint only an appearance while "translating" a sculpture into a painting. Suppose, however, that a painter possesses the exemplar from which a painting is produced. In this case the painter knows *something* about what he or she possesses, even if it does not come from the craft of the exemplar. In the *Philebus*, the painter "possesses" the words of the scribe, in creating a likeness in a painting (*eikones*) that can properly convey *pathos*. Therefore, as far as memory is concerned, it embodies the relationship of the crafter to his or her art, *in* what is created, in what is possessed by the image as *eikon*.

CHARACTER OF MEMORY

In effect, there is a tautology between image and memory in the same way that the *Theaetetus* and *Sophist* talk about being and not-being, and it hinges on memory as a possession or as a utility. In the famous question of how something can be both one and many without contradiction, the definition of image as something that both is and is-not allows for a "sharing" of type, which also allows for being and not-being without contradiction.[105] Yet, the fundamental characteristic of memory is Platonic if indeed memory *is* the wax tablet and its imprints. As Ricoeur notes, "*Eikon* and imprint is more primitive to the relations of resemblance that sets the mimetic arts into play, that a truthful or deceitful mimetic can occur only because there is a dialectic of accommodation, harmonization, or adjustment that can succeed or fail."[106] In other words, there needs to be an interpretation of the imprint.

---

104. Ambuel, *Image and Paradigm*, 5. Even more disturbing since they exact a fee for their so-called expertise.

105. Ambuel, *Image and Paradigm*, 127.

106. Ricoeur, *Memory, History, Forgetting*, 13.

Of course, by this time, one has passed from *eikon* to *phantasma*, which is more Aristotelean than Platonic, but even here, as far as the *Philebus* is concerned, the *work* of the artist still plays to *eikon*. Thus, the Janus-faced feature of memory, the looking toward of both past and future, is first based on what-is *before* it can be what-is-not, similar in fashion to the necessity of first needing to possess knowledge before identifying false belief.

This naturally leads back to what the imprint "contains," and this, too, is Platonic though it clearly has Aristotelian heirs. In his continued discussion of *eikon* and imprint, Ricoeur distinguishes the original affection contained in *eikon* and the force of the affection imparted in the imprint.[107] For Plato, however, the two are not separable. As the *Philebus* reveals, the *eikon*, the work of the painter, "contains" both the judgment of the scribe and the *pathos* of imprint. As memory *and* as image, it "captures" what-is and what-is-not. How this might work is that *in* the likeness, one has what-is-not, or in other words, by one's possession one *has* what-is-not. This trades on the Platonic mistrust of the senses and gives reason for Platonic recollection. It is only after separating *eikon* and imprint that one's use of memory becomes *phantasmata*, to say things about the senses. And it is here that most modern interpretations of theories of memory take place.

A CHRISTOLOGICAL DETOUR?

Given the Greek nature of memory, its Christian theological implications seem evident. Since Christ has a "hand" in the creation of all things, what does that mean for the image of God humans are said to possess and have by virtue of being created? Remember, that a huge ethical concern has been noted earlier in the image being a possession. But having gone through the tautology of image and memory, the linking of the image of God to the memory of God appears to be the logical next step. Admittedly, this will be conceptual since pinning down the memory of God can only ever be liminal. Thus, this is not a question of epistemology, but it can, in a way, be one of ontology because, in the end, the memory of God finds its way to theological anthropology. There must be something that *is* within human beings that accounts for the image of God. And having distinguished between possessing and having, the memory of God as possession is something imparted and latent, primordial even, that refers to God. In the previous chapter, the image of God was described in theological terms

---

107. Ricoeur, *Memory, History, Forgetting*, 50–51.

with some references to Greek terminology. Here, the book will trace how the Greek concept of image became associated with the image of God. It will take seriously *eikon* as opposed to *phantasm* (which will be important for *human* constructions of god images), and broaches what Paul states as "having the mind of Christ."

How does one get from the image of God to the memory of God? Part of the answer lies in the wax tablet. This passage clearly shows that memory is 1) an imprint and 2) physical, both features of the image of God described in the previous chapter. The parallel is striking. Just as Irenaeus describes the imprint of God in clay, so, too, Plato describes a block of wax in the soul which receives an imprint from sense perception. In addition, the state of the wax is what makes the imprint more or less durable. The better the wax, the more durable the imprint and the more durable the memory. Again, this parallels the ideal moisture content of clay in human beings so that they can hold the image of God. But can one make the argument that the *memory of God* is the image of God? For this, the memory-image tautology described in this chapter must be applied to the image of God.

The theological place to start is in the Gospel of John's Prologue: "In the beginning was the Word and the Word was with God, and the Word was God." Typically, Christian interpretation of the Word is strictly rational, that the Word represents some kind of divine intelligence or reason, which in John's Prologue was "in the beginning" and is responsible for creating all things, presumably, in a dialogue within the Godhead. However, John Sallis makes the argument that the entire Platonic corpus can be misinterpreted if one limits themselves to a strict definition of logos as rationality.[108] There is a more ancient understanding of logos that means "gathering up" or "coalescing."[109] The "*logos* belongs to a process of gathering together in which beings are brought forth into manifestness, to stand in their truth."[110] Furthermore, Socrates makes the argument that logos must be like a living being with its own body.[111] All this taken together leads one to speculate that, by logos, one is asking what is being coalesced in the incarnation of

---

108. Sallis, *Being and Logos*, 14.

109. Sallis, *Being and Logos*, 7.

110. Sallis, *Being and Logos*, 9.

111. Plato, *Phaedrus* 264c. Sallis makes the further argument that for logos to mean anything, it must have an effect, that is, the *soul* of logos is in *ergon*, the doing, or deed. Sallis, *Being and Logos*, 16.

God. At the very least, it would be some kind of image, since, as Plato in the *Cratylus* affirms, "words are images."[112]

If words are images, then what kind of image is in play here? Starting again from the theological, *eikon* is the term used for the *imago Dei*, but it is also the term used in the *Cratylus* 432c. This is significant because in chapter 1, we previously described the case of the *imago Dei* being the *perfect* image, so much so, that Christ was seen as a perfect replica of God. David Sedley, in his commentary on *Cratylus*, makes the case that indeed a portrait of Cratylus could be a perfect image of Cratylus, but only *as* portrait.[113] Ambuel, by contrast, takes Socrates at face value, and asserts that such a creation, should it be made to perfectly replicate Cratylus, would not be Cratylus and an image, but two Cratyluses.[114] It would seem, then, that theologians are on the right path to claim that Christ could be a perfect *human* replica of God, but incorrect to make the leap that in *eikon* one finds something that is perfectly copied. As Sedley points out, the medium of exemplar and copy are different and simply cannot be identical,[115] and as the previous discussion has pointed out, *eikon* states the likeness in what is different. So, what could *eikon* be referring to if theologically a perfect image is to be maintained?

It is here that memory and imprint come into play. Scholars have pointed out that Heb 1:3 refers to Christ as the "perfect or exact" imprint of God. Various Bible translations also refer to representation, as well as the very stamp of God's nature (RSV). The Greek, however, is *charakter*, not *typos*, nor *eikon*. *Strong's Concordance* 5481 cites the original use of *charakter* as a tool for engraving, which then became a "die" or "mould," before coming to mean a stamp used to impress images onto coins or a seal. Figuratively, *charakter* has come to mean exact copy, which we just described as something impossible for the meaning of image.[116] The key

---

112. Ambuel, *Image and Paradigm*, 168. Not only are words images, but so too are names, which the *Cratylus* speaks about directly (100). This play on words is also found in the *Theaetetus* as well as in sentence structure (noun + verb) in the *Sophist*.

113. Sedley, *Plato's "Cratylus,"* ch. 6, "The Limits of Etymology"; sect. 4, "Cratylus and Falsity"; loc. 1817.

114. Ambuel, *Image and Paradigm*, 80.

115. Sedley, *Plato's "Cratylus,"* ch. 6, "The Limits of Etymology"; sect. 4, "Cratylus and Falsity"; loc. 1817.

116. Ambuel makes a further note, that if a copy is exact, it cannot be an image, and if the "copy" is completely different, then it also cannot be an image. Ambuel, *Image and Paradigm*, 80n106.

is *what* is being stamped into Jesus, and Heb 1:3 says that it is God's essence (*hypostasis*, though RSV translates as "nature"), so much so that Jesus exhibits a glory that can be seen. Thus, Christ as *eikon* of God is more accurately described as imprint, which in the Greek sense is memory. Jesus possesses the coalesced "perfect" memory of God.

The intricacies of the Trinity and Christology are beyond the scope of this chapter, but a few remarks must be made if the imprint is of a hypostasis since it also asks the question of what it "contains." In the course of this book, most of the sense impressions made into the wax tablet have been of external objects, but as Ambuel notes in his discussion of *eidolon*, impressions need not be physical. He cites *Phaedrus* 250d, "that there exists no image (*eidolon*) of wisdom perceptible to the eye, only images of beauty."[117] If, however, Christ is the imprint of God, he "contains" the judgment[118] as well as *pathos* of God, both factors in what counts as being wise. How could Christ, then, represent wisdom as an image, if no images of wisdom exist? For possible answers one must first turn to Jewish sources of the much-maligned Greek-influenced use of *eikon* in the intertestamental period.

One aspect of Chris Kugler's work on Paul and the image of God traces the intertestamental use of *eikon* and the related term "likeness" in the Second Temple period. He counts twenty-two uses of *eikon* in both physical as well as spiritual senses, that is, *eikon* used to refer to body or soul/spirit.[119] He notes that all physical interpretations occur from Palestinian sources and that spiritual sources come from the diaspora, lending weight to the criticism that Greek thought influenced *eikon* interpretation. While this may be true, the fact that there is both physical (as discussed previously) as well as spiritual interpretation suggests a diversity of what *eikon* meant. In the previous chapter, this shift in meaning of *eikon* was between dissimilarity and likeness. Here, there may be further clues that hinge on the likeness found in *eikon*.

Kugler's analysis of the *eikon* of God in the Greco-Roman world can be traced through the Middle Platonic telos of "likeness to God" through to Philo's *eikon* of God. On this route, he begins with *Theaetetus* 176b where one's goal is to "escape evil" and become like god, being holy, righteous, and with wisdom.[120] This is linked to Plutarch's "becoming the Image of

117. Ambuel, *Image and Paradigm*, 72.

118. Jesus's function as Judge may be something to keep track of here (John 5:22).

119. Kugler, *Paul and the Image*, 79.

120. Kugler, *Paul and the Image*, 92. Or, justice and piety along with wisdom (Plato,

God" with the "likeness of God,"[121] the image of which had imperial functions as discussed in chapter 1 of this book. While these are clearly human
possibilities of becoming "divine," Kugler only *indirectly* makes the association of "likeness of God" to image of God in Philo when he links "the
telos of happiness" with becoming an "image."[122] It is indirect because, as
Kugler knows, Philo does not use the word *eikon* in that particular passage.
Rather, the force of the argument relies on how Philo unambiguously refers
to the "Image of God as the logos of God through which whole universe
was framed."[123] This aligns with the Plutarch passage concerning imperial
function in "becoming" like *and* that, in so becoming, the ruler is the one
who possesses God's logos, "as his likeness and luminary, intelligence in
place of a sceptre."[124] Oddly, Kugler, while translating this passage, made
no comment on what appears to be a more direct link to Philo's constant
use of *eikon*, but he does return to the logos-image linkage in Philo's defense of Plato's Forms. It is here that "Philo considers 'Forms' as 'archetypal
paradigms' that give each thing its shape,"[125] reinforcing Kugler's argument
about Middle Platonic appropriation.

By the time Kugler gets to Paul, he adds an appropriation of Jewish
Sophia tradition to Middle Platonism, linking *protokos* (firstborn) to *eikon*.
In so doing, Kugler demonstrates a wisdom Christology rather than an
Adamic one, leading to Paul's position of Christ's "'unique divine identity'
as creator."[126] As *protokos*, Christ is the divine, preexistent, Creator, in whose
image human beings are created (that is, "formed," *morphe*). In fact, Kugler
takes the meaning of "predestination" in Rom 8:29 as an allusion to wisdom
Christology since it must have occurred "in the beginning."[127] This seems to
be a more circuitous route given the rest of his analysis of Rom 7–8, which
focuses on Jewish missiological interpretation that flowed into Christian
soteriology (as far as function of image goes), not to mention that Rom
8:29 speaks of firstborn in terms of *human* creation. But by the time Kugler
arrives at Col 1:15, his argument for a wisdom Christology is a strong one.

"*Theaetetus*" and "*Sophist*," 46).

    121. Kugler, *Paul and the Image*, 93.

    122. Kugler, *Paul and the Image*, 100; referring to Philo, *Dec.* 72–74.

    123. Kugler, *Paul and the Image*, 96; referring to Philo, *Special Laws* 1.81.

    124. Kugler, *Paul and the Image*, 93.

    125. Kugler, *Paul and the Image*, 96.

    126. Kugler, *Paul and the Image*, 138; see also 184.

    127. Kugler, *Paul and the Image*, 164.

Not only is there a straightforward way of reading "he is the image of the invisible God, the firstborn of all creation," but the proximity of the words *protokos* and *eikon* makes sense contextually, which cannot be said of Rom 8:29. In the end, however, the importance of Kugler's analysis rests on his assertion of a wisdom Christology.

By assuming a wisdom Christology, it is possible to link together *eikon*, imprint, wisdom, and memory. Earlier, we picked up on the idea that wisdom had no image. Additionally, in the same section just after "likeness to God," Socrates avers that at best, a person can only approximate the righteousness of God, and that is what counts for wisdom and goodness, the supposed divine attributes that are "like god."[128] One can imagine, then, what a claim like Jesus *being* wisdom might sound like to Greek ears. It is not possible. A human being cannot be wisdom, that is, an *eikon* of God. In fact, the joke is on "you." All you must do is remember *Republic* 10, where Socrates supposes that there is some "artist" who can create everything. It seems to be the very same description given to the preexistent divine logos who creates everything, except all this person must do is twirl a mirror about, that is, create *phantasma* by reflecting images. Theaetetus thinks it a joke that anyone should be able to create everything, and the visitor agrees, adding that such a person must be playing a game, especially if charging a fee for his expertise.[129] Not that Jesus exacted any fees for his teachings, but it is clear that an "artist" who "mechanically"[130] reflects images is an imitator, a deceiver. Christ as image of God can only be an imitation, which is one of the definitions of a sophist, one who specializes in the fantastical arts.

Thus, in appropriating Jewish wisdom speculation, Paul may be implicitly arguing a theological concept of wisdom as "true" *eikon*. Not only is Sophia the creator of the *kosmos*, but as Sophia and *eikon*, she is just as the *Timaeus* describes the *kosmos*, "an image of the Intelligible, a perceptible God."[131] A perceptible God must be able to be seen, and this is what one finds in Jewish mirror language. One key text is Wis 7:26: "For she (*sophia*) is a reflection of eternal light, a spotless mirror of the working of God and an image of his goodness." As a Hellenistic Jewish text to supposedly have

---

128. Plato, *Theaetetus* 176c.

129. Plato, *Sophist* 233a—234d.

130. Plato, *Theaetetus* 176c. Rowe's translation states "in the case of craftsmen merely mechanical" to refer to the "artist."

131. Kugler, *Paul and the Image*, 92. Kugler also notes that it was not until Sophia speculation that Sophia was considered a creator of the cosmos. Cf. Kugler, *Paul and the Image*, 45.

had an internal Jewish audience,[132] it would seem that in contrast to the Greek denial of images for wisdom, the author of the Wisdom of Solomon uses *eikon* in relation to a glory that can be seen. In fact, the phenomenon of "reflecting" is more accurately translated as "beholding" in Jewish glory literature.[133] Kugler picks up on this, quoting David Litwa at length: "The semantic association of 'glory' and 'image' as well as 'image' and 'mirror' indicate that we are close to the kind of interpretation we see in 2 Cor. 3.18."[134] It is the very same kind of language one finds in Heb 1:3, that in a reflected image one sees God. Furthermore, as Kugler notes, Sophia is viewed as the "cosmogonical agent," the very one who is identified with the logos, suggesting that "the author of Wisdom understood Jewish *Sophia* and philosophical *logos* in quite similar terms."[135] Thus, in Paul, there is a christological construction of image that insists on being able to see wisdom, which interestingly takes a semantic cue from Greek (*eikon*), and incorporates Jewish Sophia.

That said, Kugler stops his appropriation of Jewish Sophia speculation at that of a divine and preexistent Christ, which gives the opportunity to link Sophia to memory by way of inheritance. Most biblical references to inheritance are those pertaining to land and wealth, but as discussed in chapter 1, Gen 5:3 states the case for an image "inherited" through sonship. Given what we know about the Greek sense of *eikon* and the philosophy behind image, begottenness is similar to bringing into being or becoming. It is through being born that an image is borne. Of course, inheritances can be passed onto any number of descendants, a point discussed later below, but regarding Christology, Jesus is the *only* begotten Son, and the *only protokos* to whom an inheritance is made. If the previous arguments about image are followed, then the "what" of inheritance is "gathered up" and passed onto the Son. In being the Word, Christ as *eikon* coalesces God's wisdom in the incarnation, that is, Jewish wisdom speculation is inherited and linked within "perfect" memory.

132. Grabbe, "Wisdom of Solomon," 1427. Grabbe claims that perhaps Alexandrian Jewish youth were the target audience, to teach them against "perverse" Greek culture.

133. Kugler, *Paul and the Image*, 134; citing N. T. Wright, *Climax*, 185.

134. Kugler, *Paul and the Image*, 134. "And all of us, with unveiled faces, seeing the glory of the Lord as though reflected in a mirror, are being transformed into the same image from one degree of glory to another; for this comes from the Lord, the Spirit" (2 Cor 3:18).

135. Kugler, *Paul and the Image*, 69. See also Wis 7:22: "wisdom, the fashioner of all things"; and Wis 9:1: "Oh God . . . who have made all things by your word."

TOWARD THE HUMAN IMAGE OF GOD

One can see the potential route for the development of a memory-wisdom imagery by combining various aspects of Jewish and Greek thought, *perhaps*, as Paul might have. First is the description of the logos in Philo's *Allegorical Interpretation*:

> God's shadow is his *logos*, which he made use of like an instrument, and so made the world. But this shadow, and what we may describe as the representation, is the archetype for further creations. For just as God is the paradigm for the image, to which the title of Shadow has just been given, even so the image becomes the paradigm of the other beings . . . that man was made according to the image when it had acquired the force of a paradigm.[136]

First, Philo does not associate light with logos,[137] so the Jewish glory element is missing here. That said, the construction of logos as an image is prominent. Just as a signet ring impresses into the wax tablet, Jesus acquires the "force" (stamp) of the paradigm, just as what the word *charakter* would imply. Second, the imprint has a referent to God in memory. Kugler argues that for Philo, a "reflection" did *not* count for seeing God because otherwise a "created thing" would mediate something of the "uncreated."[138] Whether Philo thought that Jesus was a created being is not the point here. Rather, Philo seems to be following Platonic Forms, and from an epistemological point of view, Kugler is correct. However, ontologically what is "perceptible" nevertheless leads to the Intelligible, according to Platonic recollection theory. Therefore, while Shadow does not use glory language, it still relies on the memory of the wax tablet so that, third, the idea of *human beings* as an image of the image can be constructed.

It is here that the claim made in chapter 1, that the image of God is something physical in human beings, can be combined with the claim that the image of God is memory. If memory is image and image is wisdom, then human beings "inherit" wisdom in their very creation. One can see this pattern in the Dead Sea Scrolls:

> For God's ordinance is engraved over all the iniquities of the sons of Seth. And a book of memorial is written before Him for those who keep His word. And this is the vision issuing from the

---

136. Kugler, *Paul and the Image*, 95; referring to Philo, *Allegorical Interpretation* 3.96.

137. Peltier, "Λόγος Christology," 22; quoting Guthrie.

138. Kugler, *Paul and the Image*, 136.

> meditation on the book of memorial. And he gave it as a heritage
> to mankind and to the people of the spirit. For his (man's) shape
> is modelled on the holy ones, but meditation belongs no more to
> the fleshy spirit, for it cannot distinguish between good and evil
> according to the judgement of its spirit.[139]

In keeping God's ordinances, a book of memorial is written, and this book is inherited *because* man's shape is modeled after the holy ones.[140] Furthermore, God's ordinances are "engraved" suggesting that it supersedes whatever guilt might have been passed on from the murder of Abel. As such, the "engraved words" are part of one's "modeling." If one adds to this 4Q418 81, where in v. 9, "humans are made rulers over His treasury," and v. 20, "for God has assigned a heritage to all the [living], and all those wise in heart will understand," one can see the image of God as God's memory *in* human beings.[141]

This written nature of the word in the heart has been noticed by Mary Carruthers and is a consistent theme throughout her work with Medieval memory. In building her case, Carruthers starts with ancient Greco-Roman and Jewish use. She also refers to the wax tablet but emphasizes its visual nature. What is impressed in the wax is "read" in some "eye-dependent" process.[142] While Carruthers goes to Prov 3:3, to show that faithfulness and loyalty can be "written on the tablet of the heart," in the context of this book, Prov 7:1–4, is a better example:

> 1 My child, keep my words and store up my commandments with
> you; keep my commandments and live, 2 keep my teachings as the
> apple of your eye; 3 bind them on your fingers, write them on the
> tablet of your heart. 4 Say to wisdom, "You are my sister," and call
> insight your intimate friend.

The commandments of God (wisdom) are "stored" in a process of transforming something "visual" (apple) to the fingers so that they can be written on a tablet of the heart. This aligns closely to what is found in the above

139. 4Q418 43, in Vermes, *Complete Dead Sea Scrolls*, 409.

140. Kugler argues, in agreement with other scholars, that "holy ones" is an allusion to the angels/Holy court. See Kugler, *Paul and the Image*, 78.

141. 4Q418 81, in Vermes, *Complete Dead Sea Scrolls*. Mary Carruthers points out that memory was often referred to as a treasury house, storehouse, or strongbox, something physical that contained the treasures of memory. Carruthers, *Book of Memory*, 40–41.

142. Carruthers, *Book of Memory*, 31.

analysis of the Dead Sea Scrolls. Moreover, it is wisdom that is "stored," invoking the aviary, or *arca* (wooden chest or storehouse), which Carruthers aptly points out is a storage vessel for *books*.[143] Memory is a library of books that have been written and in a theological context, the commandments or ordinances that count as wisdom, visually and literally stored in the ark of the covenant.[144] It is fitting that Carruthers's work is titled a *book* of memory, for it reflects both the memorial process of wisdom in the heart (Jewish), and also the written book of the soul found in the *Philebus*.

Paul seems to have picked up on this written nature of the heart, where he seemingly uses the same phrasing of 2 Cor 3:1–3 found in Prov 7.[145] In particular, v. 3, human beings are "letters of Christ" with an "ink" that is the Holy Spirit. As Kugler argues, this anthropological characterization is an attack on Jewish-Christian missionaries from outside the Corinthian community, who, insisting on the old covenant (stone tablets), are put into philosophical dress as shallow sophists.[146] Paul and his followers are the true philosophers, which seems to pull on the very arguments put forth in the *Sophist*. Paul is not one of those who "peddles" the word of God, asking for sums of money, who imitates philosophers and deceives people with argumentative contradictions. Paul specifically speaks of this in 2 Cor 17: "Do I make plans according to ordinary human standards, ready to 'Yes, Yes' and 'No, no' at the same time?" No. Rather, Paul points to Jesus Christ who is only yes in God's promises, who has established us "by putting his *seal* on us and giving us his Spirit in our hearts as a first installment" (vv. 19–22). This suggests that human beings are created and sealed with God's memory, that is, like a seal in wax or a tablet of the heart. Importantly, it is also with the Holy Spirit, suggesting that there is a certain *pathos* along with the imprint.[147]

143. Carruthers, *Book of Memory*, 50.

144. Carruthers notes the same imagery of the ark of the covenant as a library in referencing Deut 31:26: "Take this book of the law and put it in the side of the ark of the covenant of the Lord your God."

145. "Are we beginning to commend ourselves again? Surely we do not need, as some do, letters of recommendation to you or from you, do we? You yourselves are our letter, written on our hearts, to be known and read by all; and you show that you are a letter of Christ, prepared by us, written not with ink but with the Spirit of the living God, not on tablets of stone but on tablets of human hearts" (2 Cor 3:1–3).

146. Kugler, *Paul and the Image*, 120–26.

147. "In him you also, when you had heard the word of truth, the gospel of your salvation, and had believed in him, were marked with the seal of the promised Holy Spirit" (Eph 1:13).

CONCLUSION

Considering that the Corinthians were known to "love" wisdom, is not surprising then, that the first two chapters of 1 Corinthians deal with wisdom, one that, like the divine Sophia above, becomes a part of the human imprint. This seems to be the strand of thought missing in "Corinthian wisdom," just as some scholars claim Paul to be against Greek wisdom.[148] While this might be true concerning what wisdom consists of since Paul specifically identifies Christ as wisdom (1 Cor 1:24, 30), there still seems to be considerable Greek concepts of wisdom at play, not to mention that Paul seems to be constructing something *new* about wisdom in appropriating Jewish Sophia speculation. Surely, Christ's wisdom provides "concrete guidance for godly living, that to "learn Christ" is to develop minds that are not futile or darkened."[149] Paul, however, also says that Christians *already* have the mind of Christ (1 Cor 2:16). Now, the mind of Christ is not the same as the wisdom of Christ, which only Christ is in its entirety. Instead, humans have the *mind* of Christ, which makes *use* of the wisdom of God. In being inheritors as sons and daughters of God, we *possess* the image of God by divine fiat, but *have* the image through its use. Thus, having the mind of Christ is the result of the *ontological* properties of image that then can be *epistemologically* applied in how one "conforms" or is "renewed"[150] to Christ, the image-wisdom-memory of God. Given the theological character of memory these first two chapters, the next chapter will build the memory model in a Wesleyan anthropology of the image of God.

---

148. Kilner, *Dignity and Destiny*, 182.

149. Kilner, *Dignity and Destiny*, 75–76.

150. Note the precision of the language: "And have clothed yourselves with the new self, which is being renewed in *knowledge* according to the image of its creator" (Col 3:10 [emphasis added]).

3

A Wesleyan Theological Anthropology of Memory

INTRODUCTION

In this chapter, there will be a turn from the theoretical to the practical applications of image, memory, and theological models of anthropology. Thus, after going through the philosophical possibilities, the book returns to the theological to see how the image of God might work within the human being. To this effect, a lineage of Augustine, Bonaventure, and John Wesley has been chosen, not because these are the only theologians to have exhibited the uses of image and memory, but as a constructed vision of a Wesleyan anthropology that has some historical roots. Each of the above theologians offers something "unique" in their approach to theological anthropology, which will build into a Wesleyan approach that has tripartite aspects of the natural, moral, and political image of God.

AUGUSTINE AND DIVINE ILLUMINATION

Augustine is a monumental figure whose theology is the cornerstone for many subsequent works of theology. This book seeks to touch some of the major points of his doctrine of God, but only as necessary to memory and the image of God. Since theological anthropology is dependent on a doctrine of God, these twin "pillars" of Christian doctrine are unwieldy and in no way can be covered with sufficient depth. However, one place where many of the elements of this book come together is in Augustine's theory of divine illumination, which is at once a question of both doctrine of God and theological anthropology. Lydia Schumacher's work will be the launching point since her work involves both as she traces the history of divine illumination, while Paige E. Hochschild's work will add to it since her work addresses memory specifically with Augustine's theological anthropology.

Lydia Schumacher's work on divine illumination is an ambitious one and begins within the context of Augustine's Trinitarian theology. In short, she follows the ancient standard orthodox position of the simplicity and otherness of God.[1] This serves two general purposes. Simplicity speaks to the unity of the Godhead, which generally occupies the Catholic position in books 5 and 6 of *De Trinitate*. Here, Augustine brings up the old arguments over essence and substance found in the use of the word "person," arguing that essence is equivalent to substance.[2] In 5.2.3, God is "simple" in that only God is unchangeable essence, or substance. Yet, by 7.5.10, Augustine makes the argument that perhaps essence is the more proper word over substance. He does this to ensure that God does not "subsist" as accidents, only as relative distinctions, which was the point behind his speculation as to how God as substance might have a "manifold" quality.[3] Thus, in always coming back to a unity in the Godhead, Augustine shows the simple otherness of God that cannot be completely found in created nature.

Schumacher moves quickly on to creation in the image of God, the anthropological piece made famous by the various trinities in the human psyche. At the outset of the *De Trinitate*, Augustine states, "To have the

---

1. Schumacher, *Divine Illumination*, 29.

2. Augustine, *De Trinitate* 5.8.9; 5.9.1. Philip Schaff notes that he found it difficult to believe that Augustine would not have known the difference between substance and hypostasis, the latter of which identifies with a person. The point here is more about the unity of substance that makes for simplicity rather than Augustine's lack of discrimination. Indeed, Augustine later makes another distinction in *prosapon* and *hypostasis* in 7.6.11.

3. Augustine, *De Trinitate* 6.6.8.

fruition of God the Trinity, after whose image we are made, is indeed the fullness of our joy, than which there is no greater."[4] Being fallen creatures, however, that attainment of joy, or perhaps happiness, is only approximate or indirect, and can only be experienced through knowledge of God. Thus, even though Schumacher claims to be asking for proper theological context,[5] her project inevitably falls back to a question of epistemology, as the title of her work states. To be fair, she begins with the doctrine of God as context that leads to questions of the doctrine of creation. For example, according to Augustine, God's created order is structured by measure, number, and weight.[6] With regard to the human being, it abstractly refers to a person's actions, existence, and total potential, where the mind attaining God is to meet its measure."[7] Since God *is* measure, number, and weight, to be able to "think" like God in "abstractive or unifying acts of reasoning," the mind reflects the image of God, as impressed on human nature.[8] Thus, "forming ideas about the manner and degree to which things perform a function that is good, the mind," Augustine writes, "forms an indirect idea of the Goodness of God, which is to say that it gains insight into the wisdom (*sapientia*) of God."[9] Note the cognitive nature of interpretation as "ordered" by God, which then sets up how God might function in human psychology.

Importantly, Schumacher argues that God's "influence" is *not* externally imposed, as if God provides the mental content that would override human thought.[10] Rather, only when one "remembers" Christ does the mind recognize what has been forgotten and work to "imitate Christ" through its cognitive powers of memory, understanding, and will (the second of Augustinian trinities).[11] In "regaining" such knowledge of God, and this is key, Schumacher states that such faith is an "ongoing effort to *relearn* the use of cognitive skills given by the Son in the spirit He modeled."[12] This is a didactic process where Christ's light is the "inner teacher" one consults

---

4. Augustine, *De Trinitate* 1.8.18.

5. Schumacher, *Divine Illumination*, 25.

6. Schumacher, *Divine Illumination*, 32; referring to Augustine, *De Trinitate*, 11.11.18.

7. Schumacher, *Divine Illumination*, 34.

8. Schumacher, *Divine Illumination*, 35.

9. Schumacher, *Divine Illumination*, 38.

10. Schumacher, *Divine Illumination*, 36, 62.

11. Schumacher, *Divine Illumination*, 54.

12. Schumacher, *Divine Illumination*, 40 (emphasis added). Augustine, however, does say that learning is nothing else but to remember and recall. *De Animae Quantitate* 20.34.

in their own actions.[13] Through the process of illumination, not only is human knowledge enlightened, but so is God as the mind conforms more and more to Christ, increasingly realizing the good of God. In this "reformation" of the intellect,[14] the mind is reordered to desire and know God. Therefore, in the recovery of "forgotten" knowledge of Christ, conformity, that is, loving God, leads to the love of self, which enables love for others. This amounts to reflecting the image of God and being refashioned according to the image via consultation.

Now, Schumacher reads Augustine as claiming that "the mind that perseveres in performing its work in the Spirit of Christ that esteems the Father to be the highest good, performs its work in remembrance of Christ and thereby memorizes how to think after the manner of Christ, praying as much as it thinks."[15] It certainly seems that memory would be operative here, but technically, relearning is not memory. It could also simply be a matter of semantics, and by relearning, Schumacher may mean memory. Notice, however, that in the above statement, one performs an act of remembrance and only then memorizes (or in this case, relearns). Indeed, Schumacher says that "Augustine invokes illumination to illustrate the work of the human intellect as the *imago dei*," and that such "conformity recovers the cognitive capacity by regaining the ability to use it for its proper purpose."[16] Moreover, recovery is dependent on *imitation* of "Christ's example concerning how to think,"[17] which allows the perfection of the image. In either case, relearning or imitation, strictly speaking, is not memory, and if there really is some level of consultation with an inner teacher in a thinking process, it would at least involve the knowledge of Christ *in memory itself*. Schumacher, however, only ever indirectly refers to this, at least regarding Augustine's theories.

Remember, an important part of Schumacher's project is to establish an intrinsic cognitive capacity at work in the human mind as opposed to an extrinsic force. In keeping to a general structure of the Trinity, which she does very well, memory becomes only incidental to a process of recovering

13. Schumacher, *Divine Illumination*, 58.

14. This book does not allow an extended discussion on the ancient theories of mind but suffice it to say that various components to the mind perform different functions, of which the intellect(s) is the primary capacity for knowledge and understanding (as opposed to will, which is involved with passions, and liberty or free choice).

15. Schumacher, *Divine Illumination*, 48.

16. Schumacher, *Divine Illumination*, 58.

17. Schumacher, *Divine Illumination*, 63.

the image of God in human beings. Clearly, however, she is aware that Augustine interprets divine wisdom as Christ, that God is light, and that they serve as sources for illumination in cognitive capacity, content, process, and knowledge of God.[18] In fact, she says that "the wisdom of Christ predisposes people to affirm that there are indeed principles of order, above all, the goodness of God, but that people are not inclined to explore these principles."[19] The question, then, is, why not? A likely answer is that Schumacher wishes to steer clear of any inference to ontologism, where the cognitive content is supplied by God and interferes with or overrides human reasoning. This is something Schumacher develops later, charging Bonaventure with departing from Augustine by resorting to an extrinsic force that supervenes on human cognition[20] rather than the Augustinian way of "participation." As this book will show later, memory plays a critical role in Bonaventure's theology.

AUGUSTINE AND MEMORY

This is not to say that memory is only incidental (a part of a Trinitarian structure) for Augustine, as Schumacher's analysis seems to show. Paige E. Hochschild argues for memory's centrality in Augustine's anthropology by paying attention to the nature of wisdom and how that might relate to memory.[21] Hochschild agrees with Schumacher in that attaining God is one's measure, but since the "divine is a hidden God to which intellect rarely reaches and the sense never,"[22] there is a move from the "superlative" of a "Supreme Measure" to a "measure" as found in one who seeks after wisdom.[23] In other words, *within* a person is a "middle position" that bridges the human and the divine. Since Augustine later says that the truth comes and returns to the Supreme Measure in a clear reference to Christ, Augustine suggests that whoever comes to God through the truth has God in the soul.[24] Furthermore, one can observe "measure" if one "returns to

18. Schumacher, *Divine Illumination*, 3–7.
19. Schumacher, *Divine Illumination*, 51.
20. Schumacher, *Divine Illumination*, 144, 151.
21. Hochschild, *Memory*, 69.
22. Hochschild, *Memory*, 73; quoting Augustine, *Contra Academicos*.
23. Hochschild, *Memory*, 76–77.
24. Hochschild, *Memory*, 77.

God in their heart," another "middle position" with intellect and will.[25] Here, Hochschild does not refer yet to *memory*, intellect and will, but the foreshadowing is prescient. Such truth, or what by now is clearly wisdom to the reader, is a "divine suggestion that descends and is born within the soul, and by virtue of this, God is brought to remembrance."[26] Hochschild notes the etymology of the verb *recordor* is based in the heart,[27] reinforcing what has been previously discussed in chapter 2 of this book as wisdom written on the tablets of the heart. Consequently, wisdom, in its poetic heartfelt language, is more than just an imitation of Christ, but is a possession, making way for wisdom's association with human memory, that is, memory is what makes wisdom possible.[28]

Hochschild, however, makes the argument that Augustine, at least in chapter 10 of the *Confessions*, thinks that God cannot be possessed.[29] In introducing memory as the "embodied soul's mode of approaching God,"[30] Hochschild begins to set the anthropological foundations for memory in Augustine's thought. She claims that at this point "Augustine is not really interested in the knowledge of God so much as conformity to God in the whole person."[31] Yet, if conformity is to take place, then there must be something to which a person can conform. It is not until *Confessions* 10.42.67–69 that Augustine postulates a Mediator who "occupies" a space both divine and human, that is, the incarnated Word. For much of the rest of *Confessions* 10, Augustine finds God to be elusive in materiality, and perhaps this is the reason for moving to the idea that God is more like a felt presence. Rather than an object like a sense image, God is like "the manner of affection or *perturbatio animi*,"[32] but in a negative way, like the coin lost by the woman. The feeling of having lost something is what leads the woman to search for her lost "possession." While the coin is not present to the woman's senses, it is still contained in memory, of which the lost feeling provides the direction of searching.[33]

25. Hochschild, *Memory*, 77–78.

26. Hochschild, *Memory*, 78.

27. Hochschild, *Memory*, 79.

28. Hochschild, *Memory*, 82.

29. Hochschild, *Memory*, 147.

30. Hochschild, *Memory*, 139.

31. Hochschild, *Memory*, 141.

32. Hochschild, *Memory*, 148.

33. Augustine, *Confession* 10.28.27.

While the lost coin parable may be an apt reference for something that has been lost, it does not solve the problem of knowledge. In fact, *Confessions* 10, in general, can be seen as a version of Meno's paradox. Hochschild mentions this in *Soliloquies* where "memory is between the 'seeking' of enquiry, and the 'finding' of full understanding."[34] Similarly here, knowledge of God is somehow beyond memory[35] and not in memory before having been learned,[36] suggesting the transcendence of God. At the same time somehow, knowledge, even before it is encountered, is in memory.[37] Despite this conundrum, Augustine states that "surely my memory is where you dwell" *after* having first learned about God, that is, as far as Augustine's consciousness is aware.[38] This is important to note because in 10.26.25, Augustine broaches the topic of how forgetfulness is remembered. As with propositional memories, there is an element of detachment from an initial experience. Thus, Hochschild can say that "God is sought after through memory, like the memory of joy experienced, in a partial and fleeting manner."[39] However, Augustine also asks if happiness is in memory, and *not* in a propositional way,[40] and concludes that indeed it is "since no one can say that this is a matter outside experience, the happy life is found in the memory."[41] We have previously determined that happiness consists in the good of God and by possessing this truth we have God in our souls. It would seem, then, that a stronger argument is being made about the knowledge of God, that one may actually possess God in some way.

Logically, wisdom would be the likely candidate for what is possessed, but in *De Trinitate*, a clear distinction is made between human wisdom and divine wisdom. Already covered are the usual differences of simple versus multiple and of mutability, which generally apply to the Godhead. With respect to Christ, however, there is the special difference of natality. Augustine states that wisdom is born, and by that fact accounts for being both Son and image.[42] Much like his discussion on the body and soul in their relative

34. Hochschild, *Memory*, 98.

35. Augustine, *Confession* 10.17.26.

36. Augustine, *Confession* 10.26.37.

37. Augustine, *Confession* 10.9.16.

38. Augustine, *Confession* 10.25.36.

39. Hochschild, *Memory*, 148.

40. Augustine, *Confession* 10.20.29.

41. Augustine, *Confession* 10.21.31.

42. Augustine, *De Trinitate* 7.2.3.

distinctions of being simple and multiple, the Son is distinguishable from God the Father as image, much in the same way an image of Cratylus cannot be a perfect copy of Cratylus.[43] Such a wisdom born is contrasted with a human wisdom that is created in 7.3.4 and repeated in 7.3.5. Human beings are not born of the same wisdom as are Father and the Son; otherwise, there would be an equivalence. Yet, Augustine insists that "'humans *are* the image of God' and not simply 'after the image.'"[44] "After" designates a dissimilarity of parity or status, while image is the "approach to Him [Christ] by a sort of likeness."[45] Thus, even though there is a clear distinction between what is human and what is divine, the sense of *eikon* is in grounded in wisdom.

One can see this *eikon* language in chapter 15 where Augustine compares Christ, the Word, to human words. At first, he acknowledges the difference between the two as he has done before with respect to substance. Yet, despite whatever is *unlike*, there is yet that "word of man . . . to the image of God, that is not born of God, but made by God . . . but which precedes all the signs by which it is signified and is *begotten* from the knowledge that continues in the mind."[46] Did Augustine make a mistake in using the word "begotten" after having already stated the createdness of human wisdom? It is highly unlikely that Augustine would have thought of human wisdom in the same way as Christ, but in another sense, knowledge of Christ as source of human wisdom in the vein of divine illumination is incarnational by being enlightened with light. This book has previously described a cosmological creative wisdom that is a *physical* image of God. Here, Augustine seems to refer to such a wisdom, albeit in the human soul/ intellect, that is the pattern of the creation of human beings as fulfilled in Christ's incarnation.[47] As a result, what is proper to the knowledge of Christ can then be "born" in wisdom so that Christ is effectively both.[48]

For Hochschild, the above can only work through memory, which serves to "anchor the soul in an abiding relation to the divine life through remembering, knowing, and loving God."[49] Functionally, this is accom-

---

43. Augustine, *De Trinitate* 6.10.11. Augustine states that a perfect image would be equal to that which is image, and not its own image.

44. Augustine, *De Trinitate* 7.6.12.

45. Augustine, *De Trinitate* 7.6.12.

46. Augustine, *De Trinitate* 15.11.20 (emphasis added).

47. Augustine, *De Trinitate* 7.3.5.

48. Augustine, *De Trinitate* 13.19.24.

49. Hochschild, *Memory*, 215–16.

plished by what memory does temporally. By "fixing" a perceived object in memory, that is, "artificially giving it a beginning and an end, memory provides a stable ground for the mind's knowledge of creation since it arrests what is tending to non-being, making creation ready at hand for understanding."[50] Thus, while it appears that "wisdom cannot be attained by the embodied soul," in memory, one is able to "graft" the presence of God in the mind, unifying what is higher and lower in the soul.[51] Memory grounds a dialectic from which discourse can occur as one consults a teacher. In this fashion, one has the semblance of wisdom, which for Augustine is both a human and divine thing, a unity between practical and contemplative wisdom (*phronesis* and *Sophia*).[52]

For all of Augustine's talk of *eikon*, however, the driving force for his theology is one of *eidolon*. Part of this is responsible apophatic theology, but by making God "distant" there is literally more to be desired. Undoubtedly this has to do with the fall, which has effaced the image of God, making "the soul a place of unlikeness."[53] Yet, at the same time, Augustine says that if the soul is made after the image of God, then "from the moment when that nature so marvelous and so great began to be, whether this image be so worn out as to be almost none at all, or whether it be obscure and defaced, or bright and beautiful, certainly it always is."[54] A few moments later, he suggests that even if a defacing had occurred, it would not take away its status as image. These are positive, not negative, aspects of image. So, where does the negativity of *eidolon* come from? Augustine repeatedly states that the image of God found in human beings is not the image of the Trinity, again suggesting a negativity in image, but it is not the image itself, but the "distance" or weight of God felt *after* being imprinted. This is the point of Augustine's use of the ring in wax.[55] One can *see* the imprint only after the ring has been *removed* to even think about it. Only then is there the distance necessary for *eidolon* to work. It is not just that there is a difference between the imprint and the ring.

It is here that we enter into some speculation. If Augustine likens the imprint in wax to an *eikon*, then memory is the *physical* location of Christ's

50. Hochschild, *Memory*, 164.
51. Hochschild, *Memory*, 211.
52. Hochschild, *Memory*, 208.
53. Hochschild, *Memory*, 174.
54. Augustine, *De Trinitate* 14.4.6.
55. Augustine, *De Trinitate* 11.2.3.

impingement on human nature and is something that is *not* lost. Augustine gestures to this when he says:

> Where indeed are these rules written, wherein even the unrighteous recognizes what is righteous, wherein he discerns that he ought to have what he himself has not? Where, then, are they written, unless in the book of that Light which is called Truth? Whence every righteous law is copied and transferred (not by migrating to it, but by being as it were impressed upon it) to the heart of the man that worketh righteousness; as the impression from a ring passes into the wax yet does not leave the ring.[56]

Clearly, the book of Light refers to Christ, but the location of the imprint is on the heart. Not only is this language reminiscent of what was covered in the section on Irenaeus but speaks to the same physicality in what is a reference to memory. This image is *not* purely a mental phenomenon so easily dismissed by critiques of a rational image, as if one could switch from reading one book of truth to *the* book of Truth. No. It is the *sameness* imparted into memory, some actual content, in its *pattern*. And this is something that cannot be lost. Moreover, the image is indelibly marked on the human heart, extending to those who are unrighteous, suggesting that the interpretation of memory or pattern can either be false or true, fantastical or iconic. The image itself, however, in its iconic function, is possessed in memory as it points to God.[57]

What might such a pattern of God be like? While Augustine certainly ruminates on the various Trinitarian cognitive structures in the human mind, he writes about the "heaven of heavens" in the twelfth chapter of *Confessions*. Intriguingly, Hochschild locates it under a subheading in her book, titled "Likeness: Heaven of Heavens." Augustine initially describes it as a "nothing something, a being which is non-being" and a "realm of intellect."[58] Thus, the heaven of heavens seems to refer to a place, but also some kind of angelic being(s).[59] In either case, since God created it, it has a creaturely existence yet "knows God completely," that is, concurrently and without temporality.[60] Augustine further qualifies this creature as being

56. Augustine, *De Trinitate* 14.15.21.

57. Remember here the distinction between having and possessing.

58. Augustine, *Confession* 12.6.6; 12.9.9.

59. Hochschild, *Memory*, 175. Later in 12.11.12 Augustine conjectures a "blessed creature if there be such."

60. Augustine, *Confession* 12.13.16. Hochschild states that it "rises above the

"wisdom before everything" but not like the coeternal wisdom. Thus, the heaven of heavens is able to order their whole heart and affections to God in a *satisfied will*."[61] This certainly sounds like what Augustine desperately wants in his own mind, but according to Hochschild, memory can provide only a presence that conveys distance because of sin.[62] As such, it is an eschatological goal, though in later writings it becomes ecclesiastical. If, however, the heaven of heavens is thought of *as* a pattern of memory, then the "sameness" found in the imprint can serve as the light of divine illumination to which the will can then conform. To a degree, there is a "knowing" of God that is the knowledge of Christ.

Yet for Augustine, this inner teacher comes off as merely a consultant. Out of the dialectic setup between teacher and student, the resulting discourse enables one to think their way to God under divine influence. "The grace of illumination empowers the mind to be the direct cause of its own efforts,"[63] that yes, through illumination, one can properly shine light on the object as well as on God. In this discursive practice, memory provides the philosophical space for a "classroom" and is used as a source of knowledge. It is the enlightened intellect, however, that can participate in its imitation of Christ as one conforms themselves to the image when the will "understands" and carries out action. In this "meeting of the minds," one is persuaded to follow Christ as one's soul journeys to find rest. Indeed, the ideal of the heaven of heavens is ever far off since the will, at least in one's mortal lifetime, can never be satisfied. With Bonaventure, however, there is a slight turn that suggests at least the possibility of it.

BONAVENTURE'S THEOLOGY

To go into a thorough history of Bonaventure would be too much here, not to mention a "competing" Thomistic theology to which he has been compared. Major points of historical lineage, however, must be addressed as they bear on divine illumination and memory. For instance, in Schumacher's project, Bonaventure is portrayed as departing from Augustinianism, founding a *locus classicus* of a new Franciscan tradition because

---

mutability of time," but from this passage it is only the knowing which is with time. Hochschild, *Memory*, 175.

61. Hochschild, *Memory*, 176.

62. Hochschild, *Memory*, 177.

63. Schumacher, *Divine Illumination*, 177.

Bonaventure imports Pseudo-Dionysus and "essentialist theology" from Bonaventure's predecessors, Richard of St. Victor, Hugh of St. Victor, and Alexander of Hales.[64] Since God as Supreme Good cannot be contained, God is self-diffusive not only *ad intra*, but *ad extra* in creation, so much so that in a plurality of forms, "creatures resemble ideas as exact copies of them, and the divine ideas resemble creatures in virtue of being their exemplars."[65] This is an instance of essential univocity in the vestiges of God in creation, which Augustine and, through his intellectual lineage, Anslem and Thomas, deny. Furthermore, Alexander's finding of Avicennian abstraction in the writings of Augustine, Anselm, and Pseudo-Dionysus, lent itself to its appropriation into Victorine theology. Since it was Avicenna who claimed, "that the forms or essences God impresses on prime matter exist in the same 'absolute' mode of being as God Himself," and that "mental abstraction is to grasp the 'thing itself' as it exists in God's mind,"[66] Schumacher makes the logical leap in thinking Bonaventure does the same thing in an actualized creation. This leads to the conclusion that in divine illumination "Christ's extrinsic conditioning through the intuitive knowledge of the transcendental—the image of God—the human mind is adequate to acquire accurate and absolutely certain understanding of all things."[67] Schumacher charges Bonaventure with ontologism (a heresy of the Catholic Church), where the knowledge of Christ provides the cognitive content in an extrinsic superadded grace.

T. Alexander Giltner, who wrote his dissertation on Bonaventure's philosophy and theology of divine illumination, describes Schumacher as among the radical orthodox (concerning Bonaventure), whose defining characteristic is, following John Milbank's work *Theology and Social Theory*, a "deep distrust of modernist, post-Enlightenment thought,"[68] which is traced to the "distinctions between philosophy and theology, reason and faith."[69] The target is usually Franciscan Duns Scotus, but Giltner shows that both Milbank and Schumacher consider Bonaventure as the beginning of the Franciscan intellectual tradition. Whether that means Schumacher is "adjudicating negative and pernicious terms without pretext" is perhaps

---

64. Schumacher, *Divine Illumination*, 135.

65. Schumacher, *Divine Illumination*, 122.

66. Schumacher, *Divine Illumination*, 95–96.

67. Schumacher, *Divine Illumination*, 145–46.

68. Giltner, "Lightness of Being," 99.

69. Giltner, "Lightness of Being," 135.

going a bit far as Schumacher herself says that she does not blame Bonaventure for departing from Augustine, nor citing him to bolster his own positions.[70] In fact, she compliments Franciscan innovation as addressing their own theological concerns, in Victorine and Franciscan fashion, where the love of God is prioritized over the knowledge of God.[71] For the purposes of this book, however, it is worth noting that Schumacher appears mistaken about Bonaventure's divine illumination.

Most of the confusion can be attributed to interpreting Bonaventure's exemplarity, which Junius Johnson details is Bonaventure's attempt at answering the question of the one and the many.[72] At issue is how God's simplicity can be manifested in creation, a problem Augustine tried to answer as well. His answer was the divine ideas in the mind of God, which participates by giving form to creation, like a divine template.[73] Since only form is applied, creation is able to develop into what it was created to be, to reach its measure. Bonaventure, however, begins with an epistemological concern rather than the ontological one above: How does God know creatures?[74] Bonaventure says that "God knows creatures by means of eternal reasons which are the exemplary likeness of creatures. They are most perfectly representative and expressive, and they are essentially identical with the divine mystery itself."[75] The confusion arises out of what Bonaventure meant by essence since as covered above, Augustine made an argument equating substance with essence. If taken from an ontological perspective, it seems, as Schumacher surmises, that God is identical with what is expressed in creation. However, since Bonaventure is approaching from an epistemological vantage first, he is claiming how God knows the exemplary likenesses *within* Godself.[76] Thus, "God's knowledge through exemplary forms *is* in fact knowledge through essence," that in God, the likeness is

---

70. Schumacher, *Divine Illumination*, 152.

71. Schumacher, *Divine Illumination*, 108, 153.

72. Johnson, "One and the Many," 1–2.

73. Johnson, "One and the Many," 3; Schumacher, *Divine Illumination*, 31.

74. Johnson, "One and the Many," 3.

75. Bonaventure, *Disputed Questions*, q. 2, conclusion.

76. Bonaventure, *Disputed Questions*, q. 3, conclusion. "Without a doubt, God knows creatures; and God knows them within the divinity; and God knows them within divinity as in a likeness . . . but as a likeness, it is nothing other than the expressive truth, as was shown in the previous question . . . God knows creatures in a manner internal to the divine nature in their truth, or in that supreme light which expresses other things."

essence in totality.[77] Furthermore, as discussed in *Disputed Questions on the Knowledge of Christ* q. 3, the exemplary forms are only logically distinct from a creaturely perspective, not a divine one. This results in the maintenance of God's simplicity, making room for distinction as exemplars, much like the Trinity itself.

Importantly, the expressed likenesses are not the same essence as creaturely essence.[78] Here, Bonaventure clearly states that the creature and the Creator differ necessarily in essence,"[79] establishing what Augustine meant by substance. God and creatures do not have anything in common regarding substance, which is standard fare for most theologians. Thus, Schumacher's claim of Bonaventure insisting on creatures having identical substance with God is surprising and probably is a result of overinterpreting Avicennian metaphysics into Bonaventure. In fact, Schumacher consistently refers to Bonaventure's *univocal* concept of being,[80] but Bonaventure does not apply it to the relationship between God and creatures. As explained by Philip L. Reynolds, "Replying to the objection that there is no agreement between God and creatures, Bonaventure concedes that there is no 'likeness of univocation of participation,' for God and creatures have nothing in common."[81]

Rather, the likeness between God and creatures is analogical, either through a relational or simple resemblance. A relational resemblance likens how a sailor and teacher might be related as they guide a ship or school respectively, taking on a functional meaning.[82] This is the type of "likeness" associated with dominion language in the image of God, and clearly, there is no common substance involved. In a simple resemblance, "likeness is essentially implicated in exemplarity (whereby a creature imitates God as its archetype) and in the ordination of something to God as to its end."[83] Leaving aside for the moment creaturely imitation, the ordinal nature of

---

77. Johnson, "One and the Many," 5; see also Giltner, "Lightness of Being," 197–98.

78. Johnson, "One and the Many," 8, 10.

79. Bonaventure, *Disputed Questions*, q. 2, conclusion.

80. Schumacher, *Divine Illumination*, 123–24.

81. Reynolds, "Bonaventure's Theory of Resemblance," 237–38.

82. Reynolds, "Bonaventure's Theory of Resemblance," 219–22, 248; Giltner, "Lightness of Being," 195.

83. Reynolds, "Bonaventure's Theory of Resemblance," 220; see also Johnson, "One and the Many," 11; Bonaventure, *Disputed Questions*, q. 2, conclusion.

resemblance is an exemplary causality,[84] which following God's perfect knowledge of creatures, is representative of them. In other words, the language used here is consistent with how this book has been discussing image, but as opposed to Augustine's *eidolon* mode of likeness, Bonaventure prefers the mode of *eikon*, since sameness is the principle behind any "realness" found in analogy, either through relational or simple resemblances. How these manifest in creation is dependent, however, on Christ, the medium, or in Bonaventure's words "Triplex Verbum, the Verbum Increatum, Incarnatum, and Inspiratum."[85]

Christ as *the* image of God or "Similtude of the Father, the Uncreated Word is 'operative and expressive divine power itself' that emanates all Similtudes as the Exemplar in its creative expression."[86] Thus, "in Christ *are hidden all the treasures of God's wisdom and knowledge* (scientiae),"[87] or as Giltner puts it, "perfect knowledge and cognition of God, or Mind of God."[88] As such, the expressive power of God happens through Christ, who having perfect knowledge of Exemplars creates (*Increatum*).[89] Since the Father "begat" the Son, creation is restored (*Incarnatum*), and as inspired Word (*Inspiratum*), the eternal light reveals all, but, most importantly, reveals God. Taken together, Christ is the wisdom of God, who is necessary for human beings to understand anything. Considering that Bonaventure is talking about how a person "considers how things originate and are led back to the end [as Christ knows], and how God shines forth in them,"[90] suggests the workings of memory in Christ's function as *Triplex Verbum* in divine illumination.

84. Giltner, "Lightness of Being," 195; Johnson, "One and the Many," 7.

85. Giltner, "Lightness of Being," 161. *Triplex Verbum* appears in the *Hexaemeron* 3, Christ *en toto*.

86. Giltner, "Lightness of Being," 193–94.

87. Bonaventure, *Collations on the Hexaemeron*, 1.11 (emphasis original; referring to Col 2:3).

88. Giltner, "Lightness of Being," 195.

89. It is important to note here that God's creation is in one single act, so not in temporal sequence. Remember that the manifold nature of creation is "logical" from a creaturely point of view. Cf. Giltner, "Lightness of Being," 197–98.

90. Bonaventure, *Collations on the Hexaemeron*, 3.2.

BONAVENTURE AND CONTUITION

Since Augustinian divine illumination has been discussed previously, the principles of it do not need to be repeated here, for they generally function the same in Bonaventure's theology. However, Bonaventure's unique contribution is the ability of a "contuition" that occurs between Christ and the human mind. As Bonaventure defines it:

> For certain knowledge, the eternal reason is necessarily involved as the regulative and motivating principle, but certainly not as the sole principle nor in its full clarity. But along with created reason, it is contuited by us in part as is fitting in this life.[91]

As Giltner notes in his historical review of Bonaventure scholarship, contuition, and thus divine illumination, was primarily an epistemological issue, but as he subsequently argues, contuition is profoundly a theological issue.[92] Bonaventure is not asking about "assuaging doubt; it is about an encounter with the divine."[93] The actual question of *Disputed Questions on the Knowledge of Christ* q. 4 is whether things known with certitude are also known in the eternal reasons. Thus, certitude is already taken into account *as* it would be in the eternal reasons. Given Bonaventure's theory of resemblances, what creatures know for *certain* must be the way creation is expressed by Christ. This certain knowledge, however, is not extrinsically given, overriding human cognition and providing content as Schumacher supposes. Bonaventure rules this out.[94] Even in a hypothetical case where God's grace acts, such infused knowledge (i.e., extrinsically conditioned) would make acquired or innate knowledge impossible. Certain knowledge is also not from a purely creaturely point of view. This includes even divine "influence" that translates to human habit, for divine influence fails because it is itself not eternal or unchangeable; it comes and goes with the whims of the creature.[95]

---

91. Bonaventure, *Disputed Questions*, q. 4, conclusion.

92. Giltner, "Lightness of Being," 230.

93. Giltner, "Lightness of Being," 233.

94. Bonaventure, *Disputed Questions*, q. 4, conclusion. "In the case of certain knowledge, the evidence of eternal light concurs as the total and sole cause of that knowledge. This understanding is the least acceptable, for it allows no knowledge of reality except in the Word. . . . Since all these are false, this interpretation certainly is not to be maintained."

95. Bonaventure, *Disputed Questions*, q. 4, conclusion; Johnson, "One and the Many," 13.

Instead, a "third way" is invoked as stated above where there is a "matching" of eternal reason in the knowledge of Christ to human reason, and when the soul "contuits" in the production of a mental word, understanding results. The soul is "thinking with" *scientia* obtained from creation, and yet also the divine mind that created it.[96] This goes back to *Disputed Questions on the Knowledge of Christ* q. 2 where both a likeness of imitation and an exemplary likeness is necessary for "any knowledge of reality."[97] In the former, the creature resembles the Creator whereas in the latter the Creator resembles the created. Thus, even though Bonaventure begins with the epistemological context, he is also reaching into the ontological. Giltner, of course, rightly grounds this in Bonaventure's insistence that God's Being and knowing are identical,[98] and through expressed likeness, that is Christ, creation exists. The practical value of contuition, however, is how one knows God, and then by extension, the rest of creation.[99] The "agreement" found in certitude is the imperative for how one *shall* know creation, which is directional for human knowledge, not an absolute. Clearly, Christ is the center and locus for divine illumination,[100] but where in human cognition or the soul is such knowledge located?

BONAVENTURE, MEMORY, AND THE IMAGE OF GOD

Bonaventure uses the familiar Augustinian trinity of memory, intellect, and will as the powers of the soul that image God.[101] Bonaventure first generally states that "the divine image shines forth in the mind," likening the image to the divine light in the tabernacle. He then obliquely mentions intellects, memory, and the eye of reason before elaborating on each of the functions later in chapter 3 of the *Itinerarium*. Interestingly, before doing so, he says that by "considering these three powers, one is able to see God through oneself as through an image, which is to see through a mirror in an obscure

---

96. Giltner, "Lightness of Being," 232.

97. Bonaventure, *Disputed Questions*, q. 2, conclusion; see also Giltner, "Lightness of Being," 198.

98. Giltner, "Lightness of Being," 183; referring to Bonaventure, *Collations on the Hexaemeron*, 1.13.

99. Giltner, "Lightness of Being," 12, 223, 236.

100. Giltner, "Lightness of Being," 161.

101. Giltner, "Lightness of Being," 220; referring to Bonaventure, "Soul's Journey into God" [*Itinerarium*], 3.1, 3.5.

manner."[102] This quotation of 1 Cor 13:12 is the same passage used in *Disputed Questions on the Knowledge of Christ* q. 4 for contuition, suggesting that the intellective process of contuition is how one accesses the *imago Dei* through the soul, which is itself an image of the Trinity. Notice that Bonaventure refers to a plural intellect. Giltner makes the case that scholars have ignored Bonaventure's cognitive theory since Etienne Gilson, though Michelle Karnes's work on Bonaventure's "synthesis" of Aristotelian psychology factors prominently in his own theory of medieval imagination.[103] In any case, the specifics of a passive or active intellect are unimportant here, especially given that Bonaventure thought of them as a reciprocal unity rather than two independent psychological entities.[104] What is of interest, however, is the locus of illumination, which for Augustine was in the intellect. By contrast, for Bonaventure, illumination is in *memory*, which *precedes* anything the intellect can grasp.[105]

In fact, it is "from the activities of memory that one sees that the soul itself is an image of God."[106] Bonaventure explains three activities of memory. First, memory retains *all* temporal things, including the past, present, and future, making it an image of eternity. This concept of memory is more dynamic than one that simply refers to the past, which is only the most obvious. In addition, memory serves the "present by reception and the future by foresight."[107] Therefore, Bonaventure is setting the stage for what a person can know, i.e., stored knowledge, received knowledge, and imagined knowledge. As previously explained, directionality is important for determining *eikon* as opposed to *phantasma*. Second, memory is "informed from above by receiving and holding simple forms which cannot come from sensible images."[108] Bonaventure explains these as "axioms of science" or "everlasting truths," giving the example that in every decision is either a yes or a no. Third, "memory has an unchangeable light present to itself in which it

---

102. Bonaventure, "Soul's Journey into God" [*Itinerarium*], 3.1.

103. Karnes, *Imagination, Meditation, and Cognition*, 75–110. Giltner also blames the lack of attention to cognitive detail as the reason for Bonaventure's perceived lack of rigorous thinking compared to his contemporary Aquinas, and his anti-Aristotelian stance.

104. Giltner, "Lightness of Being," 226–27.

105. Bonaventure, "Soul's Journey into God" [*Itinerarium*], 3.1.

106. Bonaventure, "Soul's Journey into God" [*Itinerarium*], 3.2; Giltner, "Lightness of Being," 221–22. Bonaventure's explanation of the three activities of memory also come from *Itinerarium* 3.2.

107. Bonaventure, "Soul's Journey into God" [*Itinerarium*], 3.2.

108. Bonaventure, "Soul's Journey into God" [*Itinerarium*], 3.2.

remembers immutable truths."[109] The obvious implication here is Christ the light, who in the previous paragraph resides in the tabernacle. Taken together, it seems that Bonaventure is saying that *all* of knowledge, regardless of whether one realizes it or not, is contained in memory.[110] Not only is this consistent with what God must know, but "defines the soul itself as an image of God," resulting in such a closeness to God as to actually be able to grasp him and potentially possess and become a partaker of him.[111]

Thus, just as with contuition, Bonaventure's image of God is a stronger partaking of the divine than Augustinian participation. Rather than a discursive practice of consultation in the intellect, Bonaventure presents the possibility of what can actually be possessed, that is, the knowledge of God. This necessarily is based on sameness and is none other than the eternal light or truth, which is imprinted in the mind/soul.[112] Therefore, the knowledge of God *is* in memory in the proper sense as *imago Dei*, the object of faith (more on faith later). Consequently, the image of God within a person cannot be lost or damaged. As Bonaventure discusses by directly quoting *De Trinitate* 14.15.21 in *Disputed Questions on the Knowledge of Christ* q. 4: "The unjust person is *reminded* that it is necessary to turn to the Lord as to that light by which the human person is touched even when that person has turned away from God."[113] While Bonaventure does not discuss the wax imprint here, its allusion to memory seems implied.

In addition, the powers of the soul (memory, intellect, and will) are completely natural, being a part of created order.[114] Importantly, they provide the structure to compose an image. Reynolds points this feature out in the soul's "configuration" or shape (*figura*), which Bonaventure likens to

---

109. Bonaventure, "Soul's Journey into God" [*Itinerarium*], 3.2.

110. Giltner thinks that memory operates like recognition, almost in Platonic fashion. Giltner, "Lightness of Being," 222. Bonaventure says that upon hearing something one "does not perceive it anew, but rather as if he recognizes them as innate and familiar." Bonaventure, "Soul's Journey into God" [*Itinerarium*], 3.2. Recognizing here is not a kind of rational sense cognition, but is an experiential phenomenon akin to "knowing" axiomatic laws.

111. Bonaventure, "Soul's Journey into God" [*Itinerarium*], 3.2.

112. Bonaventure, *Collations on the Hexaemeron*, 21.7; 23.11.

113. Bonaventure, *Disputed Questions*, q. 4, conclusion (emphasis added).

114. Bonaventure, *Collations on the Hexaemeron*, 2.27. "Again, the creature is made in the Image of God, and this is either a natural or gratuitous (*gratuitam*) image. The former is memory, understanding (*intelligentia*), and will in which the Trinity shines forth (*relucet*)."

a triangle.[115] Each of the powers of the soul are the points of the triangle, while the lines represent a relationship. This same figure is found in the Trinity, where one "point" has a relationship with two others but altogether "encloses the whole surface."[116] Bonaventure states that the soul is an image of God "when the soul considers its Triune Principle through the trinity of its powers."[117] If "the triangle leads into the knowledge of the Trinity,"[118] then the enclosed surface represents the knowledge of God, which for this book is the memory and, in this particular context, the *pattern* of God.

Thus, Bonaventure accomplishes what Augustine could not by "matching" image to image in memory. For Augustine, the image of God could not be ontologically found anywhere, only settling for what is the most likely place in the trinity of memory, intellect, and will. Bonaventure takes a more controversial route by making knowledge of God part of the created order.[119] In principle, then, the human image of God is not lost. In fact, it is necessary for contuition to work. Of course, this takes an act of human cognition to do so, as what is in memory is presented to the intellect and then carried out by the will. Assuming contuition does happen, then "understanding," which Giltner says is a similitude of the intellect, "is the mind turning back upon itself [from] above itself, which in the sight of the mind, is a word . . . that grasps the truth of something . . . that matches the external reality and the divine similitude that is its cause."[120] In this way, God is accessed "through oneself as through an image, which is to see through a mirror in an obscure manner."[121] Yet, one has attained the eternal reasons in memory, to possess God, and in perhaps a limited fashion, in Augustine's heaven of heavens.[122]

---

115. Reynolds, "Bonaventure's Theory of Resemblance," 250–51.

116. Bonaventure, *Collations on the Hexaemeron*, 4.16.

117. Bonaventure, "Soul's Journey into God" [*Itinerarium*], 3.6.

118. Bonaventure, *Collations on the Hexaemeron*, 4.16.

119. Giltner, "Lightness of Being," 223.

120. Giltner, "Lightness of Being," 213. Later, Giltner identifies the *intellectus* with Christ (250–51), seemingly human intellect proper because it is the second power of the soul. He does mention that it can also mean "understanding." Note, however, that this book identifies Christ with memory, not with the intellect. If anything, the intellect is associated with Christ only *through* memory.

121. Bonaventure, "Soul's Journey into God" [*Itinerarium*], 3.1.

122. Both the heaven of heavens and memory are eternal, and while the conformation of the will to God is something Bonaventure ascribes to "angels" in the *Breviloquium*, it is nonetheless the end of the soul's journey to God. In this respect, memory is "halfway" there.

Only in this way can Bonaventure say that the "soul, so stamped with the divine image, had to be capable of knowing God and all things."[123]

IMAGE AND LIKENESS REDUX

That all said, the idea of participation is not without debate. Reynolds notes that Bonaventure reserved the term "participation" for univocal resemblance,[124] which has thus far been ruled out as a means of likeness between Creator and creatures. Similarly, Jinyong Choi writes that Bonaventure, being influenced by Hugh of St. Victor, who taught that image is purely quantitative while likeness pertains to nature, "construes the image as quantitative/non-participative and likeness as qualitative/participative."[125] Reynolds also cites strong evidence from John of La Rochelle, who also influenced Bonaventure and is worth quoting:

> Used in a broad sense, "likeness" refers to any sort of agreement in any category, whether it be in substance, in quantity, or in quality. And in this sense likeness is common in relation to image, for an image is an express likeness of something. This expression should be understood as configuration and as pertaining to the concept of quantity. Used in its proper sense, however, "likeness" refers to an agreement in quality or in the manner of quality. And in this sense, likeness follows image as quality follows quantity. For example, consider an image of Hercules: it is an image because it is configured in the image of Hercules or in imitation of him, and yet there is no likeness until the colors through which the image agrees with Hercules are added. Hence the natural powers of the soul constitute an image and a configuration in relation to God, while the things that come with grace are like colors that have been added to the image.[126]

According to John of La Rochelle and Hugh of St. Victor, one has what appears to be arguments against participation in a "value-neutral" image *and* how participation actually takes place. Image is merely the shape while the

---

123. Bonaventure, *Breviloquium*, 2.9.3.

124. Reynolds, "Bonaventure's Theory of Resemblance," 252.

125. Choi, "Analogy, Spirituality," 105; see also Reynolds, "Bonaventure's Theory of Resemblance," 250, 254. Both Choi and Reynolds note that nature is supernatural quality.

126. Reynolds, "Bonaventure's Theory of Resemblance," 249–50.

likeness participates by "filling in" the image. Image and likeness are two separate features, the latter of which, if Hugh is right, provides the content.

Choi traces the lineage of the separation of image and likeness from Irenaeus to Bonaventure, from the patristic to the medieval scholars, to establish Bonaventure's separation of image and likeness. In fact, he makes the argument that it was Augustine who insisted on a more participatory relationship between image and likeness to object to Marius Victorinus's position of mutual exclusivity between them.[127] Likeness became an eschatological reality achieved through a superadded grace, that of the Holy Spirit. For the most part, this analysis seems accurate, that Bonaventure follows his historical lineage in the radical distinction between image and likeness. In stipulating the distinction between image and likeness, however, it seems that by considering a "superadded" component, participation does not involve the image per se. In defining the image as value neutral or nonparticipatory, the implication is that the image is simply "objective," and that there is no "subjectivity" as well. Bonaventure appears to support this distinction:

> An image indicates a common sharing in quantity while likeness points to a commonness in regard to quality. An image indicates a certain configuration and so it suggests a figure which is either a quantity in a quality or a quality in a quantity, whereas a likeness indicates the same quality belonging to different things.[128]

But the separation of image and likeness can only be maintained if the first sentence speaks for the rest. The second sentence, however, qualifies the first, by adding how an image *contains* an element of quality or quantity (two things), whereas a likeness refers only to quality. If a structure, however, contains something, then it must participate via what it holds.

As Choi argues later, the distinctions are not truly independent of one another, but, with infused grace, the image can be reformed. Image and likeness, while spoken with distinction, are cooperative because "grace being imprinted on the formal structure of creation, *brings* the natural image participatively into the Trinitarian life which it naturally images."[129] In other words, the very creation of human capacity for God, the so-called nonparticipatory image, "is ordered as to their end (simple resemblance)

127. Choi, "Analogy, Spirituality," 8–12.

128. Choi, "Analogy, Spirituality," 62. This is coming from Bonaventure's commentary on Lombard's *Sentences*.

129. Choi, "Analogy, Spirituality," 66–67.

and thus are marks of grace."[130] As such, the infusion of grace via the Holy Spirit finds itself in the "theological virtues such as faith, hope, and charity, which take chief role in the aspiration for God."[131] And in this manner one's image is "recreated" in the possibility of enjoying God, who provides final rest and delight.[132] The Irenaean distinction between image and likeness works developmentally as one increases in likeness to God. The emphasis on likeness ultimately leads to Bonaventure's affective theology, "following Dionysius, where likeness is related to love and is spiritual."[133] Therefore, as an "affective process," Bonaventure views love as "special access to God," which in the end is a final "loving union with God" (*visio beatifica*), rather than "the consummate of human intellect in knowing God."[134] This represents the Franciscan ideal of loving God more than knowing God.

Nevertheless, the affective nature of likeness does not exist in some noumenal state divorced from the natural body. Choi tries to overcome the superadded nature of likeness by appealing to "its formal structure of creation," and how grace acts in the transitional stages of Bonaventure's *Itinerarium* to see the divine in the vestiges and the image of creation.[135] But this confuses three kinds of grace given to human beings. Bonaventure states that there is a "general grace," which sustains existence; a "gratuitously given grace," which prepares the soul to receive the Holy Spirit; and the "grace that makes pleasing," which allows for moral merit.[136] It is the latter that bestows the theological virtues, which *cannot* be received through "pleasing grace" if one first does not consent to gratuitous grace.[137] Thus, even before likeness can begin to grow there needs to be an act of the will, which exists in the so-called nonparticipatory image. Since the will acts only after it has been presented with understanding from the intellect, which itself must be presented with knowledge from memory, grace must act in an experiential knowing, not just an experiential "likeness."

130. Choi, "Analogy, Spirituality," 66.

131. Choi, "Analogy, Spirituality," 80.

132. Choi, "Analogy, Spirituality," 56.

133. Choi, "Analogy, Spirituality," 18.

134. Choi, "Analogy, Spirituality," 80.

135. Choi, "Analogy, Spirituality," 67; see also 69–72. While Bonaventure's distinctions of creation into vestige, image, and likeness are important, in the current context, they will not be discussed.

136. Bonaventure, *Breviloquium*, 5.2.2.

137. Bonaventure, *Breviloquium*, 5.4.4–5.

THE AFFECTUS

Robert Glenn Davis advances a cognitive-affective character to Bonaventure's theology based on the end goal of the *affectus*. Getting there, however, is incredibly complex. Davis notes the notorious difficulty in defining the *affectus*, something echoed by Giltner and evident in Choi. Take, for instance, William of St. Thierry, who assigns both a divine and human component to the *affectus*. The human component tends toward goodness while the divine is the Holy Spirit working in the soul.[138] As can be guessed from the discussion above, there is a cognitive component involving the will, as it is conformed to God, but then also includes "the virtues or various faculties of the soul, in a 'movement of piety, or perception, or faith, or hope, or love, or thought, or will, and so on.'"[139] For Giltner, the *affectus* "is the seat of the soul's desires, and locus of the soul's fulfillment in those desires, as willed by the soul, through the affective power of the union of love."[140] Choi wrestles with these concepts as they apply to likeness, without attempting to define *affectus*. Davis, however, embraces the diversity of how *affectus* has been defined, and chooses to let *affectus* "speak" for itself."[141] "*Affectus* for Bonaventure structures a rhetorical strategy of unsaying that marks the place of an immanent excess in language and thereby attempts to account for human beings' capacity to experience an unknowable God."[142]

For the purposes of this book, however, Davis provides a unique take on Bonaventure's *affectus* through the concept of *synderesis*. Davis traces the history of *synderesis* and its derivative term *conscientia*, concluding that the latter is more cognitive in nature and is a "natural judge" or habit concerned with moral imperatives.[143] *Synderesis*, however, is more complex. It is "the capacity of the soul to be carried into union with God and the infallible inclination toward goodness."[144] The key words here are "capacity" and "infallible." Bonaventure does not establish a "place" for *synderesis*. Rather, "*synderesis* names the affective power as it is moved naturally and

---

138. Davis, *Weight of Love*, 18.

139. Davis, *Weight of Love*, 18. Also see Davis's analysis of Douglas Langdon's take on cognition and affect (48).

140. Giltner, "Lightness of Being," 268.

141. Davis, *Weight of Love*, 18–19.

142. Davis, *Weight of Love*, 28.

143. Davis, *Weight of Love*, 54.

144. Davis, *Weight of Love*, 53.

rightly."[145] In contrast to conscience, which can be fallible due to its inter-action with reason, *synderesis* is infallible "insofar as it desires the noble good of the natural law—the obedience due to God and the respect due to one's neighbor."[146] Thus, analogously to contuition found in the intellect, conscience and *synderesis* work together to perform moral action in the will, where *synderesis* is the "spark" of conscience.[147]

Interestingly, Bonaventure says that *synderesis*, while natural, does not err.[148] By definition, this means *synderesis* is a part of human nature, but does that mean that it is completely natural or is it some divine influence? Perhaps it is both. Davis characterizes *synderesis* as "corresponding to the concupiscible and irascible powers, functioning in desiring (*appetit*) the noble good and to flee (*refugit*) evil (that is, to feel remorse over sin)."[149] This suggests human affective characteristics. At the same time, however, it is unerring and cannot be affected by free choice.[150] This conundrum is again reminiscent of the controversy over contuition. Intriguingly, Bonaventure says that *synderesis* is the "weight of the will,"[151] implying a force that drives the desire for good. Since it cannot be affected by free choice, stands apart from the cognitive in its "affectivity," and is a "natural motion [force] implanted in the soul,"[152] *synderesis* takes on a divine *quality*.

Davis eventually develops synderesis from the weight of the will to the weight of the soul, which is love. As a weight, it is "not primarily a physi-cal quantity that is analogously, or metaphorically, applied to incorporeal things. Rather, in its most literal application, *pondus* is an ordering ten-dency directing creatures toward God as their final cause."[153] It is here that Davis turns to the *Breviloquium*. He notes that while Bonaventure considers contingency (*vanitas*) as a weight (hinderance) and does not use it to refer to creatures, the use of "simile clearly implies that the *pondus* of creatures, properly speaking, is itself the presence of grace, God's action in sustaining

---

145. Davis, *Weight of Love*, 58. Davis notes Bonaventure's commentary on Peter Lom-bard's *Sentences* (155n48).

146. Davis, *Weight of Love*, 58.

147. Davis, *Weight of Love*, 54.

148. Davis, *Weight of Love*, 62–63.

149. Davis, *Weight of Love*, 59.

150. Davis, *Weight of Love*, 62.

151. Davis, *Weight of Love*, 58.

152. Davis, *Weight of Love*, 40.

153. Davis, *Weight of Love*, 82.

all creatures from reverting to nothingness."[154] Of course, this grace is the action of the Holy Spirit, the topic of part 5 of the *Breviloquium*, and as discussed above is the sustaining action of creation through a general grace. Davis mentions "actual grace" (gratuitous) and "sanctifying grace" (pleasing) in passing but moves on to how grace works for meritorious acts, one function being the ordering of affections. Here, God, ourselves, neighbor, and body must be loved with charity. As such, "love, the weight of the soul,"[155] ordered through charity, becomes "the weight of ordered inclination and the bond of perfect union."[156]

THE HOLY SPIRIT AND SYNDERESIS

Davis offers a fine analysis of *affectus* here, but in skipping over gratuitous and pleasing grace, Davis does not offer a more complete picture of *synderesis* as it applies to the Grace of the Holy Spirit. For Davis, it seems that *synderesis* is implied as it relates to the weight of the will and subsequently to love. Davis says that general grace is a weight, but this is because God has *already* participated in creating the image, and because it is "deficient" in comparison to God, the very structure needs grace to sustain it.[157] In there being a structure at all, it has been already ordered by grace for movement. Bonaventure also says that the "role of gratuitous grace is to turn a person's free will away from evil and prompt it toward good."[158] This sounds very similar to *synderesis* as it cannot err, and that it does not force choice. In fact, "free will must either give or refuse consent to such *arousal*."[159] Thus, in gratuitous grace there is an affective component that is "irrational." Upon the will's consent, pleasing grace bestows both theological *and* cardinal virtues.[160]

Therefore, while true that charity is the unifying principle as the soul's weight, it is bodily affect that effects the transformation of the image into likeness. Davis is aware of such a transformation since he is arguing through the ordering principle of *synderesis* (God, self, neighbor, body), which leads

---

154. Davis, *Weight of Love*, 83.

155. Davis, *Weight of Love*, 83.

156. Davis, *Weight of Love*, 84; see also Bonaventure, *Breviloquium*, 5.8.4–5.

157. See Bonaventure, *Breviloquium*, 5.3.1; 5.2.5.

158. Bonaventure, *Breviloquium*, 5.3.1.

159. Bonaventure, *Breviloquium*, 5.3.5 (emphasis added).

160. Bonaventure, *Breviloquium*, 5.4.2.

to the "most intimate conformity—that of the image transformed into a likeness through the infused gift of theological virtues."[161] Ultimately this leads to the transformation of the *body* through affection into that of Christ as experienced by St. Francis.[162] Transformation, however, does not happen by itself, no matter how strong or innate a weight can be. While love is the transforming and unitive principle, it is the virtues that effect the transformation. For Davis's argument, the "stumbling blocks of sin" that weigh the soul down must be rectified so that the soul is free to move upward naturally as it was created to do. In order for this to happen, however, the "pleasing grace" must work through the virtues *as* one moves from God, to self, to neighbor, and to body.

To be sure, the virtues also work affectively since they are concerned with the movement of the Holy Spirit. Interestingly, Bonaventure claims that "the human mind, distracted by cares, does not enter into itself through memory" since it is "clouded by sense images," and that no matter how enlightened one may be by the light of natural and acquired knowledge, one cannot enter into oneself *to delight* within himself *in the Lord* unless Christ be their mediator.[163] Bonaventure states that the Holy Spirit, through double procession, gives faith, through which "Christ then dwells in our hearts. This is the knowledge of Christ."[164] Furthermore, it is through belief, hope, and love (theological virtues) that one "recovers spiritual hearing and sight."[165] Thus, as these virtues are oriented toward Christ, one "sees, hears, smells, and tastes" as in a matrimony. Interestingly, the theological virtues apply to the "upper face of the soul, being the image of the Trinity,"[166] but by paying attention to the cardinal virtues, there is affective purpose to repelling vices of the "lower face of the soul," be that negative or positive appetites.[167] In the end, however, the seven virtues work together for "both action and contemplation," assisting the whole soul, where clearly action and contemplation combine to *know* the experience of God, face-to-face.

161. Davis, *Weight of Love*, 101–2.

162. Davis, *Weight of Love*, 128.

163. Bonaventure, "Soul's Journey into God" [*Itinerarium*], 4.1–2. Also, intelligence is allured away by concupiscence, and neither is there a desire for sweetness and spiritual joy. In both this section and the prologue to the *Breviloquium* Bonaventure uses John 10:9: Christ as door.

164. Bonaventure, *Breviloquium*, 1.2, prologue.

165. Bonaventure, "Soul's Journey into God" [*Itinerarium*], 4.3.

166. Bonaventure, *Breviloquium*, 5.4.4–5. However, there is only one soul.

167. Bonaventure, *Breviloquium*, 5.5.3–4.

Consequently, the cognitive-affect results in a knowledge that can only be known as experienced in the body. If in Irenaean fashion the body is what communicates with the soul as claimed in chapter 1 of this book, *synderesis* is the weight of love that "presses" on the body, directing oneself toward the shape or likeness of God. Davis may be correct in saying that "the movement of exemplarity is the affective movement to the place of the exemplar"[168] since the soul "rises" in its journeys to a place where intellect is left behind. But if indeed *synderesis* is a weight in the proper sense, something Davis denies,[169] then it is something that impacts the body, that is, leaves or imprints the "marks of grace." That imprint is the Love of the Holy Spirit or the *charakter* of God which we experience.

Thus, in a cognitive-affective union, Christ is known in and via memory. Having covered how Christ as image represents memory in chapter 2, here it is the Holy Spirit that makes Christ known. To remember something, in the episodic sense, is to "feel" something about it, that there is an actual object to which those feelings apply. Bonaventure's theology sets up this pattern for people to follow and in being clothed with the theological virtues,[170] feels its weight of *synderesis*. In receiving the "spirit of wisdom and understanding, one bears the weight of the Spirit who "instructs the prudent person."[171] In this way, one "perceives the truth" and knows wisdom, to "savor or taste its goodness."[172] Therefore, in contuition and in the cooperation of the will with *synderesis*, there is both a conformation and transformation of the human image of God. One begins to understand what the soul already remembers, or feels in the affective sense:

> That is to say, what was impressed on their hearts when they were
> created in the image of God has not been wholly blotted out. . . .
> For just as that image of God is renewed in the mind of believers
> by the new testament, which impiety had not quite abolished (for

168. Davis, *Weight of Love*, 126.

169. Davis, *Weight of Love*, 82. "It is clear, then, that *pondus* is not primarily a physical quantity that is analogously, or metaphorically, applied to incorporeal things." This is with reference to Augustine's thoughts but carries through to the ordering principle.

170. Bonaventure, "Soul's Journey into God" [*Itinerarium*], 4.3.

171. Bonaventure, *Collations on the Hexaemeron*, 1.1.

172. Bonaventure, *Breviloquium*, 5.5.9. Dominic V. Monti notes that "wisdom for Bonaventure was an experiential knowledge of God involving both an act of knowledge for apprehending divine truth and an act of affection for uniting the mind to it." He quotes Bonaventure's commentary on the third of Peter Lombard's *Sentences* (Monti, in Bonaventure, *Breviloquium*, 35.1.1).

there had remained undoubtedly that which the soul of man cannot be except it be rational), so also the law of God, which had not been wholly blotted out there by unrighteousness, is certainly written thereon, renewed by grace.[173]

JOHN WESLEY

This section builds a memory interpretation of John Wesley's tripartite image of God. With Augustine and Bonaventure, the "places" of illumination moved from the intellect to memory, respectively. Each, however, relied on Trinitarian images within the human mind, namely memory, intellect, and will. With Bonaventure, however, the seeds for a threefold path for the image of God are laid out:

> When, therefore, the soul considering the Triune Principle through the trinity of its powers, by which it is the image of God, it is aided by the lights of sciences, which perfect and inform it and represent the most blessed Trinity in a threefold way. For all philosophy is either natural, rational or moral. The first deals with the cause of being and therefore leads to the power of the Father; the second deals with the basis of understanding and therefore leads to the wisdom of the Word; the third deals with the order of living and therefore leads to the goodness of the Holy Spirit.[174]

Thus, in Wesley, there are the "building blocks" of the natural, moral, and political images of God. In what has already been argued about image and memory, all three of these parts cooperate in "cyclical" fashion to order and transform oneself in the world. In fact, by doing so, one might be able to claim, as Wesley does, to transform not only the self, but the world as well. This occurs through a memory model of the image of God.

WESLEY'S IMAGE OF GOD

Wesley is known to have a triadic structure to the image of God: the natural, the moral, and the political. According to Barry Bryant, Wesley developed this three-part structure over the course of his life.[175] First came the very

173. Augustine, "Treatise on the Spirit," ch. 48.
174. Bonaventure, "Soul's Journey into God" [*Itinerarium*], 3.6.
175. Bryant, "John Wesley's Doctrine," 144–46.

rational natural image. Then he adopts a Trinitarian hermeneutic (second development), that is: "The picture given of the God of glory was a trinitarian one, so that the image and nature of God was [*sic*] just more than the product of a trinitarian consultation, it was an image of the Trinity."[176] Hints of this can also be found in Wesley's sermon "The Image of God," since "the image of his divine Parent was still visible upon him, who had transfused as much of himself into this his picture as the materials on which he drew would allow."[177] Therefore, not only is the hermeneutic Trinitarian but so is the actual image itself (third development). The fourth and final developments are the triadic aspects of the image of God *as* the natural, moral, and political.

Wesley makes explicit reference to this trio in his sermon "The New Birth" (1760), though he picked up on these ideas from Isaac Watts as early as 1740.[178]

> "And God," the three-one God, "said, Let us make man in our image, after our likeness. So God created man in his own image, in the image of God created he him." Not barely in his *natural image*, a picture of his own immortality, a spiritual being, endued with understanding, freedom of will, and various affections; nor merely in his *political image*, the governor of this lower world, having "dominion over the fishes of the sea, and over the fowl of the air and over the cattle, and over all the earth"; but chiefly in his *moral image*, which, according to the Apostle, is "righteousness and true holiness." In this image of God was man made. "God is love": accordingly, man at his creation was full of love, which was the sole principle of all his tempers, thoughts, words, and actions. God is full of justice, mercy, and truth: so was man as he came from the hands of his Creator.[179]

First, the natural image describes primarily the soul, but also everything that might impinge upon it. Young Taek Kim, along with Kenneth Collins and Jason E. Vickers—who greatly influenced Kim's work—notes the early appearance of the natural image in his first university sermon in 1730.[180]

---

176. Bryant, "John Wesley's Doctrine," 146.

177. "The Image of God," in *WJW*, 4:292, §1. It is worth noting the importance of the words "picture" for image and "drew" as "painting." The sense is God is imprinting something onto the human.

178. Bryant, "John Wesley's Doctrine," 155. See footnotes.

179. "The New Birth," in *WJW*, 2:188, §1.1.

180. Kim, "John Wesley's Anthropology," 27; Collins and Vickers, *Sermons of John Wesley*, 29.

God as Spirit must have a spiritual component of "immortality" imaged in the soul.

Second, the political image is in line with most interpretations regarding dominion over creation. It is, however, rarely mentioned in Wesley's sermons. This leads some scholars to conclude that the main images are the natural and moral, per Randy Maddox.[181] Kim argues, however, with Collins and Vickers, that the political image is mentioned in Wesley's sermon "The General Deliverance" (1781), creating a sequence from a twofold to threefold one.[182] It seems clear, however, that Wesley was concerned for all creation, specifically written about in "The General Deliverance," "making humanity an Image of God *insofar* as the benevolence of God is reflected in human actions toward the rest of creation."[183] And while the context here is related specifically to an "ecological" dimension, the concern for creation fits a greater ethical outlook of what humanity is in relation to the world at large. Thus, in being "faithful to the order of the Creator,"[184] humanity becomes faithful stewards, a state of existential being.

Third, the image that stands out is the moral image, which for Wesley defines the relationship between God and humanity. Therefore, it is not "a function, but is a moral condition of humanity" that reflects righteousness and holiness.[185] In addition, it is not a "capacity within humanity . . . that can be employed independently of the Creator because it consists in a relationship which the creature *receives* continuously from the Creator and mediates further what is received."[186] Thus, how righteousness and holiness are effected is due in part to what a person receives and applies to a given context that would be reflective of such a relationship. Thus, the moral law given to human beings is "an incorruptible picture of the high and holy One that inhabiteth eternity," which engenders the moral image.[187]

---

181. Maddox, *Responsible Grace*, 68. This could also be because of Maddox's favored interpretation of Eastern Orthodox theology in the distinction between image and likeness. It matches with the paradigm of natural and moral images, respectively.

182. Kim, "John Wesley's Anthropology," 39; Collins, *Scripture Way of Salvation*, 23n24.

183. Runyon, *New Creation*, 14.

184. Runyon, *New Creation*, 17.

185. Kim, "John Wesley's Anthropology," 44.

186. Runyon, *New Creation*, 18.

187. "The Original, Nature, Property, and Use of the Law," in *WJW*, 2:9, §2.3.

WESLEY'S CONTEXT FOR ANTHROPOLOGY

Now, having gone through the basics of Wesley's image of God, one should note his post-Enlightenment era cultural context. Wesley would have been exposed to an interesting mixture of anthropological contexts via Locke and the Cambridge Platonists,[188] from Aristotle to Augustine and Aquinas. As Barry Bryant notes, "The general concept of a body/soul duality placed Wesley into the Platonic/Aristotelian traditions."[189] It was Aristotelian in nature because Wesley believed in a psychosomatic unity of the body and soul,[190] but also had Platonic distinctions, since the "soul, being incorruptible and immortal, was of a *nature* 'a little lower than the angels,' . . . which may, when our bodies are mouldered into earth, will remain with all their faculties."[191] Death was the separation, but survival of the soul from the body. Furthermore, while Wesley appealed to an "Aristotelian experience as the sum of remembered actions,"[192] the creation of those experiences through rational processes operated on the Platonic soul/body duality rather than one of mind/body (which is what John Locke believed). At the same time, Wesley espoused a psychosomatic unity between the body and soul,[193] even if he was unsure exactly how that happened.

That said, the interaction was of importance because the soul operated through the body,

> and the brain, on which the soul more directly depends, not less than the rest of the body. Consequently, if these instruments by which the soul works are disordered, the soul itself must be hindered in its operations. Let a musician be ever so skillful, he will make but poor music if his instrument be out of tune. From a disordered brain (such as is, more or less, that of every child of man) there will necessarily arise confoundedness of apprehension,

188. Kim, "John Wesley's Anthropology," 6, 19, 119–20, 202–3. Kim is working with the analyses of Runyon, *New Creation*; and Cragg, *Cambridge Platonists*.

189. Bryant, "John Wesley's Doctrine," 74. Bryant cites Albert Outler as placing Wesley in the Platonic tradition.

190. "On the Fall of Man," in *WJW*, 2:405–6, §2.2. "Yet the soul cannot dispense with its service, imperfect as it is. For an embodied spirit cannot form one thought but by the mediation of its bodily organs. For thinking is not (as many suppose), the act of a pure spirit, but the act of a spirit connected with a body, and playing upon a set of material keys." See also Bryant, "John Wesley's Doctrine," 74–76.

191. "The Good Steward," in *WJW*, 2:289–90, §2.8 (emphasis added).

192. Bryant, "John Wesley's Doctrine," 81.

193. Bryant, "John Wesley's Doctrine," 74.

showing itself in a thousand instances: false judgment, the natural result thereof, and wrong inferences; and from these innumerable mistakes will follow, in spite of all the caution we can use.[194]

This late sermon in 1790, less than a year from his death, is then consistent with the idea, contra Aristotle but with Irenaeus and Bonaventure, that the body informs the soul. In fact, Wesley wonders, "Suppose a soul, however holy, to dwell in a distempered body; suppose the brain be so throughly disordered, as that raging madness follows; will not all the thoughts be wild and unconnected, as long as that disorder continues?"[195] Despite this physical and Aristotelian science of the body, he was unsure of its exact interaction,[196] and "ultimately saw God as the one responsible for the immaterial acting upon the material in such a way as to result in action."[197] In other words, what appears to be taking place is a synthesis of Aristotelean psychology with Platonic anthropology. It is clear, however, that rationalistic enterprise is Aristotelian.

Furthermore, one could also say that Wesley was Aristotelian in his concept of soul because he did not believe that souls had innate knowledge like the Platonic Forms. Rather, "he denied innate knowledge because of the prominence of experience in his epistemology."[198] In this, Wesley agreed with John Locke in the concept of tabula rasa, against other Cambridge Platonists, yet was not "Lockian" because the soul, not the mind, was the blank slate.[199] This necessitates a sensory experience *before* it can be put into memory. Wesley tells of a rather bizarre (but apparently truthful) story of a toad that was living inside an ancient oak tree, and which escaped the tree when the tree was split. Wesley imagines what kind of life the toad might have had but likens it to an atheist:

> This poor animal had organs of sense; yet it had not any sensation. It had eyes, yet no ray of light ever entered its black abode. From

194. "The Heavenly Treasure in Earthen Vessels," in *WJW*, 4:165, §2.1.

195. "Wandering Thoughts," in *WJW*, 2:135, §4.3.

196. "The Imperfection of Human Knowledge," in *WJW*, 2:576, §1.13. Specifically, after wondering whether the soul was in the pineal gland or the whole brain: "How is the soul *united* to the body? A spirit or a clod? What is the secret, imperceptible chain that couples them together? Can the wisest of men give a satisfactory answer to any one of these plain questions?"

197. Bryant, "John Wesley's Doctrine," 76; referring to Wesley, "Of Action of God."

198. Bryant, "John Wesley's Doctrine," 67.

199. Bryant, "John Wesley's Doctrine," 70.

the very first instant of its existence there, it was shut up in impen-
etrable darkness. It was shut up from the sun, moon and stars, and
from the beautiful face of nature; indeed, from the whole visible
world, as much as if it had no being. . . . It scarce, therefore could
have any memory, or any imagination.[200]

A little later:

He has not the least perception of it; not the most distant idea.
He has not the least sight of God, the intellectual Sun; nor any the
least attraction toward him, or desire to have any knowledge of
his ways.[201]

Thus, not only do people not have innate knowledge, but those "living
without God" have no innate knowledge *of God* either.[202]

Because of original sin, people were born atheists, the spiritual disease
that needed to be healed (therapy) by the great Physician.

What are the diseases of his nature? What those spiritual diseases
which every one that is born of a woman brings with him into the
world? Is not the first of these *atheism*? After all that has been so
plausibly written concerning 'the innate idea of God;' after all that
have been said of its being common to all men, in all ages and
nations; it does not appear that man has naturally any more idea
of God that any of the beasts of the field: he has no knowledge of
God at all . . . he is by nature a mere Atheist.[203]

Wesley boldly claims that people are *naturally* atheists and cannot *naturally*
come to an idea of God. Wesley was probably linking this to the concept
of natural conscience which will be explained below, but the *religious* explanation is the effect of original sin on the image of God. Due to Adam's
disobedience and breaking of the moral law, the moral image was completely lost, where "moral image was knowledge of God's Moral Law."[204]
Here, Bryant offers Wesley's traducianism of the soul (in contrast to Locke's
consciousness of the mind anthropology) to account for original sin.[205] This

200. "On Living without God," in *WJW*, 4:170, paras. 3, 5. One should note that this
is a mature thought since the sermon was preached in 1790.

201. "On Living without God," in *WJW*, 4:171–72, para. 8.

202. Bryant, "John Wesley's Doctrine," 75.

203. "On the Education of Children," in *WJW*, 3:350, para. 5.

204. Bryant, "John Wesley's Doctrine," 164.

205. Bryant, "John Wesley's Doctrine," 182–86.

traducianism of souls is intended to account for *why* people have original sin, not *how*.[206] People are born in a state of atheism because of the natural propagation of soul and body that goes back to Adam in Lamarkian fashion. Therefore, the tabula rasa of the soul was not simply a blank slate, but a blank slate *with* the condition of original sin that resulted in the lack of the knowledge of God.

WESLEYAN COGNITION AND IDEAS (MEMORY)

Because this book is attempting to build a memory model of the image of God as it relates to Wesley, the fact that Wesley did not believe in innate ideas is a serious problem to overcome. Part of the problem is due to his empiricism and how memory cognitively functions in the natural world, but more importantly, the "Moral Image of God is lost and defaced,"[207] directly leading to the loss of the knowledge of God. This is the natural condition of the postlapsarian state of humanity which then suffers marred natural and political images as well. That said, memory can still be "salvaged" *because* of Wesley's empiricism and by distinguishing between the moral law and moral image.

Wesley considers the sensation of "all external objects, which have left any representation of themselves . . . to memory, as properly termed an *Idea*."[208] Thus, the content of memory consists of ideas that are the *original* impressions of external objects. Yet, Wesley distinguishes what was originally placed into memory with the image one recalls, that "the word *idea* . . . is confined to the images we have of sensible objects, and the various alterations of them by the understanding (intellect)."[209] Thus, Wesley is aware of the distinction between imagination and memory, as argued in this book. In fact, he references Locke's movement of animal spirits in the brain as a potential cause of memory, where the continued perception of an object removed is termed imagination, whereas after said perception has ceased but occurs again, that is termed memory.[210] Wesley does not of-

206. Bryant, "John Wesley's Doctrine," 183. Bryant notes that Wesley did not seek to explain how, only from the evidence at hand or human experience.

207. Wesley, *Doctrine of Original Sin*, 326.

208. Wesley, *Survey of the Wisdom*, 5:173 (emphasis original).

209. Wesley, *Survey of the Wisdom*, 5:174 (emphasis original).

210. Wesley, *Survey of the Wisdom*, 1:177. For an excellent historical view on Locke's memory system, see Sutton, *Philosophy and Memory Traces*, 167–76.

ficially adjudicate on animal spirits, preferring simply to state that external objects are perceived, can be continued to be perceived, and then can be recalled when the perceptions are gone.

Of the last, memory can be further broken down to related components of reminiscence and recollection.[211] Memory, in general, is the content of what is remembered, even those that are unprompted, and has a passive quality. Reminiscence, however, is an active process of searching that either fails or succeeds in a single movement. With recollection, the process of reminiscence is extended to content that might lead to the target memory. In this respect, Wesley seems to be following Aquinas's commentary where recollection is a "hunt for what is consequently from something prior that one does remember . . . to rediscover what had fallen away from memory."[212] This is important because recollection lays the seed for what Wesley *might* have considered to be some form of the memory of God, even though, "properly speaking, people have no idea of God."[213]

In his "Thoughts on Memory," Wesley refers to an "inward Voice" that represents "one sort of Memory, which seems more difficult to understand than any other."[214] On the surface, he appears simply to be detailing an auditory memory of tune, discourse, or poetry he had heard or spoke himself. What is curious for Wesley is that this Voice, in it "being like an echo," is *exactly* the same as the original in accent or tone. Wesley, however, knows that visual images go through some processing by the intellect, so how can this Voice be something so exact? It is possible that Wesley was hinting at a memory of God in this description, given that "Voice" is capitalized, something he does not do in other characterizations of the word.

In struggling to even arrive at the term "Voice," Wesley is demonstrating the rational process of abstraction for things of spiritual nature:

> The true abstraction seems to consist, not in forming ideas independent on sensation, but in substituting the only notions we have, which are natural, easy, and familiar, to represent those

211. Wesley, "Thoughts on Memory."

212. Aquinas, *Commentaries*, 212. By comparison, Wesley states: "Recollection seems to imply something more than simple Reminiscence: even the studious collecting and gathering up together all the parts of conversation or transaction, which had occurred before, but had in some measure escaped from the Memory." Wesley, "Thoughts on Memory," 384.

213. Wesley, *Survey of the Wisdom*, 5:176.

214. Wesley, "Thoughts on Memory," 384. Wesley uses the term "Voice" as the best approximation of his experience.

> supernatural things, of which otherwise can have no notion; in
> transferring our thoughts from the literal propriety of the words,
> by which we express them, to that analogical signification, whereby
> they are, as it were spiritualized. This seems to be the only abstrac-
> tion we are capable of, with regard to things spiritual.[215]

Thus, abstraction is not a mind thing only but has its existence as it relates specifically to instantiated ideas of sensation. Critically, this abstraction is *analogical*, which Wesley distinguishes from metaphorical and is worth quoting at length:

> Metaphor expresses an *imaginary*, analogy a *real correspondence*:
> metaphor is no more than an allusion; analogy a substitution of
> ideas and conceptions. The intention of metaphor is only to ex-
> press more emphatically something known more exactly before:
> the intention of analogy, to inform us of something, which we
> could not have known without it. Metaphor uses ideas of sensation
> to express things, whereto they have no real resemblance: anal-
> ogy substitutes our notions and complex conceptions of things,
> with which they have a real correspondence. To conclude. Words
> applied metaphorically are not understood in any part of their
> proper sense: analogical words understood in a part, though not
> the whole of their literal meaning.[216]

As examples of this important distinction, Wesley likens the "hand" of God as a metaphor, but the "power" of God as analogical. Being the responsible apophatic theologian, Wesley is making a judgment on how human beings substantiate characterizations of God. The question is, how does one characterize Voice? Is it analogical, or is it metaphoric?

In the way Wesley describes physical attributes pertaining to God, one might think that a Voice would be metaphorical, but in this instance, the Voice is analogical. In the example above, the hand of God is *imagined* in how God would use God's hands, say, in an act of creation. The Voice of God, however, is literally literal (yes, doubly literal here). First, from Gen 1, humans were "not gradually formed by God as a statue is by a human artifi-cer: But he spake the word and they were made; He commanded, and they were created."[217] Second, taking a cue from Gen 2, the formed dust is vivi-

---

215. Wesley, *Survey of the Wisdom*, 5:189.

216. Wesley, *Survey of the Wisdom*, 5:186 (emphasis added). The reader is also re-minded of Bonaventure's analogy.

217. Wesley, *Doctrine of Original Sin*, 292.

fied by the Holy Spirit, the breath of God. Therefore, in these two creation stories, Wesley has the makings for a Voice. In addition, "with the same Breath God breathed in him a living Soul, he breathed in him a *righteous* Soul."[218] Thus, the Voice is within the soul as well, at least, as it concerns original righteousness. Taken together, the evidence suggests an analogical relationship within the human soul, not a metaphorical one.

Such an analogical relationship bears a level of similarity to what is *natural*. In the above case of original righteousness, Wesley states that the human condition was "*universal* and *natural*, yet *mutable*," after having gone through the mental powers of understanding, will (liberty), and affections (will or desires).[219] This was how humanity was "created in God's own Image, consisting in knowledge, righteousness, and holiness."[220] Importantly, by "universal," Wesley meant the *entire* human being, body, soul, and spirit, and that because "it was universal, so it was natural as God had created with it." This suggests that the entire image of God is in some sense natural, and as an image, reflects an analogical relationship. It is through the analogy of the image of God that Wesley can say that God "had transfused as much of himself into this, his picture, as the materials on which he drew would allow."[221] This is precisely what this book has argued for in the language used for *eikon* and memory, which is further distinguished from imaginary metaphors or *phantasma*.

MORAL LAW VERSUS MORAL IMAGE AND THE IMAGE OF GOD

Of course, original sin broke that image through the loss of righteousness, which, due to the intrinsic nature of mutability, suffered because of Adam's liberty. Here, a distinction needs to be made between moral law and moral image. The difference between moral law and moral image is important to distinguish because it impacts the placement and function of moral law. Part of the confusion can be attributed to Wesley's thoughts on the fallen nature of humanity. The result was "the moral image was *totally* lost."[222]

218. Wesley, *Doctrine of Original Sin*, 464.

219. Wesley, *Doctrine of Original Sin*, 466 (emphasis original).

220. Wesley, *Doctrine of Original Sin*, 467.

221. "The Image of God," in *WJW*, 2:292, §1. This essentially parallels the rational description of the image of God found in the *Doctrine of Original Sin*.

222. Collins, *Scripture Way of Salvation*, 30 (emphasis original); see also Kim, "John

Scholars, however, have routinely placed the moral law with moral image. For example, Bryant states that "the moral image of God is knowledge of God's moral law."[223] Coupled with Wesley's statements that in the fallen condition or "natural condition," the locked-up spiritual senses are "as if one had them not,"[224] this suggests a loss of the moral law as well. If one does not have the knowledge of God's moral law because "it was effaced out of his heart,"[225] then, logically, there can be no moral image, which is the direct result of original sin.

Bryant notes, however, that "original sin was entirely a moral issue, not an aesthetic one."[226] Additionally, Kim and Collins state that the moral law is a part of God's created order,[227] with Collins stating that moral law was "natural" in the sense of "laws of nature" or the "Decalogue as an expression of natural law."[228] Wesley himself, referring to original righteousness, states that "the law was not written on tables of stone, but it was written upon his mind. God impressed it upon his soul, and made him a law to himself, as the remains of it even among the Heathens testify."[229] Thus, while the moral image was lost because of a moral issue, that, through a loss of righteousness and holiness the *relationship* between God and humanity was broken, the moral law is *not* lost.

In fact, this moral law is:

> Engraven on his heart by the finger of God; wrote in the inmost spirit both of men and of angels; to the intent it might never be far off, never hard to be understood, but always at hand, and always shining with clear light.[230]

While this might have been under original righteousness, Wesley also states:

> But the moral law . . . the letters once wrote by the finger of God are now in a great measure defaced by sin, yet can they not wholly

Wesley's Anthropology," 66, 78; Runyon, *New Creation*, 21; "End of Christ's Coming," in *WJW*, 2:477, §1.10. Runyon uses the words "most totally effaced."

223. Bryant, "John Wesley's Doctrine," 164. In this, Bryant agrees with other scholars, as noted earlier in the book, that the moral image consists in embodied relationships (53).

224. "The New Birth," in *WJW*, 2:192, §2.4. Also remember the toad in the tree.

225. "The Original, Nature, Property, and Use of the Law," in *WJW*, 2.7, §1.4.

226. Bryant, "John Wesley's Doctrine," 171.

227. Kim, "John Wesley's Anthropology," 201; Collins, *Scripture Way of Salvation*, 52n41.

228. Collins, *Scripture Way of Salvation*, 26n41.

229. Wesley, *Doctrine of Original Sin*, 464.

230. "The Original, Nature, Property, and Use of the Law," in *WJW*, 2:7, §1.3.

be blotted out, while we have any consciousness of good and evil. Every part of this law must remain in force, upon all mankind, and in all ages; as not depending either on time or place, or any other circumstances liable to change, but on the nature of God and the nature of man, and their unchangeable relation to each other.[231]

The combination of those two passages points to a permanent feature of the moral law. No matter how much sin has defaced it, it is still present since the moral force of the law remains in effect for all time. In other words, the moral law resides "underneath" the defacement.[232] It is an intrinsic property of natural creation that when defaced results in the defacement or loss of the moral image.

This makes more sense as Wesley moves on to the christological promise of the moral law:

> The law of God is all virtues in one, in such a shape as to be beheld with open face by all those whose eyes God hath enlightened. What is the law but divine virtue and wisdom assuming a visible form? What is it but the original ideas of truth and good, which were lodged in the uncreated mind from eternity, now drawn forth and clothed with such a vehicle as to appear even to human understanding?[233]

At the same time:

> Gospel holiness is no less than the image of God stamped upon the heart. It is no other than the whole mind which was in Christ Jesus. It consists of all heavenly affections and tempers mingled together in one.[234]

In this sequence presented, the life of God in the soul is the mind of Christ, which is the image of God stamped upon the heart, which is now renewed after Christ. There is now a cognitive component in Christ containing the

---

231. "Upon Our Lord's Sermon on the Mount Discourse the Fifth," in *WJW*, 1:551–52, §1.2.

232. Wesley makes mention of "an entire law of love which was written in his heart (against which, perhaps, he could not sin directly)." See, "Justification by Faith," in *WJW*, 1:184, §1.3.

233. "The Original, Nature, Property, and the Use of the Law," in *WJW*, 2:9–10, §2.4; see also Bryant, "John Wesley's Doctrine," 242–43.

234. "The New Birth," in *WJW*, 2:194, §3.1. Also variously said in "General Spread of the Gospel," in *WJW*, 2:491, para. 13; "On the Wedding Garment," in *WJW*, 4:147, para. 17: "That this holiness was the mind that was in Christ."

"original ideas of truth and good" that are visible; that is, Christ *is* the moral law that accounts for holiness. As such, the knowledge of Christ is *naturally* stamped upon the heart. "The 'divine mind' or 'eternal reasons' is in the souls of human persons by which the believer is able to have the 'mind which was in Christ.'"[235] Interestingly, Christ is "seen" to human understanding. What one "sees" is the light that is "the knowledge of the glory of God in the face Jesus Christ."[236] So, Wesley's oft-said phrase "the mind of Christ" not only refers to Christ himself, the express image, but also provides the content of divine illumination. In other words, Wesley is asking to see by "peering" into the mind of Christ for holiness, and in this respect, the cognitive value of the image of God is very Augustinian, as described above.

THE PARADOX

If the above is true, there is a paradox. How is it possible that in one instance Wesley claims that in the fallen condition, people do not have "the least sight of God, the intellectual Sun" (an obvious allusion to Christ), but then claim in another that the moral law is "the knowledge of thy glory of God in the face of Jesus"? Bryant states that the "image of God is not to be confused with innate knowledge,"[237] and is supported by perhaps Wesley's harshest words:

> 4. If indeed God had stamped (as some have maintained) an idea of himself on every human soul, we must certainly have understood something of these, as well as his other attributes; for we cannot suppose he would have impressed upon us either a false or an imperfect idea of himself. But the truth is, no man ever did, or does now, find any such idea stamped upon his soul. The little which we do know of God (expect what we receive by the inspiration of the Holy One) we do not gather from any inward impression, but gradually acquire from without. "The invisible things of God," if they are known at all, "are known from the things that are made"; not from what God hath written in our hearts, but from what he hath written in all his works. 5. Hence then, from

---

235. Bryant, "John Wesley's Doctrine," 243.

236. "The Great Privilege of Those That Are Born of God," in *WJW*, 1:435, §1.9. Wesley also uses "the excellent knowledge of Jesus Christ" or the knowledge of God in Christ Jesus."

237. Bryant, "John Wesley's Doctrine," 75.

> his works, particularly his works of creation, we are to learn the
> knowledge of God.[238]

Other Wesleyan scholars are also hostile to the notion of innate ideas as part of natural theology. Runyon, for example, criticizes Albert Outler, who took on a favorable Platonist view.[239] The same sentiment can be found in H. Ray Dunning and Collins where they object to the terms "natural" and "natural theology," respectively.[240] Bryant's answer ultimately is in prevenient grace, which will be explained in a moment, but in a different vein, speculates that:

> Perhaps the crucial problem in putting all of this together is not Wesley's need for a doctrine of universal revelation, or the cognitive aspect of his understanding of actual sin, *but accounting for a compulsory experience of the cognitive aspects of revelation. To say there is universal revelation through prevenient grace is one thing, but to say there is a universal consciousness of that revelation is something altogether different*, and can only be verified, or invalidated through an empirical study of anthropology.[241]

Had there been innate knowledge of God, people would be able to know something about it, and probably enough to act to procure their own natural way to salvation.[242] This, of course, is expressly prohibited by Wesley in the limits that he places on reason, that reason cannot provide faith. Perhaps, however, there is another interpretation that takes into consideration the "consciousness of universal revelation."

Going back to the distinction between analogy and metaphor, Wesley distinguishes between human knowledge of divine things with what they actually are. Commenting on 1 Cor 13:12, seeing in a glass darkly, or in a mirror:

> That a glass exhibits to us nothing of the substance of the thing represented in it: the similitude therein having no more of the

238. "The Imperfection of Human Knowledge," in *WJW*, 2:570–71, §1.4–5. Bryant cites this exact passage in his section on prevenient grace and natural theology. Bryant, "John Wesley's Doctrine," 250–51.

239. Runyon, *New Creation*, 243n9. "Christian Platonists in general had maintained this notion of innate ideas of God, and Wesley follows them since our knowledge of God and of things of God is not 'empirical' but rather intuitive."

240. Dunning, *Reflecting the Divine Image*, 51; Collins, *Scripture Way of Salvation*, 53n41.

241. Bryant, "John Wesley's Doctrine," 216 (emphasis added).

242. Bryant, "John Wesley's Doctrine," 251.

essence of the thing itself, than a mere shadow. Yet we cannot say, but there is a real likeness of the substance in the airy form. There is such a proportion between them, that the idea of a face we never saw, but in a glass, is just one, and may well be substituted for the face itself, of which it gives some real knowledge . . . as to make our conceptions of natural things just representations of the supernatural. So that the knowledge we have of them is true, and our reasonings upon them substantial, as long as they are kept within due compass of those representations.[243]

Here, Wesley seems to point to the prospect of real knowledge of the supernatural but limited to the human representations people have. Thus, what people know through reason while *not* completely known, must be based on *something* that exists, if in the positive sense through a mirror darkly. Comparatively, in the negative sense, Wesley comments that "because we have no idea of a spirit, we are naturally led to express it by a negative."[244] This is characteristically apophatic method, but despite claiming that "it may be justly affirmed, we can have no knowledge *without* ideas, yet it is most unjust and absurd to infer thence, that we can have no knowledge *beyond* them."[245] All of this is to affirm that one can have "a clear idea of God," whether by inference or intuition.

ANSWERING THE PARADOX THROUGH MEMORY

So perhaps innate ideas of God do not exist *in their fullness* because a person cannot know it completely, which is precisely what Wesley details in not being able to know godly attributes such as omniscience and eternity. Yet, eternity is represented in the knowledge of Christ, the moral law, which is necessary for the moral image. Therefore, to have some subsistence in the moral image, or, for that matter, the natural and political in their reflections of the divine, something needs to be in some form of "innate" knowledge. But since such knowledge cannot be fully known, one does not have complete consciousness of universal revelation, requiring "empirical" verification. At best, "one has deep consciousness of ignorance"[246] which drives one to search for ideas using reason.

243. Wesley, *Survey of the Wisdom*, 5:184–85.
244. Wesley, *Survey of the Wisdom*, 5:175.
245. Wesley, *Survey of the Wisdom*, 5:177–78.
246. "The Imperfection of Human Knowledge," in *WJW*, 2:584, §4.1.

Bryant notes two uses of the term "reason" by Wesley: one refers to the eternal reason, and the other to the more common use of human rationality.[247] Regarding the latter, Wesley explains the use of reason in all manner of human thinking and decision-making:

> In another acceptation of the word, reason is much the same with *understanding*. It means a faculty of the human soul; that faculty which exerts itself in three ways; by simple apprehension, by judgement, and by discourse. *Simple apprehension* is barely conceiving a thing in the mind, the first and most simple act of understanding. *Judgment* is the determining that the things before conceived either agree with or differ from each other. *Discourse* (strictly speaking) is the motion or progress of the mind from one judgment to another. The faculty of the soul which includes these three operations I here mean by the term *reason*.[248]

Importantly, reason is the faculty of the *soul* and not simply the mind, even if it is used in rational enterprises such as judgment, and subsequently, discourse. This is directly cited in Wesley's *Compendium of Logic*,[249] and paralleled and expanded upon in his remarks on pure intellect in the *Survey of the Wisdom of God in the Creation: Or a Compendium of Natural Philosophy*. It is "a simple view or survey of the ideas of sensation, just as they lie in the memory. This the Logicians have rightly termed Simple Apprehension."[250] Similarly, Wesley goes on to comment on the manipulation of these ideas (separating, comparing, enlarging, dividing) as the second operation of the intellect, that of judgment. Thus, human reason is being equated with human intellect. While Wesley does not mention discourse here, he moves on to understanding (the attainment of knowledge), which requires discourse if one is to compare objects (make a judgment) and then make further inference or deduction. Therefore, the human description of reason is Aristotelian.

According to Wesley, eternal reason is the "Nature of Things: The Nature of God, and the Nature of Man, with the Relations necessarily subsisting between them."[251] To quote further:

247. Bryant, "John Wesley's Doctrine," 51–55.

248. "Reason Impartially Considered," in *WJW*, 2:590, §1.2 (emphases original).

249. Wesley, *Compendium of Logic*, 5.

250. Wesley, *Survey of the Wisdom*, 5:188. Note that the working of intellect *depends* on memory. It is presupposed that the intellect works off prior ideas.

251. Wesley, *Earnest Appeal*, 13; see also Bryant, "John Wesley's Doctrine," 51.

> Why, this is the very Religion *we* preach: A Religion evidently founded on, and every Way agreeable to Eternal Reason, to the Essential Nature of Things. Its Foundation stands on the Nature of GOD and the Nature of Man, together with their mutual relations. And it is every Way suitable thereto: To the Nature of GOD; for it begins in knowing him, (and where but in the true Knowledge of GOD can you conceive true Religion to begin?) It goes on in loving him, and all Mankind, (for you can't but imitate whom you love:) It ends in serving him; in doing his Will; in obeying Him whom we know and love.[252]

Notice that three elements consist in a rational enterprise for religion: 1) the nature of God, 2) the nature of humanity, and 3) the relationship between them. In effect, the human instances of reason as outlined above are being used to define the meaning of Christianity. Judgments are made from the comparison of the simple apprehensions of God and human natures from which relationality is inferred. This "reasonable" characterization of Christianity can be found in Wesley's understanding of the natural image of God in one of his earliest sermons, "The Image of God" (1730):

> First with regard to his understanding. He was endued, after the likeness of his Maker, with a power of distinguishing truth from falsehood; either by a simple view wherein he made the nearest approach to that all-seeing Nature, or by comparing one thing with another (a manner of knowledge perhaps peculiar to himself) and often inferring farther truths from these preceding comparisons.[253]

Thus, in this early development of the natural image, Wesley is proposing the natural image as a way to *know* God, because thinking creatures analogously reflect the rational agency of God in their mind. In addition, people are endued with a will and liberty. Contrary to a will as executor of understanding, "Wesley's concept of will is related to the attributes of emotions [passions and affections],"[254] which is consistent with the medieval distinction between will and liberty, where liberty refers to free choice, "a power of self-determination."[255] In each of these mental capacities, there is a kind of knowledge at work. The intellect judges content; the will has emotional content; and liberty directs the understood content to godly ends.

---

252. Wesley, *Earnest Appeal*, 13 (emphasis original).

253. "The Image of God," in *WJW*, 4:293, §1.1.

254. Kim, "John Wesley's Anthropology," 32; see also Maddox, *Responsible Grace*, 69.

255. Kim, "John Wesley's Anthropology," 37.

And this was perfect under original righteousness as the image of God was intended to function morally.

But despite the moral law being defaced, the content of the law remains intact. Thus, in principle, the moral interpretive frame also remains intact, suggesting a glimmer of some kind of "innate" idea that can be known. Critically, this moral law is described as "a copy of the eternal mind, a transcript of the divine nature."[256] In the law being a transcript, it is written in nature and as a copy, there is a dependency on the exemplar which is the eternal mind of God. In fact, Bryant makes a more general argument that the language of "transcript" encompasses a Trinitarian hermeneutic, or the second development of Wesley's doctrine of the image of God mentioned above.[257] This suggests a broader understanding of what is "written" to include the Father and Holy Spirit (discussed below), but as it pertains to the moral law in its postlapsarian condition, it is "misread."

Thus, the problem is not that the moral image has been lost per se, but that the errors in reading the transcript is a function of impaired memory. If indeed the moral law is "only" effaced and that some knowledge of it remains (by the grace of God), then it is much like the parable of the lost coin that Augustine mentions. It may be possible that there is a recognition of something that was forgotten, of a knowledge lost. And it is reason that provides a potential route to begin but finish the process of recovering that lost knowledge.

If the eternal mind is a transcript (in the sense of it being read) of the divine just as eternal reason concerns God, humanity, and the relations between them, then the implication is that an image of God is a memory of God, a part of which is, and begins with, Christ the moral law and the mind of Christ. It is here that that process of "re-inscription"[258] also begins, in what amounts to Wesley's definition of recollection.

256. "The Original, Nature, Property, and Use of the Law," in *WJW*, 2:10, §2.6. Bryant also shows the important theology of Charles Wesley's hymns with which John generally agreed. He notes the appearance of "transcripts" in 1742, eight years before "The Original, Nature, Property, and Use of the Law" in 1750, and subsequent Trinitarian development of the image of God by at least 1770. Bryant, "John Wesley's Doctrine," 148–49.

257. Bryant, "John Wesley's Doctrine," 148.

258. Some think that be by re-inscription, Wesley is talking about a new inscription over the old in the vein of having humanity created anew. This is certainly possible, but in the interpretation of this book, the re-inscription is a "bringing to the fore" of what always had lain underneath any effacement. By re-inscription, the same content of the law is *retraced* so that it can be properly read.

PREVENIENT GRACE OF THE HOLY
SPIRIT AND MEMORY

Bryant notes that "the Moral Law had to always work in conjunction with the Holy Spirit."[259] As powerful as the knowledge of Christ is, it can be accessed only *after* the working of the Holy Spirit. Kim states that the Holy Spirit (grace of God) gives humanity the mind that was in Christ,[260] and this is true in a "two-fold operation of the Holy Spirit—having the eyes of our soul both *opened* and *enlightened*,"[261] to see and *hear* what one naturally could not. The conditions for access and understanding happen prior to knowledge, that is, the Holy Spirit gives faith, which the "testimony of the of the Spirit in is an inward impression on the soul."[262] This results in knowing that as a child of God, Christ loves me and through his atonement is reconciled to God. Yet, this action of the Holy Spirit occurs *before* conscious awareness. Wesley's rationale is that one must be holy before being conscious of it, but that loving God is a prior commitment, which itself can happen only after realizing that God first loved us.[263] In this way, "natural theology" is informed by the Holy Spirit, which without, becomes a psychological "content problem."

Bryant also puts the re-inscription of the moral law within the purview of prevenient grace by remarking: "Prevenient grace provides the knowledge necessary to make one cognizant of sin, which means it has more to do with the conviction of sin than with its forgiveness."[264] Since the moral law works with the Holy Spirit, there certainly is an "activation" of knowledge by the infusion of the Spirit. Thus, for Bryant, this combination of the moral law and the Holy Spirit becomes "Christ-consciousness" or human conscience,[265] as considered by Wesley in both "The Witness of the Spirit" and "The Witness of Our Own Spirit." In this context, conscience

---

259. Bryant, "John Wesley's Doctrine," 244.

260. Kim, "John Wesley's Anthropology," 17.

261. "Scripture Way of Salvation," in *WJW*, 2:161, §2.1 (emphases original).

262. "The Witness of the Spirit Discourse One," in *WJW*, 1:274, §1.7. Wesley reaffirms this twenty years later in a second discourse.

263. "The Witness of the Spirit Discourse One," in *WJW*, 1:274, §1.8. "Now we cannot love God till we know he loves us. . . . Since, therefore, this testimony of his Spirit must precede the love of God and all holiness, of consequence it must precede our inward consciousness thereof, or the testimony of our spirit concerning them."

264. Bryant, "John Wesley's Doctrine," 253.

265. Bryant, "John Wesley's Doctrine," 248.

must be prevenient because of the superadded nature of the Holy Spirit. There is some room for an alternate interpretation here.

Wesley was not fond of the term "conscience," since it leads people to consider a "vulgar," "natural conscience," independent of God's influence. Rather, conscience is "properly called preventing grace"[266] and is a "supernatural gift of God."[267] In this Wesleyan scholars are agreed that there is no such thing as a "natural conscience," allowing only the term "natural," as Wesley does, since it is found in human beings.[268] If indeed, Wesley thought that "natural conscience" was exclusively superadded, he does himself no favors by allowing some version of natural conscience:

> Certainly, whether this is *natural* or superadded by the grace of God, it is found, at least in some small degree, in every child of man. Something of this is found in every human heart, passing sentence concerning good and evil, not only in all Christians, but in all Mahometans, all Pagans, yea, the vilest of savages.[269]

Perhaps this is more of rhetorical gesture, and that *if* there is some conscience, it is because "no person . . . is wholly void of the grace of God."[270] If this is the case, then how would conscience be considered natural but as part of the created order, whether moral law is considered merely a ceremonial form of the law "written on the hearts by the Finger of God" or an "eternal Moral Law" engraved on the hearts of men and angels?[271] In either case, the language is the same, pointing to a valid form of conscience, at least as far as "heathens" are concerned, which is different from a Christian conscience.[272]

266. "Scripture Way of Salvation," in *WJW*, 2:156, §1.2.

267. "On Conscience," in *WJW*, 3:482, 484, §1.5, 9; see also Bryant, "John Wesley's Doctrine," 247.

268. Runyon, *New Creation*, 32; Collins and Vickers, *Sermons of John Wesley*, 40; Kim, "John Wesley's Anthropology," 99–102. Maddox thinks that the condition of the fall left "conscience without a standard." Maddox, *Responsible Grace*, 81.

269. "The Heavenly Treasures in Earthen Vessels," in *WJW*, 4:163, §1.1 (emphasis added).

270. "On Working Out Our Own Salvation," in *WJW*, 3:207, §3.4.

271. Bryant, "John Wesley's Doctrine," 243; see also Collins, "John Wesley's Platonic Conception," 117–18.

272. The reader is reminded that indeed glimpses of God could be attained from creation, which logically would mean that there is some form of relationship between God and creation discerned. Yet, this does not mean a natural salvation.

A Christian conscience bears *affective* knowledge mediated by the Holy Spirit and does not need the moral law to work.[273] When Wesley strictly discusses the Holy Spirit in its prevenient role, it *is* the nature by which one will know and *feel* God's love. When Wesley mentions "a measure of light, some faint glimmering ray, which, sooner or later, more or less, enlightens every man that cometh into the world,"[274] Wesley is not talking about the human conscience as such. Rather:

> There is something of an *infinitely higher kind*: Some motions of his Will, which are more strong and vigorous than can be conceived by men, and although they have not the nature of human passions,—yet will answer the ends of them. By grief, therefore, we are to understand, *a disposition in God's will, flowing* at once from his boundless love to the persons of men, and his infinite abhorrence of their sins. And in this restrained sense it is here applied to the Spirit of God in the words of the Apostle.[275]

Furthermore:

> There can be no point of greater importance to him, who knows, that it is the Holy Spirit which *leads us into all truth and into all holiness*, than to consider with *what temper of soul we are to entertain his divine presence*; so as not either to drive him from us, or to disappoint him of the *gracious ends for which his abode with us is designed*; which is *not the amusement of our understanding*, but the conversion and entire sanctification of our hearts and lives.[276]

Thus, in Wesley consistently referring to the heart or soul being stamped, impressed, or sealed *by the Holy Spirit*, he seems to be "intuiting" the force of the impact generated by the Holy Spirit and on the soul, awakening the spiritual senses. Consequently, one feels in it the "distance" created after impact, which is characteristic of the function of conscience. Like a hammer striking an anvil, the Holy Spirit echoes within the soul, allowing one to see and, importantly, to hear what one could not.

Within this context, the Holy Spirit is one characterization of the Voice mentioned above and results in the memory of God. In several places, Wesley refers to a Voice or to an act of hearing:

273. Bryant, "John Wesley's Doctrine," 244.

274. "On Working Out Our Own Salvation," in *WJW*, 3:207, §3.4.

275. Wesley, "On Grieving Holy Spirit," 608 (emphasis added).

276. Wesley, "On Grieving Holy Spirit," 607 (emphasis added).

> And herein we remain till the Second Adam becomes a quicken-
> ing Spirit to us, till he raises the dead, the dead in sin, in pleasure,
> riches or honours. But, before any dead soul can live, he "hears
> (hearkens to) the voice of the Son of God": he is made sensible of
> his lost estate and receives the sentence of death in himself.[277]

> While he is calling, "I beseech thee, show me thy glory!" he hears a
> voice in the inmost soul, "I will make all my goodness pass before
> thee, and I will proclaim the name of the Lord; I will be gracious
> to whom I will be gracious, and I will show mercy to whom I will
> show mercy." And, it is not long before "the Lord descends in the
> cloud, and proclaims the name of the Lord." Then he sees, but not
> with eyes of flesh and blood, "The Lord, the Lord God; merci-
> ful and gracious, long-suffering, and abundant in goodness and
> truth."[278]

> It is the Ear of the Soul, whereby a sinner hears the Voice of the
> Son of God and lives; even that Voice which alone wakes the Dead.
> Son thy Sins are forgiven thee.[279]

While it is conceivable that the Voice of the Son of God refers to Christ, and
perhaps knowledge of Christ and the moral law, it seems that it is revealed
by Scripture or, as the first passage alludes, the Holy Spirit. Together with
how this Voice functions as an echo above, one is able to recollect, that is,
remember God since it is the Holy Spirit that gives faith. Once received,
one is able feel the love of God shed abroad in the heart, and having been
recognized as loved, is enabled to love God.[280] Thus, this is not simply a
remembrance of God, but also a remembrance of the self as stimulated by
holy conscience. It is as if the shallow impressions on wax (defacement)
have been "re-inscribed." So, in this prevenient renewal of the image of
God, one also feels the conviction of sin. Intriguingly, when one looks at
how original sin destroys human nature in Wesley's *Survey* vol. 5, Wesley
curiously omits the category of memory in his explanations of the corrup-
tions of the understanding, will, affections, conscience, and memory.[281]

277. "Awake, Thou That Sleepest," in *WJW*, 1:145, §1.9.

278. "The Spirt of Bondage and of Adoption," in *WJW*, 1:260–61, §3.2.

279. Wesley, *Earnest Appeal*, 4–5.

280. A few paragraphs later, after the hearing section in *Earnest Appeal*, there is a
clear attestation of affective valence. One is able not only to hear, but to "taste" and feel
God. Wesley, *Earnest Appeal*, 5.

281. Wesley, *Doctrine of Original Sin*, 481. After the section on conscience (sect. 4),

However Wesley *does* warn "that when you are with the Physician, O forget not this disease."[282]

And why this warning against forgetfulness? It is here that this book makes a synthesis with Bonaventure. Bryant mentions the similarity between Wesley's concept of the Trinitarian image of God and those of the medieval mystics, Bonaventure being one of them.[283] For Wesley, original sin results in:

> A corruptible body that presses down the soul. It very frequently hinders the soul in its operations; and, at best, serves it very imperfectly.[284]

This is contrasted with:

> It is certain he had such strength of understanding as no man ever since had. His understanding was perfect in its kind; capable of apprehending all things clearly, and judging concerning them according to truth, without any mixture of error. His will had no wrong bias of any sort, but all his passions and affections were regular, being steadily and uniformly guided by the dictates of his unerring understanding; embracing nothing but good, and every good in proportion to its degree of intrinsic goodness. His liberty likewise was wholly guided by his understanding: He chose, or refused, according to its direction. Above all (which was his highest excellence, far more valuable than all the rest put together) he was a creature capable of God, capable of knowing, loving, and obeying his Creator. And in fact he did know God, did unfeignedly love and uniformly obey him. This was the supreme perfection of man.[285]

This lengthy quote is nothing other than original righteousness, but the fascinating aspect is that it is a result of the power of self-motion. Furthermore, self-motion is an innate principle that is part of the natural image along with understanding, will, and liberty.[286] Due to its triadic structure, Wesley's image of God is usually framed in terms of understanding, will, and liberty. But while scholars may mention self-motion, the potential

---

there should be one for memory, but there is no heading for it.

282. Wesley, *Doctrine of Original Sin*, 517–18.

283. Bryant, "John Wesley's Doctrine," 151.

284. "On the Fall of Man," in *WJW*, 2:405, §3.2.

285. "The General Deliverance," in *WJW*, 2:439, §1.2.

286. "The General Deliverance," in *WJW*, 2:438, §1.1.

consequences of inclusion in the natural image needs expansion.[287] In particular, if the Holy Spirit confers righteousness as the breath of God, then within a person, there is another kind of conscience and of memory, that of *synderesis* described previously in the section on Bonaventure.

THE HOLY SPIRIT AND *SYNDERESIS*, CONSCIENCE, AND CONTUITON

According to Wesley, the Holy Spirit is an ordering already present within the created individual as that "free grace which 'formed man of the dust of the ground, and breathed into him a living soul,' and stamped on that soul, the image of God."[288] Since a "free grace" is designed to order humanity, it acts much like the principle of self-motion conferred at creation described above. In this respect, self-motion is like *synderesis* as found in Bonaventure. Whereas Bonaventure links it specifically to a matter of the will,[289] Wesley takes a broader approach to encompass all other cognitive faculties. Generally speaking, however, Wesley's and Bonaventure's approaches can align in the will representing a desire for God and good, or the *affectus*. But, in following Bonaventure's theology of *synderesis*, the weight of the Holy Spirit acts as the memory of the free grace that impressed its stamp on creation. This is like Bonaventure's general grace and the purview of *synderesis* and Wesley's prevenient grace. Therefore, self-motion falls in line with Davis's more traditional reading of *synderesis* (which cannot err) and weight of the will (due to sin), which needs to be removed so that people can "naturally" incline in an ascent to God, something Wesley frequently mentions under original righteous.[290]

Ultimately, however, evidence in Wesley's system must be appropriated because he does not distinguish between conscience and *synderesis* despite what is "naturally" human and divinely empowering. When Wesley uses the term "conscious" both in its vulgar variety and its divine one, he

287. For example, Kim mentions it as part of the natural image but does not comment, and Bryant notes that it is a part of the spirit. Kim, "John Wesley's Anthropology," 28–29; Bryant, "John Wesley's Doctrine," 152.

288. "Salvation by Faith," in *WJW*, 1:115, introduction, para. 1; Kim, "John Wesley's Anthropology," 19.

289. Eardley, "Medieval Theories of Conscience," §3.1.

290. Wesley, *Doctrine of Original Sin*, 465–68. The converse, of course, is that because of original sin, people are inclined to evil.

is conflating the terms "conscience" and *synderesis*. He mentions the Greek *synderesis* in conjunction with his definition of conscience:

> Conscience, then, is that faculty whereby we are at once con-science of our own thoughts, words, and actions; and of their merit or demerit, of their being good or bad; and, consequently, deserving either praise or censure. And some pleasure generally attends the former sentence; some uneasiness the latter: But this varies exceedingly, according to education and a thousand other circumstances.[291]

While Wesley could have read Bonaventure, it is more possible that he read Aquinas and St. Jerome. Jerome defines *synderesis* as "that by which humans *feel* shame and embarrassment at their sin, but also the power to correct. It is the spirit that knows the soul interiorly, suggesting a cognitive or intellectual faculty."[292] Aquinas describes *synderesis* as a "natural habit said to incite to good, and to murmur at evil, inasmuch as through first principles we proceed to discover, and judge of what we have discovered."[293] Clearly, there is a conscious judgment *of* a process that takes understanding. Thus, insofar as conscience involves a human act, even a Christian one, it is mutable and fallible, though influenced or convicted by divine witness. Thus, the idea of *synderesis* as memory remains intact in the conviction of sin as it is recollected. It is possible, then, for Wesley to be excused from not making the distinction between conscience and *synderesis* if he is taking it to mean a rational human process.

Nevertheless, there are, in essence, two aspects of "conscience" at work, one divine and one human. Here, Bonaventure's contuition aligns with Wesley's scales of assent. The historical background of Wesley's scales of assent cannot be discussed, but Bryant explains Wesley's scales of assent in depth and in context with Locke's degrees of assent.[294] The crux of the matter was divine revelation, and Wesley's mother, Susanna, was instrumental in advising a young Wesley on the matter:

> I insist upon it that the virtue of faith, by which through the merits of our Redeemer we must be saved, is an assent to the truth of

---

291. "On Conscience," in *WJW*, 3:481, §1.2–3.

292. Davis, *Weight of Love*, 47.

293. Aquinas, *Summa Theologica*, 384, q. 79, art. 12.

294. Bryant, "John Wesley's Doctrine," 45–49.

whatever God hath been pleased to reveal, because he hath revealed it, and not because we understand it.[295]

Furthermore, "the truth of revelation is assented to on the basis of the work of the Holy Spirit, and not on reason alone."[296] It is faith based. If what was said above of Wesley's "*synderesis*" is true, then just as contuition is an "agreement" between *synderesis* and conscience in Bonaventure's system, so, too, are divine revelation and conscience in Wesley's system. In both systems, there is a rational process that "confirms" what God knows. And in both systems, there is a conjunction of the knowledge of God in the intellect and the Holy Spirit of the will. Thus, it appears that Wesley, to a good degree, combines both these aspects of conscience in a cognitive-affective way that also combines both divine and human in one of participation.

With conscience, there is the "acceptance" of that conviction of the Holy Spirit that has sealed you, that God loves you, and allows for the understanding of moral law, or the knowledge of Christ, "the *pattern* of our great Master."[297] This is gratuitous grace. Pleasing grace, or sanctifying grace, is then the reception of all the virtues that then order human life in conformity to the "Standard of Christian Perfection."[298] Altogether, in an act of contuition one gradually recovers the "whole image of God,"[299] as one "walks as Christ walked."[300] One is attempting to peer into the mind of Christ, to *feel* it, or what Wesley terms as experimental knowledge. In this respect, memory is "hidden" but at the center of Wesley's natural, moral, and political images as one moves through them. That is:

> And first, we are sealed by the Holy Spirit of God, by our receiving his real stamp upon our souls; being made the partakers of the divine nature, and meet for the inheritance of the saints in light. This is indeed the design of his dwelling in us, to heal our disordered souls, and to restore that image of his upon our nature, which is so defaced by our original and actual corruptions. . . . But by the renewal of our minds in the image of Him that created us, we are still more capable of his influences; and by means of a daily

---

295. S. Wesley, "Nov. 10th, 1725," 25:183.

296. Bryant, "John Wesley's Doctrine," 62.

297. "On Working Out Our Own Salvation," in *WJW*, 3.208, §3.5 (emphasis added).

298. Wesley, *Christian Perfection*, 14, §2.13.

299. "The Heavenly Treasures in Earthen Vessels," in *WJW*, 4:164, §1.3.

300. "Reason Impartially Considered," in *WJW*, 2:592, §1.6.

intercourse with him, we are more and more transformed into his likeness, till we are satisfied with it.[301]

And as one moves through the aspects of the image of God, human beings recapitulate the way human beings were intended to be ordered, which Wesley (with an additional item, in contrast to Bonaventure's fourfold way) might regard as 1) love of God, 2) self-knowledge, 3) love of neighbor, 4) *transformation of the world*, and 5) perfection of the body. It is the inheritance (memory) of divine wisdom put into godly action.

CONCLUSION

If there is a summary of a memorial process and ethic in Wesley's image of God, the following three quotes might be it:

> The beauty of holiness, of that inward man of the heart which is renewed after the Image of God, cannot but strike every eye which God hath opened,—every enlightened understanding. The ornament of a meek, humble, loving spirit, will at least excite the approbation of all those who are capable in any degree, of discerning spiritual good and evil. From the hour men begin to emerge out of the darkness which covers the giddy, unthinking world, they cannot but perceive how desirable a thing it is to be thus *transformed into the likeness of him that created us. This inward religion bears the shape of God* so visibly *impressed* upon it, that a soul must be wholly immersed in flesh and blood when he can doubt of its divine original. We may say of this, in a secondary sense, even as of the Son of God himself, that it is the "brightness of his glory, the express image of his person"; απαυγασμα μα της δοξης . . . αυτον "the beaming forth of his" eternal "glory"; and yet so tempered and softened, that even the children of men may herein see God and live; χαρακτηρ της υποστασεως αυτου, "the character, the stamp, the living impression, of his person," who is the fountain of beauty and love, the original source of all excellency and perfection.[302]

And:

> I rejoice, because the sense of God's love to me hath, by the same Spirit, wrought in me to love him, and to love for his sake every

301. Wesley, "On Grieving Holy Spirit," III.1 (612).

302. "Upon Our Lord's Sermon on the Mount Discourse the Fourth," in *WJW*, 1:531–32 (emphasis added).

> child of man, every soul that hath made. I rejoice, because he gives me *to feel in myself "the mind that was in Christ"*: simplicity, a single eye to him in every motion of my heart; power always to fix the loving eye of my soul on Him who "loved me, and gave himself for me," to aim at him alone, at his glorious will, in all I think or speak or do; purity, desiring nothing more but God.[303]

And:

> On this condition he hath entrusted us with our souls, our bodies, our goods, and whatever other talents we have received: But in order to *impress this weighty truth on our hearts*, it will be needful to come to particulars.
> And, first, God has entrusted us with our soul, an immortal spirit, made in the Image of God; together with all the powers and faculties thereof—understanding, imagination, memory, will, and a train of affections, either included in it or closely dependent upon it; love and hatred, joy and sorrow, respecting present good and evil; desire and aversion, hope and fear, respecting that which is to come.[304]

In these respective quotes, there is the application of the natural, moral, and political images through the weight of memory, which is iconic in nature as it is impressed on the physical body. In this the Holy Spirit activates the pattern of Christ. In Wesley's model, however, compared to Bonaventure or Augustine, the specific conformation to the likeness of God is found in the image of God that is the mind of Christ. To look at the glory of God in the face of Christ is to try to remember the memory of Christ, as more than just an idea of Christ, but to plumb the eternal depth of divine wisdom. To do so is to taste the goodness of the Lord.

303. "The Witness of Our Own Spirit," in *WJW*, 1:310, para. 16 (emphasis added).
304. "The Good Steward," in *WJW*, 2:284, §1.2 (emphasis added).

4

Memory, the Image of God, and Neuroscientific Prospects

INTRODUCTION

Thus far, the first three chapters have argued for 1) the physicality of the image of God, 2) the image of God in human beings as the memory of God, and 3) a Wesleyan interpretation of memory in the natural, moral, and political images of God. This chapter considers how the memory of God, and therefore the image of God, *may* be physically embodied. In other words, this chapter builds on the theological assertions of the previous chapters into what could be *plausible* instantiations of memory and the image of God, particularly if Christians are said to have been sealed by the Holy Spirit and have the mind of Christ. Given the cognitive-affective context of the previous chapters, neuroscientific research will be used to describe those theological possibilities.

The focus of the chapter will be on the brain, and the centerpiece of memory's physicality will be on the memory engram, first coined by Richard Semon but then elaborated on by Endel Tulving and Daniel Schacter. The engram serves as a *general* and plausible physical basis for the image of God that is related to but not restricted to how memory works in Tulving's general abstract processing system proposed in 1983. Then, recent research using a technique called optogenetics will elucidate how engrams are created and function in memory. Once the existence of engrams has been established, the theological significance of engrams will be discussed. Taken all together, this chapter attempts to take the theological language of the image of God and memory to its resemblance in neuroscientific literature. In so doing, the scientific overlay provides a possible natural description for the image of God that is more than something strictly theological.

PHILOSOPHICAL GROUND-CLEARING

Embedded in this chapter is the perennial debate over the interaction between science and religion. A detailed discussion into this debate is beyond the scope of this book, but some reason should be given as to why science is even included and to clearly state the reasons for using it in describing the image of God. This chapter *is not* a scientific paper intending to discover the image of God in the brain as if some network or assemblage of neurons already exist on which hypotheses can be tested. After all, one can rightly critique that *if* there is a stable structure of neurons for the image of God in the memory structures of the brain, then it should be scientifically testable. Only after testing can one confirm or disaffirm theological claims. The ability to perform science, however, is not the relevant issue here and is not the reason for its inclusion in this book. A rather small but important distinction is being made and explained below.

In describing the image of God as the memory of God, much of the analysis has come from the "academic" writings of churchmen and scholars, somewhat like a scientific literature review. But this cannot overlook the fact that they were informed by the *narrative* of creation involving the godhead. This was shown in the analysis of Genesis in chapter 1 and by Paul's appropriation of wisdom speculation in chapter 2, pointing to the Father and Son respectively. Furthermore, the Greek concepts of image and memory were added to the analysis through Platonic stories of the wax tablet, the aviary, the scribe, and painter. In this respect, Colleen Shantz is correct to state that the image of God has a "poetic character."[1] After all, much of this book has tried to bring forward the *language* of the image of God and memory. For example, Irenaeus wrote that Christ and the Holy Spirit were the metaphorical "hands" of God in fashioning human beings,

1. Shantz, "In Divine (Mental) Image," 51–52.

giving them "fingerprints." The language of sealing or stamping of the Holy Spirit which leave behind both the imprint as well as felt force of its impact contributes to the *pathos* or "feeling" of bearing the image of God in human flesh. Indeed, the image of God and memory can be poetic.

In describing the image of God as poetic, however, Shantz claims that "*imago Dei* has never been a central doctrinal thread in the systematic tapestry," making the image of God and its narrative quality "poorly calibrated for systematic theology . . . and difficult to assimilate into scientific discourse."[2] Having situated the image of God in a theological anthropology between a doctrine of God and a doctrine of creation, this book argues not only for the centrality of the image of God, but for a "systematic theology" built around memory, even if it is not a complete one. Furthermore, just because something is poetic does not necessarily mean that it *cannot* be put into scientific discourse. For instance, when Susan Eastman quotes Janet Martin Soskice, that "models and metaphorical theory terms may be reality depicting without pretending to be directly descriptive,"[3] she is trying to "find new ways of pointing to and expressing [Paul's] meaning and, along the way, find pointers that look intriguingly similar to some other expressions of the self in the ancient world."[4] This chapter follows Soskice in attempting to convey a theological reality, but grounded in scientific expression.

And this is where the distinction between presuming theology and presuming science must be made. This chapter does not presume the accuracy of science, or even what science does, to then accurately reflect theology. Rather, the image of God as memory is the presumptive theological claim antecedent to scientific claim. Does this mean that no scientific work is being done or integrated into theology? No, in the domain of a theology of nature (not to be confused with natural theology), theology is revealed in science, in which it is able to "translate" the poetics of narrative into physical descriptors. This trades on one of the primary claims of the book, that the image of God is physical, and saying that is to ask a basic question: What would a scientific description of the image of God "look" like? In a way, this extends Anthony James Shelton's view that the brain is the physical interface or window between the divine and human.[5] Rather than

---

2. Shantz, "In Divine (Mental) Image," 51–52.

3. Eastman, *Paul and the Person*, 131.

4. Eastman, *Paul and the Person*, 4.

5. Shelton, "Window to God," 37.

intelligence, however, this chapter is about memory. So, as will be detailed below, the "what" of memory, that is, a memory trace or engram, *could* be how the image of God is represented in the brain, not that it necessarily is.

BASIC NEUROSCIENCE AND MEMORY

Before getting into the details of how theology and neuroscience relate, it will be helpful for the reader to know some terms in the orientation of the brain. This taxonomy will be general at first, but when details are called for, increasingly more specific. Broadly speaking, the cerebrum can be sectioned into the frontal, temporal, parietal, and occipital lobes. As the name implies, the frontal lobe is towards the forehead, extending back to approximately the middle of the skull. Similarly, the temporal lobe begins near one's temples extending towards the back of the brain where the occipital lobe is located. The parietal lobe sits above the temporal lobe and behind the frontal lobe. Since the brain is divided into two hemispheres, it can also be described in spatial terms; the medial, lateral, dorsal, and ventral refer to the middle, side, top, or bottom of the brain. Bringing up the rear, literally, is the cerebellum, which is located below the occipital lobe. Lastly, the entire cerebrum "sits" on the brainstem, which then exits the skull in the familiar spinal cord. These are only some of the terms used and oftentimes are combined to give greater location specificity. For example, the medial temporal lobe (MTL) describes an area of the brain that is nearer to the midline of the brain in the temporal lobe. Similarly, the dorsolateral prefrontal cortex (DLPFC) describes an area near the top and to the side of the front part of the brain. In concert with the parietal lobe, the MTL and DLPFC function in memory creation and retrieval, specifically *episodic* memory.[6]

Episodic memory usually refers to a remembered "episode," that has a subjective feeling accompanying the recalled event. Within MTL, the hippocampal formation and adjoining regions have been crucial for intact episodic memory, as patient H. M. and numerous following studies have demonstrated.[7] As far as retrieval is concerned, however, an increasing

6. Slotnick, *Cognitive Neuroscience of Memory*, 47.

7. Corkin, "What's New." It is worth noting that because of H. M., other forms of memory were discovered. Even though H. M. could not form new memories, he could still remember childhood facts and become more efficient at tracing patterns and rudimentary learning.

number of studies have pointed to the parahippocampus (alongside the hippocampus) because it appears to process the context information germane to episodic memory.[8] Taken together with item information coming into the perirhinal cortex (another MTL region important for familiarity judgments), the hippocampus "builds" relevant features of stored material and their contexts into an "episode" that is spatiotemporally remembered. In effect, the hippocampus acts as a "binder" of information that counts for a successfully "retrieved" memory in addition to its function in memory formation.[9]

Assumed in memory formation are *semantic* memories, the classic pairing to episodic memory, which are the "abstracted words, concepts, and rules stored in long-term memory."[10] Often times, this memory is referred to "as factual information learned over a long period of time,"[11] such as definitions of words, but where the specific learning episode is not involved (cannot be remembered). Considering that objects have multiple features (form and motion, for example), and that they can be associated with human motor skills, it is unsurprising that multiple cortical areas (ventral occipitotemporal, lateral temporal, ventral premotor) are involved, some being modality specific (visual, auditory, language). Other forms of memory include working; short-term; and, broadly speaking, implicit.[12] As with semantic memories, these other forms of memory have contributions from other areas of the brain, including prefrontal (both lateral and medial), the angular gyrus, and basal ganglia and cerebellar regions respectively. In addition, some cortical regions of the brain already mentioned function differently for different memory tasks (for instance, the DLPFC), that is, in the construction of memories, it is not only the content that matters, but the *process* of encoding, consolidating, and retrieving a memory.[13] All these together count for what can be termed memory.

---

8. Slotnick, *Cognitive Neuroscience of Memory*, 48–49; Rugg and Vilberg, "Brain Networks," 256; Moscovitch et al., "Episodic Memory and Beyond," 108 (here, it is "view-specific scene representation").

9. Slotnick, *Cognitive Neuroscience of Memory*, 48–49; Simons and Spiers, "Prefrontal and Medial," 638.

10. Bower, "Brief History," 22.

11. Slotnick, *Cognitive Neuroscience of Memory*, 2.

12. A. Martin and Chao, "Semantic Memory in Brain," 195–97.

13. Each of the steps of memory formation has its own debates. For example, there is a debate about memory transfer. Just where is memory "stored" once consolidated, and does it need the function of the hippocampus? Evidence seems to suggest that the

THEOLOGY AND NEUROSCIENCE

Previous attempts at linking specific neurobiology to theology have been made, notably, by Carol Rausch Albright and James B. Ashbrook, in an ambitiously titled book, *Where God Lives in the Human Brain*. They argue that the structures of the human brain create a meaning-seeking mind that encompasses the universe, of which "God is the 'self-evident' and 'dynamic source' of *all reality* as experienced and expressed by human beings."[14] Albright and Ashbrook shine a spotlight on neurobiology by adapting Paul D. MacLean's triune brain in different ways of understanding God.[15] The reptilian brain or primal mind contributes to human survival. The paleo-mammalian brain or emotional mind (limbic involvement) forges the connection of relatedness and meaning through memory and empathy. The neomammalian brain or rational mind organizes meaning by ordering and categorizing information in the neocortex for understanding (meaning-seeking). More specifically, the frontal lobes contribute to "intentional processes of a conscious brain in understanding a God who is purposeful."[16] Together, the entire brain integrates concepts and constructs how humans understand God. In this humanizing endeavor, Emily Dickinson's line of "The Brain is just the weight of God" finds itself in the cosmic order of an "anthropomorphism" of God.[17]

While Albright and Ashbrook's book is provocative and ambitious in combining neuroscience, psychology, and theology, it is somewhat outdated in neurobiology and only broadly covers theological concepts. In some ways, this is unavoidable since a central claim is how the brain itself "fits" and works within a cosmic order. In fact, by arguing for a unitary function of understanding God in the brain, Albright and Ashbrook planted the seeds for the outdated use of neurobiology, despite their attempts at its integration. The triune model is supposed to have delineated functions/behaviors to specific parts of the brain, but more recent neuroscience involves

---

hippocampus is involved in all episodic memory regardless of the age of memory. The alternative, however, is to suppose there are cortico-cortical instances of memory storage.

14. Albright and Ashbrook, *Where God Lives*, xxviii.

15. Albright and Ashbrook, *Where God Lives*, 51–53.

16. Albright and Ashbrook, *Where God Lives*, 133.

17. Albright and Ashbrook, *Where God Lives*, xiv, 109, 163–64. See the full text of Emily Dickinson's poem "The Brain—Is Wider Than the Sky" at https://www.litcharts.com/poetry/emily-dickinson/the-brain-is-wider-than-the-sky; quotation at line 9.

whole networks integrating different parts of the brain. That said, critically, they apply the categorization of brain structures to the image of God.

In each of the three "parts" of the brain, the image of God is given a descriptive function. The reptilian brain, for example, functions in hierarchy, territoriality, watchfulness, persistence, to not only keep one alive, but to reflect the ever-present, "unchanging" God.[18] The paleomammalian brain in its emotional/relational capacity is like a nurturing parent God. And the neocortex in its divisions of left and right hemispheres, bring forth images of a logical, purposeful God and of an "emotional," all-encompassing, interlinking God respectively.[19] All of the above are considered "images" by Albright and Ashbrook, yet at the same time, they are none of the above.[20] Surely, this is simply a careful apophatic measure, but clearly, the authors are not squeamish about thoroughly humanizing the *imago Dei*, as only the mind can call forth in any given dimension.[21] This would be necessary for those fully committed to being God's co-creators.

Patrick McNamara takes a slightly different approach, acknowledging first that "empirical facts with which religious scholars have been grappling with for decades, or better, centuries, simply cannot yet be adequately handled by current models of the Mind/brain in the cognitive neurosciences."[22] That said, McNamara's central argument of changes in the self[23] is broadly applied to various religious experiences rather than to theology, whether they stem from pathological conditions or religious practices. In short, a "decentering" phenomenon occurs to temporarily take the current "executive self" offline while attempting to rebuild a new self in comparison to an ideal self.[24] Space does not allow for a philosophical discussion or a detailed neurobiological analysis of the self as it lies beyond the scope of this book. To McNamara's argument, however, religiosity involves the "orbital frontal, right temporal, limbic system (amygdala), and serotonin (valence) and

---

18. Albright and Ashbrook, *Where God Lives*, 63.

19. Albright and Ashbrook, *Where God Lives*, 128–31.

20. Albright and Ashbrook, *Where God Lives*, 69.

21. Albright and Ashbrook, *Where God Lives*, xxix. "It is the humanness of our brain that shapes all that matters to us, whether we call that God, or Nature or Life or History or Destiny or Evolution."

22. McNamara, *Neuroscience of Religious Experience*, x.

23. McNamara, *Neuroscience of Religious Experience*, xi–xiii.

24. McNamara, *Neuroscience of Religious Experience*, 44–58.

dopamine (reward) system."[25] In the end, religious experience, induced or otherwise, allows for the transformation of the self.

McNamara's theories are impressive in the functional aspect of our religious selves, but in being neuroscientific, considerable space is left for the theological. For example, in following his decentering argument, McNamara points to dreams as a potential source of God concepts. While people dream, they create supernatural agents who interact with them.[26] Drawing on the work of Pascal Boyer and Justin Barrett, McNamara agrees that God concepts from dreams fit the definition of being "minimally counterintuitive" or a result of a "hyperactive agency detection device" (in our brain). They can, after all, be omniscient since they are products of one's own mind but have no body. Thus, these "self" creations, or God *images*, might compete, even when awake, with the current self until it regains executive control.[27] Through this temporary "yoking up" to the God image, the self is enriched with control over its executive functions. McNamara claims that this process takes time so that the self experiences "prolonged periods of God-related decentering,"[28] presumably for the better, but always a bit dangerous. What might be interesting is that religious people ritualize this in focal periods of time.

Notice, however, that like Albright and Ashbrook, McNamara is not advocating an ontology for these images of God. Perhaps this is because he does not want to imply causality. Scientific authors have stated to some degree that a correlation of some region of the brain to a behavioral outcome does not imply the causation of the observed phenomena. Furthermore, as Stanley B. Klein argues concerning *memory*:

> There is simply no other way to reliably know what a mental state, qua mental state, entails. While experience eventually may prove grounded in events taking place at the neural, molecular, atomic, or subatomic level, reducing our phenomenology to the motion, shape, and size of its constituents (or knowledge thereof) cannot provide the information we acquire in virtue of having the experience.[29]

25. McNamara, *Neuroscience of Religious Experience*, 127.

26. McNamara, *Neuroscience of Religious Experience*, 196, 204.

27. McNamara, *Neuroscience of Religious Experience*, 204–5.

28. McNamara, *Neuroscience of Religious Experience*, 205.

29. Klein, "What Memory Is," 7.

So, while Albright, Ashbrook, and McNamara take seriously the interplay between theology and neuroscience in possible models, they echo Shantz in "poetic" fashion. Various images or concepts of God resist systematization and result *out of* human evolution. The theology comes after the science.

THE "POETIC" MEMORY ENGRAM

To be fair, this book does not address evolution, but it does try to place theology first in interpreting the science. In so doing, it takes human beings at face value and how theology and memory might work within a person rather than trying to hypothesize a theology in human evolution. Is this then merely poetic? This chapter has tried to answer that question in the negative, that in holding fast to theology, prospective answers can be found through science. *One* reasonable possibility is the memory engram, which has characteristics consistent with Platonic memory and theological language.

Historically the memory engram goes back to Richard Semon who first coined the word "engram" in his 1921 publication *The Mneme*. He defined it as "the enduring though primarily latent modification in the irritable substance produced by a stimulus."[30] Semon further defined the engram later as "the result of engraphic action, and implies an altered disposition of the irritable substance towards a recurrence of the state of excitement produced by the original stimulus."[31] Engrams are fixed "in their totality," that is, various sensory modalities and excitations in various locations make up a "simultaneous engram-complex or engram-store."[32] In fact, Semon theorized in Galtonian fashion that different parts of the brain would have larger engraphic effects based on sensory modality specialization and gave the possibility that functionally, engram localization would be distributed in an interdependent fashion.[33] These engrams are laid down

---

30. Semon, *Mneme*, 12.

31. Semon, *Mneme*, 89. By *engraphic*, Semon means a sensory stimulus that excites the irritable substance.

32. Semon, *Mneme*, 91.

33. Semon, *Mneme*, 120, 128–29. Semon goes on to quote C. von Monokow, seemingly agreeing with his assessment of Semon's theory: "The working areas for the later acquired engram-complexes (Semon), that is, what we describe as 'perceptions,' 'presentations,' 'memory images,' etc., must, although differently distributed, extend far beyond the proper somatic cortical areas *over the entire brain surface like a wide-spread fibrous tent.*

in layers in a time-dependent fashion. After a stimulus has been removed, a "synchronous phase" gives way to an "acoluthic phase," which is the residual fading of the excitation of the irritable substance.[34] As such, it is possible for new engram complexes to be *unique* as the engram is not simply a passage of one engram to another (X → Y), but (X + Y) held together by the acoluthic "temporal glue."[35] Taken together, engram formation comprises Semon's law of engraphy or how memories are laid down and are ready for recall, or ecphory.

Semon's defines ecphory as:

> By the ecphory of an engram we understand the passage of an engram from a latent to a manifest state, or as we might say, the rousing into action of a disposition created by the original excitation and characterized as a permanent but usually latent change in the organism.[36]

Note that here Semon is referring to a single engram, but since memories are composed of multimodal detail, the engram-complex is activated. Because of this interdependence of engrams, activation of one latent engram can activate other engrams, whether it is the original stimulus or a derived one (either internal or mnemic). Semon calls this "coalescence" of engrams a homophony.[37] The most salient feature of homophony, however, is its creation of *new* engrams. As Daniel Schacter, James Eich, and Endel Tulving comment, Semon went against the prevailing strengthening view of memory (repetition makes stronger memories) and proposed that each repeated stimulus created a new engram (in another layer).[38] This means that rather than the same engrams being activated for a memory, new engrams

---

... *A certain local element, however, is essential to all functions*, even the highest, namely, that which serves as physiological basis for the immediate realization, or, as Semon would say, the ecphory of various acts" (129 [emphasis added]).

34. Semon, *Mneme*, 22; see also Schacter et al., "Richard Semon's Theory," 729.

35. Schacter et al., "Richard Semon's Theory," 730.

36. Semon, *Mneme*, 138.

37. Semon, *Mneme*, 154; Schacter et al., "Richard Semon's Theory," 734.

38. Schacter et al., "Richard Semon's Theory," 735; referring to Semon, *Mneme*, 165. It is worth quoting Semon here (all capital letters in the original text): "THE FUNDAMENTAL DIFFERENCE LIES IN THE FACT THAT REPETITION OF A STIMULUS DOES NOT STRENGTHEN AN ALREADY EXISTING ENGRAM, BUT GENERATES A NEW ENGRAM, AND THE MNEMIC EXCITATIONS RESULTING FROM ANY SUBSEQUENT ECPHORY OF THESE ENGRAMS ARE IN HOMOPHONY." Semon, *Mneme*, 169. Semon was very adamant about this feature of ecphory.

are created with each recall. As such, depending on the context, different engram-complexes will be recalled in Semon's law of ecphory.

In reading about Semon's memory engrams, the reader should find the familiar ancient stories about memory as previously described in the book. Although Semon does not mention either Plato or Aristotle—and for that matter neither do most memory scientists (and if so, only a general remark)—the connection between the engrams and Plato is clear. Both talk about a process that makes a change to an impressionable material. In the *Theaetetus* it was wax, while for Semon, it was neurons (and arguably synapses). Furthermore, Semon refers to the engram as "a permanent record that has been written or engraved on the irritable substance."[39] This, too, aligns with the language of memory in its theological context, where the Holy Spirit writes or engraves on the tables of the heart. Thus, even though Semon was proposing a "scientific" theory of memory for his time, it paralleled the ancient understanding of memory. In fact, it could be said that Semon's theory of memory is "poetic" in nature since it was completely theoretical with no evidence for the existence of engrams in the brain.

THE SCIENTIFIC UNDERSTANDING OF ENGRAMS

Taken together, engraphy and ecophory form the basis for Endel Tulving's episodic model of memory called the general abstract processing system (GAPS). It is "general" in that it can fit multiple models of memory; abstract in that the details of its components, save for the interaction between engram and retrieval cue; a processing system in that the memorial process is of more interest than its underlying structures; and systematic in that a number of components interact to make an integrated whole.[40] Engrams represent the encoding of information in "feature bundles,"[41] giving strength to the idea of neural networks, while "retrieval" represents the memorial experience. Tulving is careful to distinguish between retrieval and ecphory. With ecphory, the encoded material is brought together with the retrieval cue to be transformed into ecphoric information, from which the original engram is reencoded. This process occurs before "conversion," which denotes the successful process of accessing an engram and cue in experiencing the memory, whether that is through a narrative or some

---

39. Semon, *Mneme*, 24.

40. Tulving, *Elements of Episodic Memory*, 130–34.

41. Tulving, *Elements of Episodic Memory*, 160–61.

other means of communication. As one can see, Tuvling has expanded on Semon's theories. At the time GAPS was proposed (1983), however, data on the neuroanatomy of memory was comparatively light. It is unsurprising then to see some of the "gaps" in GAPS be filled with new knowledge. One advancement of GAPS is the localization of engrams cells and engram networks as initially proposed by Semon and found in rodents. To be clear, these experiments have been performed only in animals, to which analogous structures and processes exist in the human brain.

The key techniques that allow for such cell type specificity in animals studies are optogenetics and pharmacogenetics and are mentioned here as technical references leading to the memory engram. With optogenetics and pharmacogenetics, specific populations of cells can be labeled with light-sensitive channel proteins (channelrhodosin 2, ChR2) or drug receptors respectively, with viral vectors or in the germ line transmission of transgenes.[42] Thus, by using genetic manipulation, specific neurons in a heterogenous population can have genes turned on (gain of function) or off (loss of function) using light or drugs.[43] Moreover, the process is reversible. It was through optogenetics, which allowed for the discovery of specific memory cells, or engrams, in fear-conditioned mice.

In an optogenetic experiment on mice, members of Susumu Tonegawa's lab were able to demonstrate specific dentate gyrus cells (DG) in the hippocampus to be active during specific conditioned fear contexts (foot shock).[44] In their setup, transgenic c-fos-tetracycline activator (tTA) mice were virally infected with a tetracycline response element (TRE) connected to the ChR2-EYFP gene (EYFP, enhanced yellow fluorescent protein). C-fos is an intermediate early gene indicative of recent neuronal activity. Mice fed a diet with doxycycline (Dox) will block the TRE in c-fos expressing neurons and prevent ChR2 expression. When Dox is withheld, c-fos driven expression of tTA will bind to the TRE, activating ChR2 expression. In principle, this method would label activity dependent cells under a fear conditioning context (both c-fos and ChR2 positive), which could then be tested with gain of function light activation. Under "natural" circumstances, a mouse will learn the difference between the home cage (context A) and the foot shock associated with a tone (context B) of another cage. These trained mice will exhibit freezing behavior in context B, with active

42. Adolphs and Anderson, *Neuroscience of Emotion*, 134–40.
43. For a review, see Kasparov, "Optogenetics."
44. Lui et al., "Optogenetic Stimulation."

double-positive DG neurons. These neurons are not active when placed back in context A. With light stimulation, however, these neurons become active in context A, and the mouse exhibits freezing behavior. Moreover, another set of experiments showed that light activation was for specific contexts, revealing different DG neurons for different contexts (context C, open field fear conditioning). Together with other data where freezing behavior was *extinguished* by silencing, these showed that specific cells in the hippocampus are part of memory recall, the *engram cells*.[45]

Engram cells are dynamic in their creation and their maturation and dematuration. Engram cells are first generated from neurons that initially are more excitable than their neighboring neurons. Sheena A. Josselyn's lab was able to show that by microinjecting CREB via HSV vector (a transcription factor for protein synthesis) into subpopulations of lateral amygdalar (LA) neurons, mutant mice exhibiting deficits in fear memory could be rescued with a fraction of LA neurons.[46] Moreover, there was a high degree of colocalization of recent-activity neurons (arc protein) with CREB induced neurons, suggesting that these neurons were "selected" in fear memory as opposed to other neurons. Subsequent experiments using chemical and optogenetic tools replicated the CREB results, showing a more general excitability as the factor in neurons that "win" competition for a memory trace.[47] Interestingly, while an engram cell might be chosen, it may be "silent," meaning that the potential for its activation remains, but that "natural" cues do not activate the engram.[48] Rather, only after artificial stimulation does the engram become active. The study also found that silent engrams had low spine density and that only mature engrams had high spine density. This not only showed the dynamic range of engram cells, but also provided the basis for a systems consolidation of memory, that other cortical areas such as the medial prefrontal cortex (mPFC) have their own engram cells *to* which memory consolidates.

Indeed, the authors promote a systems consolidation of memory (at least for fear memory), where the hippocampus and mPFC coordinate storage of memories by first activating "silent engrams" in the DG into mature

---

45. Tonegawa et al., "Role of Engram Cells."

46. Han et al., "Neuronal Competition." The reader should note that here, the amygdala, a region just in front of the hippocampus, is being tested. The amygdala is widely known to be involved in emotional responses.

47. Yui et al., "Neurons Are Recruited." A caveat is that cells infected were *random*.

48. Ryan et al., "Engram Cells Retain Memory."

engrams (high spine density), which signals through to the mPFC silent engrams via the hippocampal circuit. Together with basolateral amygdalar input, the mPFC develops mature engrams, that for long-term storage by-passes DG engram cells which have gone silent.[49] As mentioned previously, this transfer of memory "storage" is contested. In fact, a graph analysis of functionally connected regions in fear conditioned mice tested one and thirty-six days apart, showed that some hippocampal regions remained coupled, particularly to the thalamus and neocortex (perhaps even more so), even though overall magnitude of signal decreased.[50] Thus it appears that the hippocampus remains engaged in long-term memory rather than in the simple transfer of memory to other brain regions. Strikingly, however, after thirty-six days, the number of connections to the mPFC and thalamus markedly increase, lending some weight to the "transition" of memory to the neocortex. In addition, the authors show a "small worlds" architecture that has a central core of the anterior cingulate, the prelimbic cortex, and the nucleus reuniens. Together, they form as "hippocampal," mPFC, and thalamic hub system important for the fear memory trace. In this way, "engram ensembles" are created based on how they are connected by an "engram index," lending much strength to a networked nature of memory.[51]

CONCLUSION

As of 2021, one hundred years will have passed between Semon's publication and recent research on engrams, but despite the passage of time, Semon's theory of memory has garnered much attention as researchers continue to elucidate how memory might work. Optogenetics have revealed silent engrams, that even artificial stimulation of silent engrams can "reawaken" "forgotten" emotional memories. Indeed, it is through ecphory and ecphoric information that a particular memory becomes "activated" from a "latent" state. This is very reminiscent of the image of God language in chapter 3, where the pattern of God, the image of God, is made known by the Holy Spirit. Importantly, the engram then, becomes not only a scientific theory of memory, but also a theological.

In becoming theological, the memory engram also fits within the definitions of *eikon* described in previous chapters. As a total engram complex,

---

49. Tonegawa et al., "Role of Engram Cells," 495.

50. Wheeler et al., "Identification of Functional Connectome."

51. Josselyn and Tonegawa, "Memory Engrams."

the image of God within human beings is reference to God but is only ever liminal and only through Christ, the wisdom of God. As such, human beings possess the image of God through the creative act of imprinting. Engrams are representative *eikons* like those in wax that can "hold" the *pathos* of God *as* the work of Christ and felt through the Holy Spirit. This is not to be confused with engrams that are "used" (having engrams) by human beings, which moves the discussion towards *phantasma*. Thus, if engrams are viewed like the image of God as divine fiat, they are also "inherited," in the theological sense. Interestingly, a large portion of Semon's work was dedicated to how engrams could be inherited. It was also probably the reason why his work in general was not seriously considered until more recently.[52] Nevertheless, the prospect of the image of God as engram seems intriguing because here at the end of chapter 4, the choice of the engram or engram complexes as the image of God offers a way for God to be "anchored" in the human being.

Now, is this all just poetic license of scientific data? That the science described does not do any work in the theological system argued for? In the end, the answer seems dependent on where one places the emphasis, on the theology or on the science. But for those who place more weight on the theological, the engram complex or pattern, however it may be distributed or connected, gives rationale for how the image of God might be instantiated within human beings. It also allows for some *theological* work to be done where doctrines clash and mingle in ourselves. One does not need to go all the way to a tiny scribe and a tiny painter within oneself to realize that. Rather, one can look to engrams within Tulving's GAPS. Is the image of God then a kind of god of the GAPS? Now perhaps *that* is poetic.

---

52. Schacter et al., "Richard Semon's Theory," 739.

Conclusions

Memory, Theology, Neuroscience, and Anthropology

THE CONCLUSION TO THIS book is admittedly a modest one compared to the amount of material offered to explain theological and philosophical views on memory. The basic conclusion is that God "naturally exists" as memory within a person, by the sheer force of creation that imparts God's marks, which are the impressions of Christ and movement of the Holy Spirit, the "two hands of God." This means that memory is instantiated in some way, which this book argues is the image of God. This makes theologians squeamish as it seemingly violates the radical distinction between God's nature and human nature. Yet, some modern theologies, in attempts to explain theodicy or evolution, have chipped away at traditionally divine characteristics. Process theology argues for two "parts" to God, one primordial and one consequent, which together show how God evolves with creation. Intriguingly, God's primordial nature is how God remembers creation as time passes, the consequent being transferred into the primordial. This seemingly violates God's simplicity, immutability, and impassibility. Other models of God proffer a "middle knowledge" of God, that while God knows all possibilities whether real or not (unicorns, for example), God does not know actual outcomes since they are dependent on the choices creation makes. This seemingly violates God's omniscience and omnipotence.

This book, however, tries its best to respect the unbridgeable gap that will always exist between humanity and God, as Augustine tries to do. However, the key to the actualization of creation lies in Bonaventure's theory of resemblance, where creation is what God *knows*, not the actual substance

154

of divine nature. As a result, whatever exists as the memory of God in the brain is theoretical in whatever God decides to create, to which one has limited access. This is known from the philosophy of memory and image. There is never total recall or a one-to-one correlation with any experience. It is a consequence of the creation of images. But in the creation of such icons, there is that *Bildwissenschaft* that gestures to something prior, which theologically is God the *Bildhauer*. Sometimes Bonaventure refers to God as the Eternal Art, and human beings are creation of that Art that bears God's signature. Historically that signature has been neatly tucked away in the immaterial soul, and while that might be true in what results in noetic phenomena, it cannot be of a Cartesian variety. To say that God has created a human being with God's memories, God's wisdom even, is to say that, yes, there *could be* in nature the brain structures, neurons, and even synapses that network together to instantiate those memories of God.

In this respect, Richard's Semon's memory engram or engram complex was offered as potential physicality for the image of God in the human brain. Since the existence of latent engram cells have been shown through optogenetics, there is the possibility of latency in the human memory God, at least from a theological perspective. In claiming that human beings are *created* as the image of God, the human body retains the "fingerprints" of God, as Irenaeus suggests, and are like imprints one finds in a wax tablet. Engrams act as physical "signatures," where memory engrams have the capacity to be stimulated. This presents the possibility of religious experiences, and theologically speaking, being accessible to the movement of the Holy Spirit.

This book has consistently relied on the language used to indicate memory. It was established by Plato and Aristotle, which was then followed into theological use. To be sure, Augustine, Bonaventure, and Wesley did not say that the image of God was memory per se. At best, they relied on the natural image of the soul, the mind in particular, where memory was only one aspect of the image of God. Even here, memory was seen more as a power or capacity rather than an instantiation of God's memory. Thus, it was necessary to point out the philosophical heritage that made its way into words like "impressed," "stamped," or "sealed," as they were used in the theology of Augustine, Bonaventure, and Wesley. Given that the language used by theologians referred to memory, how the Trinity reflects memory in the theological models was examined.

Here, two facets were combined into a cognitive-affective synergy resulting in an experiential knowledge of the *memory* of God. The knowledge of Christ, as medium, represented the "object" of cognition that was *the* image of God. Philosophically, Christ "fit the mold" as the impression in the wax of the human body. But as demonstrated by Bonaventure and Wesley, the affective component highlighted the power of the Holy Spirit in actually making that knowledge known. In fact, some recent work by James Jones argues that "the insistence that virtually all metaphors are grounded bodily might provide additional insight into the functioning of religious language."[1] This can come in the form of spiritual senses, which are "the neurologically grounded embodiment of our cognitive processes."[2] Thus, we know God via experiential knowledge carried through the physical body that bears the markings of God. Jones offers two possibilities: that through our bodies "we conceptualize a spiritual sense as a sense of our cosmic embodiment and interconnection with all that exists and/or an embodied perspective is to conceptualize a spiritual sense as a sense of our own existence that has become transparent to its ultimate source."[3] This book argues both, that while Christ might have been knowledge, its access was available because the Holy Spirit opened the spiritual senses.

This book has also focused on memory as the image of God, but also how it might apply to a Wesleyan theological anthropology. The apostle Paul clearly says that Christians *have* the "mind of Christ" (1 Cor 2:16) and that "renewing the spirit of the mind, in putting on a new self, created according to the likeness of God in true righteousness and holiness" (Eph 4:23–24). In memory we have a Janus-faced impetus, one that "looks" inward to the *possession* of Christ, the knowledge of God, and one that looks outward to the world as one *feels* what it means to *have* Christ. In remembering God, one can explain how "Christ becoming the likeness of humanity allows humanity to become likeness God, as God intended,"[4] when God created humans as God's impressions. There is a telos yet to be achieved, and to "put on Christ" (Rom 13:14) is to clothe oneself in the cloak of virtues, given, received, and reflective of the moral law that was stamped on the heart. In this way, the image of God branches into an anthropological dignity and a christological destiny when compared and remembered, and then *emerges* as the "new" self.

---

1. Jones, *Living Religion*, 97. Jones also states that "an embodied theology is not a theology of the body," but this book approaches this in what memory can provide.

2. Jones, *Living Religion*, 148.

3. Jones, *Living Religion*, 148.

4. Kilner, *Dignity and Destiny*, 72.

Bibliography

Adolphs, Ralph, and David Anderson. *The Neuroscience of Emotion: A New Synthesis*. Princeton, NJ: Princeton University Press, 2018. Kindle.

Albright, Carol Rausch, and James B. Ashbrook. *Where God Lives in the Human Brain*. Naperville, IL: Sourcebooks, 2001.

Ambuel, David. *Image and Paradigm in Plato's* Sophist. Las Vegas: Parmenides, 2007.

Aquinas, Thomas. *Commentaries on Aristotle's "On Sense and What Is Sensed" and "On Memory and Recollection."* Translated by Kevin White and Edward M. Macierowski. Washington, DC: Catholic University of America Press, 2005.

———. *Summa Theologica*. Translated by the Fathers of the Dominican Province. N.p.: N.p., n.d. Kindle.

Arendt, Hannah. *The Life of the Mind*. San Diego: Harcourt, 1978.

Augustine. *On the Trinity*. CCEL, 1887. From *Nicene and Post-Nicene Fathers*, edited by Philip Schaff, translated by Arthur West Haddan, revised and annotated by William G. T. Shedd, 1st ser., 3. https://ccel.org/ccel/schaff/npnf103/npnf103.iv.i.html.

———. *Saint Augustine's Confession*. Translated by Henry Chadwick. Oxford: Oxford University Press, 2008.

———. "A Treatise on the Spirit and the Letter." CCEL, 1887. From *Nicene and Post-Nicene Fathers*, edited by Philip Schaff, translated by Peter Holmes and Robert Ernest Wallis, revised by Benjamin B. Warfield, 1st ser., 5. https://ccel.org/ccel/schaff/npnf105/npnf105.xi.i.html.

Augustine, Daniela C. "Image, Spirit, and *Theosis*." In *The Image of God in an Image Driven Age: Explorations in Theological Anthropology*, edited by Beth Felker Jones and Jeffrey W. Barbeau, Wheaton Theology Conference Series, 173–88. Downers Grove, IL: IVP Academic, 2016. Kindle.

Balthasar, Hans Urs von. *Seeing the Form*. Edited by Joseph Fessio and John Kenneth Riches. Translated by Erasmo Leiva-Merikakis. Vol. 1 of *The Glory of the Lord: A Theological Aesthetics*. San Francisco: Ignatius, 2009.

Barth, Karl. *The Doctrine of Creation, Part 1*. Vol. 3.1 of *Church Dogmatics*. Edited by G. W. Bromiley and T. F. Torrance. Translated by J. W. Edwards et al. 1958. Reprint, New York: T&T Clark, 2010.

Bernecker, Sven. *Memory: A Philosophical Study*. Oxford: Oxford University Press, 2009. Kindle.

Bieber Lake, Christina. "Carrying the Fire, Bearing the Image." In *The Image of God in an Image Driven Age: Explorations in Theological Anthropology*, edited by Beth Felker Jones and Jeffrey W. Barbeau, Wheaton Theology Conference Series, 136–53. Downers Grove, IL: IVP Academic, 2016. Kindle.

Blomberg, Craig L. "True Righteousness and Holiness: The Image of God in the New Testament." In *The Image of God in an Image Driven Age: Explorations in Theological Anthropology*, edited by Beth Felker Jones and Jeffrey W. Barbeau, Wheaton Theology Conference Series, 66–86. Downers Grove, IL: IVP Academic, 2016. Kindle.

Boetcher, James Arnold. "An Analysis of Some of the Major Roles of Emotion in the Soteriology of John and Charles Wesley and Its Implications in Relationship to Contemporary Research on Emotions." PhD diss., Middlesex University, 2019.

Bonaventure. *Breviloquium*. Translated by Dominic V. Monti. Bonaventure Texts in Translation Series 9. New York: Franciscan Institute, 2005.

———. *Collations on the Hexaemeron: Conferences on the Six Days of Creation; The Illuminations of the Church*. Edited by Dominic V. Monti. Translated by Jay M. Hammond. Bonaventure Texts in Translation Series 18. New York: Franciscan Institute, 2018.

———. *Disputed Questions on the Knowledge of Christ*. Translated by Zachary Hayes. *Works of Saint Bonaventure* 4. New York: Franciscan Institute, 1992.

———. "The Soul's Journey into God." In *Bonaventure: The Soul's Journey Into God. The Tree of Life. The Life of St. Francis*, translated by Ewert Cousins, 53–116. Classics of Western Spirituality: A Library of Great Spiritual Masters. New York: Paulist, 1978.

Bower, Gordon H. "A Brief History of Memory Research." In *The Oxford Handbook of Memory*, edited by Endel Tulving and Fergus I. M. Craik, 1–32. Oxford: Oxford University Press, 2000. Kindle.

Brunner, Emil. *The Christian Doctrine of Creation and Redemption*. Vol. 2 of *Dogmatics*. Translated by Olive Wyon. Philadelphia: Westminster, 1952.

———. *Man in Revolt: A Christian Anthropology*. Translated by Olive Wyon. London: Lutterworth, 1957.

Bryant, Barry Edward. "John Wesley's Doctrine of Sin." PhD diss., King's College, 1992. https://kclpure.kcl.ac.uk/portal/en/studentTheses/john-wesleys-doctrine-of-sin.

Burnyeat, M. F. "Plato on the Grammar of Perceiving." *Classical Quarterly* 26 (1976) 29–51.

Bynum, Caroline Walker. *Jesus as Mother: Studies in the Spirituality of the High Middle Ages*. Berkeley: University of California Press, 1982.

Carruthers, Mary. *The Book of Memory: A Study of Memory in Medieval Culture*. 2nd ed. Cambridge: Cambridge University Press, 2013.

Chappell, Sophie-Grace. "Aristotle." In *The Routledge Handbook of Philosophy of Memory*, edited by Sven Bernecker and Michaelian Kourken, Routledge Handbooks in Philosophy, 396–407. London: Routledge, 2019.

———. "Plato." In *The Routledge Handbook of Philosophy of Memory*, edited by Sven Bernecker and Michaelian Kourken, Routledge Handbooks in Philosophy, 385–95. London: Routledge, 2019.

———. "Plato on Knowledge in the *Theaetetus*." *Stanford Encyclopedia of Philosophy Archive*, May 7, 2005; last revised Nov. 21, 2019. https://plato.stanford.edu/archives/spr2021/entries/plato-theaetetus/.

Choi, Jinyong. "Analogy, Spirituality, and the Beatific Enjoyment of God: Bonaventure and the Doctrine of Image and Likeness." PhD diss., Boston College, 2019.

Coleman, Janet. *Ancient and Medieval Memories: Studies in the Reconstruction of the Past.* Cambridge: Cambridge University Press, 1992.

Collins, Kenneth, and Jason E. Vickers, eds. *The Sermons of John Wesley: A Collection for the Christian Journey.* By John Wesley. Nashville: Abingdon, 2013.

Collins, Kenneth J. "John Wesley's Platonic Conception of the Moral Law." *Wesleyan Theological Journal* 21 (Spring 1986) 116–28.

———. *The Scripture Way of Salvation: The Heart of John Wesley's Theology.* Nashville: Abingdon, 1997.

Corkin, Suzanne. "What's New with the Amnesic Patient H. M." *Nature Reviews Neuroscience* 3 (Feb. 2002) 1–10.

Cragg, Gerald R., ed. *The Cambridge Platonists.* New York: Oxford University Press, 1968.

Curtis, Edward M. "Image of God (OT)." In *The Anchor Bible Dictionary*, edited by David Noel Freedman et al, 3:389–91. New York: Doubleday, 1992.

Davis, Robert Glenn. *The Weight of Love: Affect, Ecstasy, and Union in the Theology of Bonaventure.* New York: Fordham University Press, 2017.

Deretić, Irina. "ΨΥΧΗ as Biblion: Cognitive Dispositions and Pleasures at *Philebus* 38E12–40." *Theoria* 2 (2009) 69–80. https://doiserbia.nb.rs/img/doi/0351-2274/2009/0351-22740902069D.pdf.

Dunning, H. Ray. *Reflecting the Divine Image: Christian Ethics in Wesleyan Perspective.* Downers Grove, IL: InterVarsity, 1998.

Dyrness, William. "Poised between Life and Death." In *The Image of God in an Image Driven Age: Explorations in Theological Anthropology*, edited by Beth Felker Jones and Jeffrey W. Barbeau, Wheaton Theology Conference Series, 47–65. Downers Grove, IL: IVP Academic, 2016. Kindle.

Eardley, Peter. "Medieval Theories of Conscience." *Stanford Encyclopedia of Philosophy*, Jan. 19, 2021. https://plato.stanford.edu/entries/conscience-medieval/.

Eastman, Susan. *Paul and the Person: Reframing Paul's Anthropology.* Grand Rapids: Eerdmans, 2017.

Fantino, Jacques. *L'homme, image de Dieu, chez Saint Irénée de Lyon.* Paris: Cerf, 1986.

Felker Jones, Beth and Jeffrey W. Barbeau, eds. *The Image of God in an Image Driven Age: Explorations in Theological Anthropology.* Wheaton Theology Conference Series. Downers Grove, IL: IVP Academic, 2016. Kindle.

Gaiger, Jason. "The Idea of a Universal *Bildwissenschaft.*" *Estetika: The Central European Journal of Aesthetics* 51 (2014) 208–29. DOI: 10.33134/eeja.124.

Giltner, T. Alexander. "The Lightness of Being: Illumination in the Philosophy and Theology of Saint Bonaventure." PhD diss., St. Louis University, 2018.

Gonzalez, Michelle. *Created in God's Image: An Introduction to Feminist Theological Anthropology.* Maryknoll, NY: Orbis, 2007.

Grabbe, Lester L. "The Wisdom of Solomon." In *The New Oxford Annotated Bible New Revised Standard Version with the Apocrypha*, edited by Michael D. Coogan, 1427–28. New York: Oxford University Press, 2010.

Han, Jin-Hee et al. "Neuronal Competition and Selection during Memory Formation." *Science* 316 (Apr. 20, 2007) 457–60.

Harte, Verity. "Desire, Memory, and the Authority of the Soul: Plato, *Philebus* 35 C–D." In *Oxford Studies in Ancient Philosophy*, edited by Brad Inwood, 46:33–72. Oxford: Oxford University Press, 2014.

Hefner, Philip. *The Human Factor: Evolution, Culture, and Religion*. Theology and the Sciences. Minneapolis: Fortress, 1993.

Hochschild, Paige E. *Memory in Augustine's Theological Anthropology*. Oxford Early Christian Studies. Oxford: Oxford University Press, 2012.

Hutabarat, Reymand M. "Exploring Karl Barth's View on the Image of God." *International Journal of Philosophy and Theology* 3 (June 2015) 122–28.

Irenaeus. "Adversus Haereses." CCEL, 1885. From *Ante-Nicene Fathers*, edited by Philip Schaff, 1. https://ccel.org/ccel/schaff/anf01/anf01.

———. *Demonstration of the Apostolic Preaching*. CCEL, 1920. Edited by Armitage Robinson. https://ccel.org/ccel/irenaeus/demonstr/demonstr.

Johnson, Junius. "The One and the Many in Bonaventure Exemplarity Explained." *Religions* 7 (2016) 1–16.

Jones, James. *Living Religion: Embodiment, Theology, and the Possibility of a Spiritual Sense*. New York: Oxford University Press, 2019.

Josselyn, Sheena A., and Susumu Tonegawa. "Memory Engrams: Recalling the Past and Imagining the Future." *Science* 367 (Jan. 3, 2020) 1–14.

Justin Martyr. *On the Resurrection, Fragments*. CCEL, 1885. From *Ante-Nicene Fathers*, edited by Philip Schaff, 1. https://ccel.org/ccel/justin_martyr/on_the_resurrection_fragments/anf01.

Karnes, Michelle. *Imagination, Meditation, and Cognition in the Middle Ages*. Chicago: University of Chicago Press, 2011.

Kasparov, Sergei. "Optogenetics." In *Primer on the Autonomic Nervous System*, edited by David Robertson et al., 689–91. 3rd ed. London: Academic/Elsevier, 2012.

Kilner, John Frederic. *Dignity and Destiny: Humanity in the Image of God*. Grand Rapids: Eerdmans, 2015.

Kim, Young Taek. "John Wesley's Anthropology: Restoration of the Imago Dei as a Framework for Wesley's Theology." PhD diss., Drew University, 2006.

Klein, Stanley B. "What Memory Is." *WIREs Cognitive Science* 6 (Jan./Feb. 2015) 1–38.

Kourken, Michaelian. "Generative Memory." *Philosophical Psychology* 24 (2011) 323–42.

Kugler, Chris. *Paul and the Image of God*. Lanham, MD: Fortress Academic, 2020. Kindle.

Lossky, Vladimir. *In the Image and Likeness of God*. Edited by John H. Erickson and Thomas E. Bird. Crestwood, NY: St. Vladimir's Seminary Press, 1974.

Lui, Xu, et al. "Optogenetic Stimulation of a Hippocampal Engram Activates Fear Memory Recall." *Letters to Nature* 484 (Apr. 19, 2012) 381–87.

Maddox, Randy L. *Responsible Grace: John Wesley's Practical Theology*. Nashville: Abingdon, 1994.

Martin, Alex, and Linda L. Chao. "Semantic Memory in the Brain: Structure and Processes." *Current Opinion in Neurobiology* 11 (2001) 194–201.

Martin, Dale B. *The Corinthian Body*. New Haven, CT: Yale University Press, 1999.

McDowell, Catherine. "In the Image of God He Created Them: How Genesis 1:26–27 Defines the Divine-Human Relationship and Why It Matters." In *The Image of God in an Image Driven Age: Explorations in Theological Anthropology*, edited by Beth Felker Jones and Jeffrey W. Barbeau, Wheaton Theology Conference Series, 29–45. Downers Grove, IL: IVP Academic, 2016. Kindle.

McFarland, Ian A. "What Does It Mean to See Someone: Icons and Identity." In *The Image of God in an Image Driven Age: Explorations in Theological Anthropology*, edited by Beth Felker Jones and Jeffrey W. Barbeau, Wheaton Theology Conference Series, 157–72. Downers Grove, IL: IVP Academic, 2016. Kindle.

McLeod, Frederick G. *The Image of God in the Antiochene Tradition*. Washington, DC: Catholic University of American Press, 1999.

McNamara, Patrick. *The Neuroscience of Religious Experience*. New York: Cambridge University Press, 2011.

Milford, Stephen. "Substantive or Relational? The Counterfeit Choice in the *Imago Dei* Debate." *McMaster Journal of Theology and Ministry* 20 (2018–19) 84–117.

Moscovitch, Morris, et al. "Episodic Memory and Beyond: The Hippocampus and Neocortex in Transformation." *Annual Review of Psychology* 67 (2016) 105–34.

Pannenberg, Wolfhart. *Anthropology in Theological Perspective*. Translated by Matthew J. O'Connell. Edinburgh: T&T Clark, 1999.

Peltier, Robert V. "Λόγος Christology in the Prologue of John's Gospel: A Rejection of Philo of Alexandria's Logos Philosophy." Master's thesis, South African Theological Seminary, 2019.

Peters, Karl E. "The Image of God as a Model for Humanization." *Zygon* 9 (1974) 98–125.

Petrusek, Matthew. "The Image of God and Moral Action: Challenging the Practicality of the Imago Dei." *Studies in Christian Ethics* 30 (2017) 60–82.

Plato. "*Meno*" and "*Phaedo*." Edited by David Sedley. Translated by Alex Long. Cambridge Texts in the History of Philosophy. Cambridge: Cambridge University Press, 2010.

———. *Plato's "Philebus."* Translated by R. Hackforth. Cambridge: Cambridge University Press, 1972.

———. *Philebus*. Translated by Benjamin Jowett. Coppell, TX: N.p., 2022.

———. "*Theaetetus*" and "*Sophist*." Edited by Christopher Rowe. Cambridge Texts in the History of Philosophy. Cambridge: Cambridge University Press, 2015.

Reynolds, Philip L. "Bonaventure's Theory of Resemblance." *Tradito* 58 (2003) 219–55.

Ricoeur, Paul. *Memory, History, Forgetting*. Translated by Kathleen Blamey and David Pellauer. Chicago: University of Chicago Press, 2004.

Robins, Sarah. "Representing the Past: Memory Traces and the Causal Theory of Memory." *Philosophical Studies* 173 (2016) 2998–3013.

Robinson, Richard. "Forms and Error in Plato's *Theaetetus*." *Philosophical Review* 59 (Jan. 1950) 3–30.

Rugg, Michael D., and Kaia L. Vilberg. "Brain Networks Underlying Episodic Memory Retrieval." *Current Opinions in Neurobiology* 23 (2013) 255–60.

Runyon, Theodore. *The New Creation: John Wesley's Theology Today*. Nashville: Abingdon, 1998.

Ryan, T. J., et al. "Engram Cells Retain Memory under Retrograde Amnesia." *Science* 348 (2015) 1007–13.

Sallis, John. *Being and Logos: Reading the Platonic Dialogues*. Bloomington: Indiana University Press, 2019. Kindle.

Schacter, Daniel L., et al. "Richard Semon's Theory of Memory." *Journal of Verbal Learning and Verbal Behavior* 17 (1978) 721–43.

Schumacher, Lydia. *Divine Illumination: The History and Future of Augustine's Theory of Knowledge*. West Sussex, UK: Wiley-Blackwell, 2011. Kindle.

Sedley, David. *Plato's "Cratylus."* Cambridge Studies in the Dialogues of Plato. Cambridge: Cambridge University Press, 2003.

Semon, Richard. *The Mneme*. New York: Macmilllan, 1921.

Shantz, Colleen. "In the Divine (Mental) Image: Theological Anthropology and the Structure of Cognition." In *Theology as Interdisciplinary Inquiry: Learning with and from the Natural and Human Sciences*, edited by Robin W. Lovin and Joshua Mauldin, 50–67. Grand Rapids: Eerdmans, 2017.

Shelton, Anthony James. "A Window to God? A Theological and Philosophical Appraisal at the Crossroads of Religious Experience and Neuroscience." PhD diss., Princeton Theological Seminary, 2007.

Simons, Jon S., and Hugo J. Spiers. "Prefrontal and Medial Temporal Lobe Interactions in Long-Term Memory." *Nature Reviews Neuroscience* 4 (Aug. 2003) 637–48.

Slotnick, Scott D. *Cognitive Neuroscience of Memory*. Cambridge: Cambridge University Press, 2017.

Sorabji, Richard. *Aristotle on Memory*. Chicago: University of Chicago Press, 2004.

Sutton, John. *Philosophy and Memory Traces: Descartes to Connectionism*. Cambridge: Cambridge University Press, 1998.

Thielicke, Helmut. *Foundations*. Edited by William H. Lazareth. Vol. 1 of *Theological Ethics*. London: A&C Black, 1966.

Tonegawa, Susumu, et al. "The Role of Engram Cells in the Systems Consolidation of Memory." *Nature Reviews: Neuroscience* 19 (Aug. 2018) 485–98.

Tulving, Endel. *Elements of Episodic Memory*. Oxford Psychology Series. New York: Oxford University Press, 1983.

Vawter, Bruce. "Genesis 1:1—11:26: The Book of Origins." In *New Catholic Commentary on Holy Scriptures*, edited by Reginald C. Fuller et al., 166–205. Camden, NJ: Thomas Nelson and Sons.

Vermes, Geza, trans. *The Complete Dead Sea Scrolls in English*. London: Penguin, 1997.

Weinandy, Thomas G. "St. Irenaeus and the *Imago Dei*: Importance of Being Human." *Logos: A Journal of Catholic Thought and Culture* 6 (Fall 2003) 15–34.

Weissenbacher, Alan C. "Born-Again Brain: Neuroscience and Wesleyan Salvation." PhD diss., Graduate Theological Union, 2016.

Welz, Claudia. "*Imago Dei*: References to the Invisible." *Studia Theologica* 65 (2011) 74–91.

Wesley, John. *Christian Perfection: A Sermon*. 2nd ed. Bristol, UK: Gooding, 1743.

———. *A Compendium of Logic*. 2nd ed. London: n.p., 1756.

———. *The Doctrine of Original Sin: According to Scripture, Reason, and Experience*. Bristol, UK: Farley, 1757.

———. *An Earnest Appeal to Men of Reason and Religion*. 6th ed. Bristol, UK: Pine, 1765.

———. "Of the Action of God and Creatures." *Arminian Magazine* (1786) 276–77.

———. "On Grieving the Holy Spirit (1733)." *Methodist Magazine* 21 (Dec. 1798) 607–13.

———. *The Sermons of John Wesley: A Collection for the Christian Journey*. Edited by Kenneth Collins and Jason E. Vickers. Nashville: Abingdon, 2013.

———. *Survey of the Wisdom of God in the Creation: Or a Compendium of Natural Philosophy*. Vol. 1. 3rd ed. London: Fry and Co., 1777.

———. *Survey of the Wisdom of God in the Creation: Or a Compendium of Natural Philosophy*. Vol. 5. 3rd ed. London: Fry and Co., 1777.

———. "Thoughts on Memory." *Arminian Magazine* (July 1790) 383–84.

Wesley, Susanna. "From Mrs. Susanna Wesley, Nov. 10th, 1725." In *The Oxford Edition of the Works of John Wesley*, edited by Frank Baker, 25:183–85. Oxford: Oxford University Press, 1980.

Wheeler, Anne L., et al. "Identification of a Functional Connectome for Long-Term Fear Memory in Mice." *Plos Computational Biology* 9 (Jan. 2013) 1–18.

Wright, Stephen. *Growing into God*. Edited by Jean Mayland. London: Churches Together in Britain and Ireland, 2003.

Yui, Adelaide, et al. "Neurons Are Recruited to a Memory Trace Based on Relative Neuronal Excitability Immediately before Training." *Neuron* 83 (Aug. 6, 2014) 722–35.

Subject Index

Scripture Index

Made in United States
North Haven, CT
15 May 2024

52548824R00104